Dope Black Boy 2
Rich Black Man

Dope Black Boy 2 Rich Black Man

GUIDE TO CHANNELING A YOUNG HUSTLER'S AMBITION INTO THE DEVELOPMENT OF AN EMPOWERED SUCCESSFUL MAN

Christopher Freeman and Marcellus Womack

Dope Black Boy 2 Rich Black Man.

Copyright © 2015 by Christopher Freeman and Marcellus Womack
All rights reserved. No part of this book may be used, reproduced, scanned, or distributed in any printed or electronic form without written permission.

Printed by CreateSpace Independent Publishing Platform, North Charleston, SC
Cover Art and Design by Phat Chik Dzine

Library of Congress Cataloging-in-Publication
Data is available upon request

ISBN: 9781517143244
ISBN: 1517143241
Library of Congress Control Number: 2015914545
CreateSpace Independent Publishing Platform
North Charleston, South Carolina

Printed in the United States of America
10 9 8 7 6 5 4 3 2 1

Contents

INTRO

Hustler's Ambition

Across from the Gateway mall, on the north side of Jacksonville, Florida, is the Norwood Indoor Flea Market. Inside are dozens of urban vendors for clothing, music, food, barbering, hairstyling, tattoos, and more. At the back of the indoor flea market is a custom graphics T-shirt shop. Many patronize it or walk right past as if all is normal, but I can't. My heart literally drops every time I walk past and look inside at the T-shirts.

Dozens of T-shirts in various colors cover the walls of the shop. Printed on most of the shirts is a picture of a young black male. There are numerous faces of young black males, and above each face is the fatal caption "In Memory Of" and "R.I.P." Often following their name is a brutally cold and short interval of time, representing a precious life petrifyingly bridged by a hyphen: 1977-2004, 1987-2009, 1995-2011, 2000-2013. It appears that the owner shows respect to every order made for these T-shirts honoring loved ones who have passed away, by making sure one T-shirt remains hanging in the store. There are dozens of slain black male faces, all left to hang in a store. With local and national media headlines displaying the faces of this same demographic of murdered young black males daily, what is the message being sent?

Society historically honors a "soldier's death." The highest degrees of iconic status are rewarded to men who have brutally died fighting for a courageous cause—beloved men like William Wallace (Braveheart), Leonidas of the 300 Spartans, Martin Luther King Jr., Malcolm X, and most noteworthy Jesus Christ. Society even resonates with the "made it from the bottom to the top" underdog stories of notorious criminals, who relentlessly fought to make their mark in this world, while constantly facing an unavoidable death or incarceration—men such as Billy the Kid, Jesse James, Al Capone, Frank Lucas, and even the fictional phenomenon Scarface. Their willingness to fight and face death to fulfill their mission is the fundamental principle of a hustler's ambition.

The definition of a martyr is one who dies, sacrificing his or her own life in a gallant pursuit. We love a fighter who dies fighting for his beliefs. It's the ultimate storyline behind what humanity most cherishes, celebrates, and worships. The most powerful nation on the planet was anchored at the start of its Revolutionary War by Patrick Henry's famous words, "Give me liberty or give me death." If freedom by any means, including death, is the fabric for what has driven our civilization's infatuation with heroes since the beginning of time, why is it so hard for society to empathize with this exact sentiment among young black males all over this country?

Who has embodied this heralded revolutionary spirit in the face of death more than the young black male in Urban America? What war of unbearable multi-century economic, socio-cultural, and politically unjust proportions rivals that of the war a young black male ferociously fights in Urban America? Even in the midst of the count-less numbers of black-on-black killings that are beyond unfortunate and catastrophic, why are so few able to recognize this as an ambitiously misguided reaction to the deeply centered pain of feeling wronged and disadvantaged, with no source of real help? A pain to such an unconscious, yet visibly symptomatic, extent that young black boys are recklessly expediting the process to manhood, by choosing to die fighting for an internal revolutionary cause. Ironically, they are then labeled senseless hooligans and idiotic rebels with no cause.

The global media is captivated by this ongoing warfare. Amidst this turmoil with-in inner-city hoods all across America—like Chicago, New York, Los Angeles, Atlanta, New Orleans, and Jacksonville—we all haphazardly salute the heroism of a young black murdered male who has proven he could walk through the valley of death in all its tragic finality. This salute is reflected through every T-shirt, tattoo, national headline, or highly publicized court trial for a murdered young black male. We know their life experience somehow put them in the line of fire, similar to the one faced by our greatest heroes during their last moments. Unfortunately, what may haunt our entire society even more is that we may have a stronger infatuation for a person's drive to be the "killer."

Aggression and killer instinct demonstrated in a competitive, metaphoric, or lit-erally violent way are qualities men are encouraged to have in gaining power, respect, wealth, success, and greatness. Some of the greatest men in the Bible were killers, such as Moses, Paul, and King David, who first gained notoriety as a child, after slay-ing the giant Goliath. Society celebrates and rewards a man's ability to demonstrate overpowering killer instinct in sports, business, religion, and politics. It's still intriguing to me that the most intelligent political leaders in the world still resort to handling the most serious conflicts by overpowering the opposing country or group through massive killings and war.

Even today, this barbaric mind-set and ability is behind what really makes a country most respected. The financing power to back these war activities is the real strength behind a country's economy. We have a highly sophisticated structure for humanity, which, if simplified to its lowest form, is humans killing humans for power. History repeats this vicious cycle of nations going to war, oftentimes fighting against people of similar or the same descent.

However, when a group of people finds a cause to rally behind for a self-serving agenda, there's always a collective reason for rationalizing horrific acts such as violence and murder. There's also a convoluted scheme that we choose to naively support if those activities help support "the cause." To right a wrong, by doing wrong, because you're right, is right and not wrong. As twisted as this sounds, it's the main lesson our world teaches every young male who is to ever become a man: Aggressively secure your freedom, through a mission to gain power and wealth, with no real regard for human life.

Is war between countries not a glorified version of gang banging between sets? Is the Israel-Palestine conflict not similar to the Bloods vs. Crips beef? Are foreign relations' tactics to amass more land and oil much different from a dope boy's hustle game to take over more blocks to sell crack? Is capitalism anything other than a hustler's ambition? Who are we fooling by overly stereotyping young black males engaged in street activity as if they're the scum of the earth and out of control? We ridicule them as if the pursuit of building any other powerful regime in this world, mostly based on greed, isn't a carbon copy of the exact same thing. A young hustler in the streets is cut from the same ambitious yet erratic cloth of every other idolized man, president, and king throughout our history who has ordered to kill for what they wanted.

So a message to the young black male with strong desires to empower yourself through the streets is:

"YOU ARE NOT CRAZY! "

Regardless of the path, we all do everything in life ultimately to be fulfilled and happy. You are no different. For anyone to say they don't understand your inner motive would be to naively exploit their own existence as a hypocrite and liar. You're not animalistic, inferior, stupid, incapable, unloved, nor hopeless. You are fearless, superior, intelligent, talented, and secretly idolized by the world for your raw expression of your personal will to win. You are built with the same gene for greatness as the greatest men and leaders who have ever lived. You have identified within yourself one of the greatest qualities a man can possess, a "hustler's ambition." This hustler's ambition is the core building block for driving mankind.

However, young black man—when you're involved in a life of crime, drugs, and violence, you are playing a vicious game that you will always lose. You become a suicidal soldier, fighting against your own culture, which defeats the entire point of being a soldier. Regardless of the world's violent historical pattern for men achieving greatness, you as a black male have been displaced in a situation far too great to conquer with similar inhumane illegitimate tactics. You do not own this society, and you do not currently control the power structures that manipulate this human game. Above all, you may have a higher calling of greatness; you may be able to rise above these tactics, by channeling this common human spirit of ambition in a way that does not always revolve back to self-destruction.

It is said that deep within a person's eyes you can find their soul. Back at the indoor flea market T-shirt shop, I've had chilling moments where I have looked into the eyes of slain black males in jpeg pics, centered on T-shirts. I received a different message of heroism when I contemplated the value of these forever-gone, yet saluted sons of our community. As I looked deep into the eyes of framed past moments on dozens of T-shirts, I felt the depths of each of their souls telling me:

"Bruh, LIVE your life! It's obvious mine was ended too soon. The only heroism I want you to get from me on this T-shirt is that I was a part of a sacrifice, so that you WON'T be on a T-shirt like this anytime soon. Living is the shizznit! Don't take your opportunities for granted or get caught up in death traps! There is nothing I can do at this point, except give you this dose of realness; but you are ALIVE to do so much more. I have attained freedom in death, but you can attain freedom in LIFE. You are free to make the most of every single LIVING breath in your body, despite your circumstances, by living out the fullest, most positive LIFE you can and by being the greatest person you can be. You are my hero because you can courageously impact the world now! Make the most of all your talents, and don't let anything stop you from happily LIVING your LIFE as a FREE MAN!"

Mr. Freeman

Before I met Christopher Freeman, I had first heard about him from a good female friend of mine. Being a Marketing/PR Consultant, she knew my client base included several beauty supply stores in Jacksonville. She called me one day and said, "Marcellus, I just got some fiyah hair from this guy who has the best hair I've ever seen!"

I replied, "Really, where at?" She told me he sold it to her out of his trunk on the north side, and she described him as a cool dude who had been a d-boy but was now selling hair after doing time in prison. I thought to myself, "Okay, a young hustling brotha, who after doing time has found a quick lick for selling a little hair weave out the trunk. That's wazzzup."

However, a couple of weeks later I began to hear more and more stories from other ladies all over Jacksonville. They were losing their minds over this now mythical guy Chris, who carried this quality virgin hair, superior to anything on the market. The local buzz grew to a level that rivaled the excitement generated by the new Jordans hitting stores for the first time, or when Steve Jobs announced the release of the first iPhone. It seemed like every black lady in Jacksonville from the beauty salons, work offices, and clubs, to Facebook and Instagram were all talking about Chris and his supply of "Beautiful Hair!"

It's no secret that black women drive the hair extensions market. After studying numerous consumer patterns in the urban market regarding the beauty industry, I'm convinced that black women drive the economy. Recession or not, black women have proven they're going to make sure their hair looks good. The unchallenged reality, however, has always been that despite this high demand and customer loyalty from black women for such hair products, the beauty supply store market is predominantly owned and controlled by non-blacks. Thus, my initial response to Christopher Freeman's story was amazement. I thought, "This young BLACK brotha has uncovered the glitch to the urban beauty supply matrix, by establishing a booming presence for providing pure virgin hair better than anyone else."

It wasn't long before some of the beauty supply owners I worked with began expressing their extreme concern for this new competitor, who came out of nowhere and was rapidly building a huge customer base at their expense. Amidst an already highly competitive market, these beauty supply owners quickly saw their market share declining at an alarming rate, as Chris expanded to a storefront business named "Beautiful Hair 4 U." The other beauty supply owners began desperately seeking out more of my consultation for creative marketing promotions that could help keep their businesses afloat. It was at this point that I had to step back and marvel at the growing success of this young black man, who had converted his street hustler's ambition to a successful legitimate business enterprise that was "taking names and kicking some serious beauty supply butt."

It made me proud to witness the business acumen of Mr. Christopher Freeman, a young black entrepreneur and former dope boy from the hood, who was outsmarting an entire market of established beauty supply chains by strategically implementing the most savvy business techniques. This included international sourcing, upscale branding, viral guerrilla marketing, profit maximization, quality management, and numerous other tactics that could easily be used in an Ivy League business case study competition.

I was slightly torn about creating various promotions for the other beauty supply owners, knowing their main purpose was to offset the avalanche of one black man's ferocious entry into the market. So I made a vow to myself to refrain from any direct promotional attacks or sharing of any critical information regarding Chris and Beautiful Hair 4 U.

As competition within the local beauty supply market over virgin hair extensions became even more intense, I became concerned with how Chris would be able to fully conform to the business world without resorting back to street tactics if push came to shove. How would he handle competitive disputes, which were unavoidable now that he was the new target in such a hostile business environment?

I would hear about uncool tactics used against him, including calls made to U.S. Customs, maliciously accusing Chris of importing illegal substances as opposed to hair products. Being from the inner city south side of Chicago, I know that most people with a street upbringing are conditioned to react by applying a street code mentality to such issues. My hope was that Chris would not revert back to any irrational street tactics that could put his business and freedom at risk. I often thought about reaching out to Chris to, at least, show some brotherly support and respect for his emergence into the market, but I'd convince myself that the time for us to connect would occur naturally if it was meant to be.

That time came sooner rather than later. I was informed of a business issue that had arisen between Chris and a mutual party we both worked with, non-related to beauty supply stores. I took it upon myself to help resolve the issue by calling Chris. The first ten minutes of this call was shrewd and potentially confrontational. Chris was semi-heated about a situation in which he felt he was disrespected. However, after the initial dialogue, we reached a higher understanding of resolve and mutual respect for each other.

The next hour was an incredibly bonding conversation in which we discussed our own personal stories. For Chris this included his past life in the streets as a dealer and doing time in prison, before turning his life around and launching his virgin hair business, Beautiful Hair 4 U. We also discussed family life, business, marketing, the beauty supply industry, politics, international affairs, challenges in today's black youth culture, collective black empowerment, and ideas for greater unity in the black community. It was not long before I set up a meeting with Chris at a Starbucks, to discuss how I could contribute to helping Beautiful Hair 4 U reach even greater heights.

Christopher Freeman & Marcellus Womack

A couple of new stores and successful promo campaigns later, we found ourselves ready to co-write a book that could inspire other young black males to achieve success in the same ambitious manner in which Chris has. Chris was a high school dropout, juvenile offender, who became a major drug dealer in the dope game. Chris then was caught by the Feds and became a convicted felon, who had to serve two prison sentences for a total of over seven years between 2001-2011.

After Chris paid his debt to society, he made a personal vow to never again engage in a criminal lifestyle. Chris reprogrammed his mind and channeled 100 percent of his hustler's ambition to becoming a successful business man. No longer shackled by a misguided mind-set or illegal street trade, Chris is now able to excel through every facet of LIFE as an unstoppable embodiment of his last name...FREEMAN!

What greater gift than to be young, gifted, and black? What better story does the world admire than for one to convert extreme struggle into ultimate triumph, starting with nothing and immaculately taking one's life situation from the bottom to the top? *Dope Black Boy 2 Rich Black Man* is an enlightening guide for young black males, showing how to channel a hustler's ambition into an empowering force that can catapult a man to ultimate success.

This book gives the proper perspective for directing inner masculine-rooted desires into productive outlets for pursuing true greatness. Chris and I unite as one voice to speak directly to the mind, body, and soul of the young black male—as well as anyone with a deep-seated concern for exploring solutions to the young black male's plight. *Dope Black Boy 2 Rich Black Man* provides life tools for actively pursuing being the best!

Young black male, regardless of your current situation, you are ingeniously sculpted by the hands of God to LIVE LIFE to the fullest as a FREE MAN. Let this book and Christopher Freeman's experience help guide you along your journey towards the fulfillment of your most incredible dreams.

CHAPTER 1

Personal Responsibility

From my observations and experiences, it is important that we initially address personal responsibility. A critical part of being a man is taking on personal responsibility, which is grounded by YOUR character and discipline. Personal responsibility relates to handling YOUR business. It means taking control of YOUR life and making choices. It also means accepting responsibility and holding YOURSELF accountable for the consequences after making that choice, good or bad. The way life works is very clear: the decisions YOU make ultimately determine your reality. Make good decisions, and good things eventually happen. Make bad decisions, and eventually bad things happen and catch up with YOU.

During childhood, we begin developing crucial habits, good or bad, that shape our foundation for making decisions that will forever impact our lives. That's why it's so important to begin focusing on the consequences to your actions at an early age. Morality leads to knowledge, which leads to self-control, which leads to righteous perseverance. Without proper development of these character traits, you will always look for the quick way out. Many reckless habits, which got me incarcerated, started from bad habits I developed as a child. You don't just wake up and become a felon locked up in federal prison. It takes years of habitually neglecting the consequences to high-risk actions, which take years and sometimes your own life to pay off.

Fight Night

Growing up on the north side of Jacksonville, what I remember most throughout grade school is getting into fights all the time. I was one rebellious, fighting little kid. I was smaller than most other kids growing up, so I always felt like I had to defend myself on sight, whenever someone approached me the wrong way. I would also be quick to jump if someone messed with a family member, especially with my younger brothers. As the oldest of four, I've always been willing to do any and everything for my younger brothers Jacoby, Ebony, and Mitch. I took pride in being the Big Brother and "Big Homey." I would quickly turn any potential altercation into a rumble.

I loved to have fun and play as a kid, but I had a lightning quick temper and adrenaline rush like no other when it came to throwing those thangs. I wasn't a bully at all though. Usually, I would only choose to fight when standing up for myself or when I was committed to holding down others. I felt it was my responsibility to make sure we were never violated or disrespected without dishing out some get-back and hurt.

As a child, I grew up with my mom and stepdad, initially. Although I didn't have a relationship with my biological father, my stepdad did what he could to play the role. However, he was real corny and lame to me. As a young, naive hothead, I rarely valued his perspective and couldn't relate to him at all. My mom was gone a lot, running the streets; so I stayed with my grandparents often. Grandpa was always working, so Grandma had to hold it down most of the time.

One day I was at the mall with one of my homeys. We ran across some boys we had a little beef with at school. We approached them and then proceeded to fight right in the middle of the mall. We were punching one of the boys on the ground; and when it was time to run away before security came, my homeboy snatched his chain. We got caught and were charged with strong-armed robbery. I was only 13 years old.

I was sent to the juvenile detention center, along with my homeboy. That fight led to a life in the streets, where we both would eventually pay the price by doing time. My homeboy is now doing 22 years in prison.

If you want to show your aggression by fighting all the time, society has a cruel way of removing you from the regular world to isolated areas where that's the only thing you can do to survive. "You want to fight? Cool! Let's see how you handle yourself among 50 other kids in juvey who love to fight all day." Those boys in juvey were rough. To prove I wasn't a punk, I was always fighting in there as well.

When we got back to school after the mall altercation, the boys we had fought were threatening to kill us. My mom was concerned and didn't want me to go back to the school. She pulled me and my younger brother Jacoby out and sent us to live with my grandma by the Jacksonville Beaches. I started going to a school out there and soon began getting in trouble again.

I was tired of this kid at school messing with Jacoby, so one day I jammed him up in the hallway and threw him into the lockers with all my might. His collar bone broke; and when I was sent to the principal's office, they decided they had had enough of me. I was expelled from school. I rarely attended school after that and ended up dropping out at the beginning of 9th grade.

Dope Boy Magic

After dropping out of school at the age of 14, I began hanging out more in the streets, running around with my older cousin Weegie. Weegie was a dope boy, and I was always interested in how he would maneuver around the neighborhood selling drugs and making money. One day we were outside my grandma's house, and he had to go inside. He didn't want to bring the crack rock he had on him inside, so he asked me to hold it.

At first I was just going to chill outside the house until he came back; but down the street was the Canterbury Court Apartments, where everyone was dealing drugs. It was like a flea market for drugs, with all the dealers and addicts making exchanges left and right. I would always go around there and watch all the dudes selling, including Weegie.

As I looked towards the spot where all the action was going down, I began to get anxious. For the first time, I could go into the apartment complex holding something. Finally, I couldn't resist the temptation of temporarily having what all the other dope boys had, and I walked down the street into the area.

When I got there, a lady approached me and asked, "Hey, are you holding?" Then she said, "I got $20." With no hesitation, I sold her the rock I was holding for Weegie. I was amazed at how easy it was to make that $20. It literally took about 10 seconds.

My cousin Weegie came back out of Grandma's house and asked, "Where's the rock?"

Still in awe from my transaction, but now a little nervous as reality set in on how I no longer had the rock he told me to hold, I said, "I sold it."

Weegie said, "Man, you did what? You better give me my $10."

I paused for a second and said to myself, "Bet I can give him this $10 and keep $10 for me." So that's exactly what I did. Weegie took the $10, and my mind began turning 100 miles per hour. That money was so easy to make, like magic! Show up with some dope, and "waaala" people giving you money appear. I had to get in on some more of this action. I said "Weegie, give me another rock to sell." He did. I went back to the same place and did the same thing again.

I turned $10 to $20, $20 to $40, and then ended up being able to get me a bag of about 10 rocks each. By the time I was 15 years old, I was making $200 a day. I would serve throughout the day, put $100 in the stash, and buy a bag of 10 more rocks. I became infatuated with learning how I could stack money by copping low and selling high. I was more passionate about selling drugs than I had ever been about any subject in school or any other activity I did as a child. This was the lick! I had way more money than all the other teens around my age going to school every day. At that point I could care less about a high school prom or graduation. I had my eyes on that re-up I could flip enough to soon graduate to "balla" status.

Ballin'!

I began copping all the new Jordans whenever they dropped, $1,000 chains, plus all the freshest gear and brand names I could find. Soon I had put enough money aside to buy my first car, which was a Starburst Blue Bonneville. Mind you, all of this I had to hide from my grandparents because they didn't know what I was doing. I was only 15, so I had to let that car sit until I turned 16.

By 16 I had stacked enough money to cop another car, and I got a Cadillac Deville Yellow Short Dog, a pimped-out whip similar to the other dope boys I admired. I was always looking up in admiration to the big dudes that I would buy the rocks from. They were doing it real big in my eyes. My barber introduced me to the big dope boy that would sell to all the little dope boys in my area. He would sell me the $10 rocks that I could make double from. I looked up to him because he had a Lexus with rims and other cars with candy paint, hydraulics, booming sound systems, and all the works.

He and all the other major dope boys around the way were the men who inspired me. I never really knew my real dad, I wasn't living with my step dad anymore plus he was a square to me, and my granddad worked all the time. So those big-time dope boys represented everything I thought a man could successfully be in life. They had serious respect and popularity in the hood. Everybody knew they were the man! They had all the fly chicks with the pretty little up-dews riding around in the passenger seats of their latest ride, while they were rocking all the jewelry with the icy gold teeth. I would just look in awe like, "Cot dang I wanna be just like them when I grow up." I aspired to be just like all of them. I'd pick up things from each one to emulate until eventually I became my own major dope boy version of them.

Getting money and getting rich was how I started measuring my success. I worked hard to move dope and make thousands of dollars a week. After grinding out to flip product in making as much money as possible, I began to flex with even more material possessions to show how great I felt I was becoming. I started getting gold teeth all over my mouth, Rolex necklaces that weighed up to 9 ounces, Versace glasses and apparel, plus everything else I could grab a hold of and stunt with.

After I flipped my first ¼ kilo when I was 17, I went on a spending spree, buying new cars. I went from a Cadillac Deville to copping a Regal, painting it a flip flop candy green, & sitting it on 30s and vogues. Afterwards, I purchased a Dayton sitting on all gold rims. I wasn't even old enough to put it in my name, so I had my older cousin sign for my cars as I bought them in cash. I was making a lot of money and refused to be stopped.

In 50 Cent's classic debut album, "Get Rich or Die Tryin," one of the lines he said was "Don't chase the women, chase the money, and the women will follow." With all my new fancy possessions, I quickly learned this was true, as the females began going crazy. I'd go to teen parties and be the life of the party. As a young, fly d-boy, girls were attracted to the interesting fast lifestyle I lived.

Even the nerdy 4.0 G.P.A.-type pretty girls in high school were fascinated with my life and the way I was living. To see a person their age with so much money was mind-blowing to them. I would pull up to their high schools, with the "flip flop" ride, the bass on blast, bumpin' UGK. The chicks couldn't resist. "Snatch & Grab" is what I would call it, living a lifestyle where I was running through as many beautiful females as possible.

At the peak of my hustling, I was making over $50,000 a month profit. I had become one of the major dope boys in my area and "Dat Dude" all the other dope boys looked up to. As Rick Ross said in his first hit, "Every Day I'm Hustlin'." That was my motto. Every day I would wake up, pour me a shot of Remy, roll me a blunt, and get straight to grind mode. I would cook up a quarter of crack, ride down to my main hub in Jacksonville, which was Mayport, and hit all the spots and sellers I needed to for that day. Throughout much of the day, I was conducting meetings with current and new plugs as well.

I was also "Blowing Money Fast!" My splurging had grown to a point where I was spending, on average, $1,000 a day. I would hit the mall daily. I was the jewelry stores' top customer. I would cop everything from Rolexes, Franco chains, and Cuban links. I also stayed coppin' and poppin' tags. I never wore the same gear twice. I never washed clothes either. I just had a big pile of new clothes in bags and boxes of unopened kicks.

Then I would hit the club every night and put on a bottle-poppin' show for the city. Every night was full of a lot of drugs, sex, and hardcore hip hop (in place of Rock & Roll). I had a plush 3-bedroom home in a nice area of Jacksonville at the time called Sandalwood, with serious whips in the garage and driveway. I had all this before I turned 21. I was living the dope boy American dream.

This superficial success gets to your head; I started feeling like I was the best and built for this. Everyone was jockin and so impressed that I was able to make money and stunt in a way most couldn't. I began thinking I was invincible. This fueled a false sense of greatness within me, and I was delusional in my dominant mentality. This pushed me further into wanting to ball out. My goal then became to stunt the hardest. I wanted to stunt on everybody, by pulling up to the hottest spots in the baddest whips, looking the flyest in the best VIP sections, copping the most expensive champagne bottles, and being surrounded with the baddest women.

Catch Me If You Can

I knew this lifestyle came with a cost, but I thought I could be the one exception to avoid it. Most hustlers in the game eventually get caught or killed. I saw it happen time and time again. However, I thought I could beat the streets and the fatal hands of time. I knew the Feds/DEA were on me. I would see them posted up around my crib as well as various spots I would hit up. But I was so high on weed most of the time, in addition to being super high on myself, that I always thought I could out-maneuver them. I was so cocky that it got to the point where I almost wanted to go knock on their car windows before I left anywhere to remind them to come follow me, like "Catch Me If You Can!"

One of my main tactics to evade the Feds was to just out-race them in the fastest whips. I bought an '87 Buick Grand National just for the strategic purposes of racing from the police. This was the fastest car I ever had. The FBI eventually banned this car, because dudes were souping them up and getting away from the cops on the highway. I was one of those dudes. I had souped-up my Grand National something serious, with a new transmission and turbocharged engine. There were several times where I had to blow the spot quick, and I was straight getting my Dale Earnhardt Jr. on. Pedal to the metal; 0-100 real quick. Ghost!

During this time, I was also getting arrested frequently. My record was far from clean. But I had so much money that I could hire the best lawyers, who would always find a loophole to get me off. I spent well over $200,000 on lawyer fees and bonds. That became a monthly expense that I knew came with the territory of my level of hustling.

But every move I made, thinking I was getting away with something, was just a deeper step into an inevitable quicksand of incarceration. The DEA had been building a case on me for quite some time. One day out of the blue, they approached me at a restaurant while I was dining with my wife and arrested me on a drug conspiracy charge. I GOT CAUGHT...and for the first time, I had no way out.

My lawyers made it very clear to me that the gig was up. The only real viable option I had was to cop a plea. In 2001, with my wife at the time pregnant with our first child, I was sentenced to do 6 years and 6 months in prison. I was only 22.

It Ain't My Fault

In the beginning of my prison sentence, I did not take personal responsibility for the crime. I was convicted of a drug conspiracy charge, which means I didn't have direct contact with the informant. So in my mind, I didn't do anything wrong. I felt the rules of the game were set up so "they have to all-out catch me red-handed," and they didn't. But I learned you don't have to believe in karma for karma to believe in you.

Everything that I did do wrong in the streets ended up catching up with me that very moment I was sentenced, handcuffed, and brought to the FCI Jesup Prison in Georgia, where I did 4 years and 9 months from 2001-2006. During my first conviction on conspiracy, there were numerous crimes I had committed in selling drugs, for which I never got caught. I got the conspiracy charge because I chose to live a lifestyle that was heavily involved in criminal activity.

We try to justify our actions by trying to stick to some moral code. Even when living a life of crime, every man wants to live by a code that reflects some sense of honor. One of my rules when hustling was that I would never sell crack to a pregnant woman. But guess what? I sold crack to mothers with children. I'm sure there were plenty of times their kids did not have a good Christmas, dinner for Thanksgiving, or a TV set to watch their favorite cartoons on, all because I capitalized on their mother's destructive addiction to crack cocaine.

My rationale would be "if I don't do it and make a serious come-up off these addicts, someone else will." But the problem is, I did it; so all of the consequences fell on me. I made crazy money by selling drugs that made people crazy and out of control, so I could live a crazy wild life, which all led to losing my freedom and being locked up in a crazy jungle called prison. Ironically, my mind was too crazy and twisted to take full responsibility for my crazy actions that put me in this crazy place.

I would blame anyone but myself for being locked up. The punk judge, prosecutor, cops, system, and of course "the man." Was I alone in thinking this way? Not at all. I began to notice the majority of inmates felt the same way. Hundreds of criminals locked up in this one federal penitentiary, but it was hard to find one man that could admit they were in the wrong and deserved to be removed from society. Everybody was in the joint supposedly because of outside factors other than themselves.

A turning point for me in prison was when I finally started processing how irresponsible it sounded to hear inmates try to justify the crimes they committed. "Man my ole lady was putting a lot of pressure on me, and I had to get my kids them school clothes." This was the reason an inmate gave me for why he ran up in a bank with an assault rifle. He needed to rob the bank of thousands of dollars, all to do some back-to-school shopping for his kids? After receiving life plus thirty years, I'm sure his kids have clothes on their back. But he's missing out on their lives and unable to give them much of anything in prison. The harsh reality is that he will never see the light of day as a free man again. On top of that, his ole lady stopped visiting him and got engaged to another man.

After hearing countless excuses like these from other inmates, I realized that if I didn't start taking responsibility for my actions, I would continue to live a delusional life like these guys. Not taking personal responsibility severely cripples a male from learning from his mistakes and properly rebuilding his moral foundation as a man for controlling his own life. I realized that I hadn't fully become a man yet, because I wasn't holding myself accountable for the wrong decisions I constantly chose to make all my life.

Self-reflection is necessary to dig deep and ask "Why." Why am I so prone to making decisions that have ruined my life? Understanding is the key to accepting responsibility because you gain a clear grasp on why you should and should not do certain things, which improves your ability to make right decisions in the future.

Aggression

Why was I so aggressive as a young boy? Why did I feel the need to fight all the time to prove my worth? When I was first released from prison, I had to see a psychiatrist, who told me the source of my pain was a subconscious anger directed at my mom. When they told me this, I was like "what the heck is this fool talking about? I love my mom." But I could not argue that there had always been a rebellious energy within me that drove me to fight all the time. What was I really fighting?

My mom had me when she was very young, 17. She was always going out, so I was with my grandma all the time. I was with her so often that I would call my mom "Tina" and my grandma "Mom." I'm sure I did this because I would just use the same names they used that I heard so often. Just this dynamic alone reflects how disconnected I was from a traditional mother-son relationship. My mom was always gone, and my grandma practically raised me. It could definitely be the case that I had a deep-seated anger towards my mom for not being there—a deep resentment I didn't even know about. It only surfaced in situations where I felt rejected by others, and that's when I would fight.

Poverty, parental neglect, and growing up under harsh circumstances can quite naturally affect the way we react to life. Those experiences as a child do shape the perspective through which we see the world and our place in it. I am very aware that I can be stingy at times, to the extent where I never pull out a lump sum of money. This is because whenever I pulled out money around my mom as a child, she would take it. So I didn't trust my mom the way a child normally should. It also reinforced a stigma within me that whatever I had, someone else was going to find a way to take it. That included not only material possessions but also my pride and respect. So in retrospect, I did fight, mostly to protect myself and what was mine—whether it was my jacket, my money, my self-confidence, or my pride.

Many young black males are labeled for lacking self-control. But some of the negative conditions we are forced to live under are totally unimaginable to the average person: never knowing your real dad; mom rarely being home; never having air-conditioning; living in an apartment infested with rats and roaches; crackheads running from drug dealers that they owe, on the playground you play at; or young boys you know being killed in cold blood. The psychological effects of a broken home and all the other ills within this kind of environment lead to extreme turmoil and inner conflict with a black child who experiences this daily.

Also in identifying with the aggressive manner in which society celebrates a man with power, a young black boy is tormented with how to break out from under such drastic barriers into full-fledged manhood. This is an internal fight like no other. So when it fully expresses itself as a child that fights all the time, it's quite understandable.

These circumstances are a lot to mentally process as a young boy. As it continues to eat us up inside, our emotions run wild because we can't logically explain it, but we have to release that fiery energy. This is done through fighting and other violent measures that clearly show we have lost control. Our only way to cope with the situation at hand is by eliminating the filter between our feelings and actions. We just impulsively react with violence from feeling offended and upset. However, it is never an excuse. Never! You're always the sole controller of your destiny and the outcome of your life. Whatever happens to you is ultimately because of YOU!

Looking back at all those fights I had as a kid, were they a gain or loss? In every situation we encounter in life, it will either add to our ultimate well-being or take away from it. When I would fight I would gain some respect, some cool points; and it was a confidence booster for believing I could defend myself well against others. On the surface I was empowered, and it appeared to be a gain. But the problem was, the more I fought, the more I was labeled a troublemaker in school. That led to teachers not wanting to deal with me and vice versa.

How could I learn and empower myself intellectually under those conditions? With this type of confrontational and disruptive behavior, how could I continue to learn all the important skills of reading, writing, and math at higher levels? What did my fighting reputation lead to? It led to more detentions, suspensions, and eventually being expelled.

School is the track kids are placed on to learn and mature into responsible productive adults. We're given 12 grades to refine our trajectory for being responsible and productive. I chose to buck the education system by continuously fighting and misbehaving, which led to blindly choosing to operate in the real adult world with real responsibilities, despite not having the adult skill sets or maturity to handle them.

This is too often the problem with our young black males, very similar to teenage pregnancy for young black girls. Choosing to be too grown too quick, we throw ourselves off track from the delicate safety net built for our learning and development during our youth, and naively throw ourselves into an adult lifestyle that brings about serious adult consequences that we aren't ready to be held accountable for.

Dropping out of school and choosing to chase fast money through a life of crime is equivalent to a phrase I heard rapper 50 Cent use—"flying on a private jet with no wheels." "It's a nice comfortable flight at first, but when it lands it will crash." You can only fly so long before you have to get back on solid ground. The problem is, that particular lifestyle has absolutely no way to safely land. You will crash, and in the very slim likelihood you survive, you will permanently hurt.

Power of Choice

In a perfect world, we could do anything we wanted. Whatever we said would go, and we'd never be wrong. Let's say everyone could, in fact, have their way and we could do whatever we wanted without consequence. Can you imagine the lawlessness? Some people commit crimes and say they were doing what they had to do to take care of their kids and family, or just doing what it took to survive. The truth of the matter is, no one has to do anything they don't want to do. When a person decides to commit a crime, that is a choice. The consequence of that choice is your own. YOU own it!

Master the art of being proactive versus reactive. This means dictating what you want the outcome of the situation to be before an uncontrollable outcome is dictated upon you. This is a very important life skill that will keep you out of unnecessary trouble as a child and adult. Being proactive is in fact very similar to being reactive. The only difference is that you envision the outcome in your mind first, so that you can do the reacting ahead of time. This means taking a few extra seconds to think and play out in your mind the consequences for all the options available. Then evaluate which option serves your highest good. One of the keys to life is avoiding and diffusing situations that can potentially turn into a problem.

Young black male, let's say you go to a predominantly white school; and during the middle of lunch, a white kid calls you a "nigger." You have at least three main options:

1) Punch the crap out of the kid, and make an example out of him
2) Turn away and ignore the kid as if he isn't even there
3) Confidently address the kid without fighting, and educate him on why you won't tolerate such name calling.

With Option 1, you definitely make your presence felt and release some anger that many believe is justified for such racism, but you could easily face being suspended and labeled a bad kid that can't control his emotions. Option 2 keeps you out of trouble, but doesn't deal with the situation in a way in which it won't happen again. This gesture may be mistaken as a weakness and motivator for the kid to continue making such racist attacks.

However, with Option 3 you can avoid an automatic suspension for fighting yet address that kid face to face. You can let him know he's using a racist term that has absolutely no power over you, but it's totally unacceptable to use that word anywhere within your presence. You can inform him that you would like to have a three-way convo with an authority figure to see if the kid has the balls to tell them what he said. Let them know that, for their sake, it's much better that the authority figure handle them versus the alternative, which is you whuppin' his behind! You can also let them know that shooting him the fade is something you're confidently capable of doing. But that would be the worst-case scenario, if it came down to it.

This is how to be proactive in not relinquishing your power—by initiating wise reactions that will deliver the best-case scenario for you, considering all possible outcomes. Marcellus' son Simeon took this exact approach at 10 years old in the 5th grade when he was confronted with this exact same situation. I was very proud to hear he handled it in this manner. After the white kid was disciplined by the teacher and his parents, the kid sincerely apologized. He told Simeon, "I'm sorry about yesterday. If I had known what that word really meant, I would've never said that to you." It seemed sincere and, most importantly, that kid never called him that word again. That's what you call going above and beyond to overcome ignorance in demonstrating a responsible superior mind-set.

The Trayvon Martin killing and court trial was one of the most disturbing tragedies I've ever seen unfold in all my life. For a young black teenager to be walking in a neighborhood where he's residing and be racially profiled, stalked, and murdered without the killer being convicted is beyond belief. One of the most sickening parts to the coverage was the way many in conservative media tried to paint Trayvon as a "thug." They tried to describe his lifestyle as one that may warrant being a possible threat to society, as if to say he could've put himself in a predicament where being killed by a grown man stalking him was an understandable option.

Many brought up the fact that he had on a "hoodie" as if that is gangster apparel. I will never forget a picture I saw of Trayvon, which made me sick to my stomach. Trayvon was lying dead on the ground at the murder scene, but his eyes and mouth were wide open. All this media talk about the gangster apparel and infamous "hoodie" he had on was ridiculous. I was able to see for myself that he had on some skinny jean khakis tapered at the ankle and an urban couture-type shirt with a fashionable hoodie, all laced with some clean white Jordans.

Anyone who is familiar with modern-day youth culture is aware that this type of apparel is about as non-gangster and non-threatening as any article of casual clothing can get. Skinny jeans are at the top of the debate in the hood for not being manly enough to wear once you pass a certain adult age. You definitely don't get a "hood pass" for wearing them. And as ridiculous as it is to label someone gangster because of a "hood" on their sweater, Trayvon's sweater looked like one that could easily be found in the most suburban trendy H&M-type shop.

Beyond sad, as I looked at the picture of Trayvon, his open eyes spoke to me the way the young black males did on the T-shirts at the indoor flea market. Trayvon's message to me was:

"Bruh, the only way I can explain this senseless killing that ended my life is ... it's not my will but God's will! It's God's will to use me as an example to bring light to injustices on so many levels. I did everything I was supposed to do in the face of those unfortunate circumstances. I know you are a father to a son; and just like my dad, I know there's nothing more you would want than for your own son to come back home. Let your son know that if he's ever faced with the same adverse situation I was faced with, his calling can be different from mine. I made this sacrifice just like Jordan Davis and many others, so that other young black males wouldn't have to. There is another choice. They can choose to use other powers they have within them to assertively avoid such ignorance. Educate them on how they can mentally overpower any situation just as effectively, if not more effectively than any physical tactic. It's all in the power of choice."

Young black male, there are times when you will feel like you have to fight. Part of being a man in this world is being prepared to fight when, in fact, you have to and there is no other option. Very similar to Trayvon, whom we salute to the fullest in our culture for what he had to endure that day to forever live in our hearts and history books for justice. However, young black male, one of the most powerful skills you can develop is learning how to control your emotions, because most issues you face are not life-threatening.

When you are feeling an unexplainable pain or struggle within you, that's an emotional intelligent indicator, triggering you to do something different. This is often the best source for pursuing life at a level of high passion and self-preservation most useful in cultivating success. At the root of that inner fire and anger is the power to move mountains and create sheer greatness.

Despite the many challenges within urban black culture, blacks have relatively low suicide rates in comparison to other ethnic groups in America. This reflects a very high emotional IQ to be able to emotionally cope with anything from poverty, drugs, high incarceration rates, absentee fathers, hundreds of years of historical oppression, and much more, while still "choosing" to live and not give up. We are warriors and fighters who are adored all over the world because of this well-known ability to survive and thrive in producing some of the greatest people in human history. You have the power within to become one of these people as well.

With this being said, we must become much wiser in recognizing that strength is not always demonstrated with our physical power and willingness to beat someone up or take their life. Despite society's celebration of physical manpower, there is a disproportionate level of punishment handed out to young Black Americans following the same path. So it's paramount that we take full responsibility for our actions. We must master the art of channeling our emotions through our mental power and discipline, to logically overcome turmoil—whether that is at home, in school, playing sports, on the job, or in the streets. Develop the ability to diffuse situations by applying strong thinking and verbal skills to handle issues.

Martin Luther King Jr. once said, "Don't let anyone take your manhood." He was by far one of the greatest men and fighters to ever live. However, he fought with the power of his mind, morals, character, voice, and self-control, as a non-violent warrior for civil rights. Manhood equates to personal responsibility. Don't let anyone take away your ability to be responsible, disciplined, and forward thinking. With all the adversity we've encountered as a black race, can we ever afford to be irresponsible?

Don't let the world fool you or mis-educate you into forgetting that, as a young black male, you're a descendent of the very first African black man to father this entire planet. It's in your DNA to be an excellent and responsible father. Before you can be a responsible father and husband, you must be a responsible son, as well as a responsible student, colleague, co-worker, athlete, and any other role you take on.

What kingly heir would settle for being less than 100 percent man? Be 100 percent man by being 100 percent responsible. Young black male, take pride in knowing you're becoming a strong black man by taking responsibility for your actions. Freedom and true success is always a choice of the mind. We're born leaders and kings with an entire culture and state of destiny anxiously waiting for our collective greatness to break through. Let's empower ourselves and hold ourselves fully accountable for handling our business and getting the job done.

CHAPTER 2

Own Mind

What is the greatest luxury possession we could ever have? a Bugatti, a 100-bedroom mansion, a yacht the size of the Dallas Cowboys football stadium, or how about a private island? I believe our most valuable possession is something we already have, and something we should already own. Our greatest luxury possession is our OWN MIND. Our own unique perspective, intelligence, vision, imagination, rationale, and awareness ultimately create our reality. Before we do anything in life, we always justify on some level, within our own minds, whether or not we're capable of doing it and if it's worth doing. The primary driver for doing anything in life begins and ends with our OWN MIND.

We have 100 billion cells all connected within our brain to support the decisions we make. There is a popular theory that we only use 10 percent of our brain. However, scientists confirm that we use virtually every part of the brain, and that the brain is active almost all the time. I personally think the 10 percent theory applies to how much of our mind we normally decide to take full ownership of.

For example, let's say you own a luxury car and always ride in it with a friend. Only 10 percent of the time you drive and decide where to go. You normally choose to go somewhere not too far and rarely use any of the car's features. However, your friend drives the car 90 percent of the time with you in the passenger seat. He chooses to drive all across the country. He's putting heavy mileage on the car, driving from city to city while making use of all the car's features, like the booming audio system, satellite radio, GPS, air-conditioning, Bluetooth, Xbox, convertible top, mini-refrigerator, and Jacuzzi (yeah, I forgot to mention it's a luxury Hummer stretch limo).

I don't think it would be fully accurate to just say "you're only using 10 percent of your ride." No, your plush ride is being put to serious use. But it's your friend doing all the joy riding unsparingly, while making use of all the ride's fancy features. You're just sitting in the passenger seat. The car you own is being fully used and maybe even abused, you're just not the one driving it. In this case it would be more accurate to say, "You're only choosing to control where you go in the ride 10 percent of the time." But trust your car is going "somewhere" and being used in 'some way" with someone else in control.

This is exactly how our mind works. As long as we're alive, our brain is always working at full capacity at doing "something." Whether that's creating ways to make more money, cleaning, playing sports, driving, singing, reading, talking, texting, sleeping, chilling, or even being lazy and doing nothing. Whatever we're doing or not doing, the mind is working non-stop to do or not do it. So the problem is not our brain working; the problem is that we must take full control over how we want our mind to work. Do we assume full power over controlling our minds, or do we mostly give away this power to other forces outside of ourselves to ultimately control how we think?

Back in the Game

In 2006 I was released from prison. My mind-set was, "I'm about to get back to hustling I just got to be smarter and more careful." Unfortunately, I viewed those 4 years and 9 months I spent in prison as just a temporary setback to getting back to the dope boy hustle, while starting new legit businesses in order to eventually transition out of the game. I had made a lot of drug connects across the country while locked up and used them to operate. I had $12,000 stashed away that I came back to. I jumped right into a brand new 2006 Charger and got it poppin' again.

I knew I couldn't go back to being the major dope boy because of the tight watch the DEA and my probation officer had on me. So I operated low key as the "plug" and middleman who connected sources to each other. I didn't touch the drugs, I just bridged the connects and got paid off each lick. I also started a Home Care Company. A lady I knew, who was a certified nurse, worked there managing the care for senior citizens.

Close to 1 year after being out of prison, I was snitched on by a blood cousin, who was a smaller dealer that I had plugged in to a connect. In 2007 I was arrested for drug distribution and violating my probation. I was sentenced to 5 years in prison at the high-security Coleman U.S. Penitentiary in Florida.

Mind Reprogramming

The first time I was locked up, I was in a medium-security prison. The high-security prison I went to for the second time was much different. The prison was a lot dirtier, and the inmates were much more violent. It was the worst kind of ghetto prison you could imagine. At various times riots would break out, guards were attacked, and inmates were murdered. It was a war zone, where you had to protect yourself at all times.

Losing my freedom again for the second time and having to live under such hostile conditions began to weigh on me. Unfortunately, it took another prison sentencing for me to really begin to reconsider my ways. I recognized that I needed to really get right, so I would never have to lose my freedom again.

After 2 years, I was offered the option to enroll in the Modified Therapeutic Community (M.T.C.) within the Residential Drug Abuse Program (R.D.A.P.). R.D.A.P. is a voluntary one-year program that offers group and individual therapy to federal prisoners with substance abuse problems. Many inmates are interested in this program because, once completed, 18 months is taken off your sentence.

I had smoked weed and was an alcoholic for much of my life before prison, but that was not my main reason for volunteering. Although I had been a heavy drinker and smoker, I had gotten over those urges and had determined those bad habits were acts of irresponsible depression that contributed to losing my freedom. My main interest was the Modified Therapeutic Community (M.T.C.) portion of the program. I was told M.T.C. was designed to reprogram your mind and help you with your thinking skills to make significant changes for the good in your life. I knew this was totally what I needed.

I desperately wanted to change my life and stay out of prison once I got out. This offered me the opportunity to make a permanent change towards bettering my life by changing the way I thought. I wanted to learn how to master my mind and reprogram myself into a whole new person, while terminating every negative troublesome trait of the old Chris that led to my incarceration. I wanted to start driving my own mind, so I could begin controlling my own destiny. I signed up!

The M.T.C. program required me to fly to another federal prison in Herlong, California, about 50 miles outside of Reno, Nevada. Once flown there, I was 1 of 120 other inmates from all over the country who had also volunteered. We all lived together in one dorm separate from all the other prisoners on the same prison compound. They kept us all together exclusively as a unit for our program activities and lodging, but outside of those times, we also had to intermingle with the general prison population.

My first experience in the program was a session in which all the M.T.C. volunteer inmates were told to grab a chair and make a circle. We all picked up a chair and got in our own racial group. I grabbed my chair and sat next to all the blacks. The Hispanics sat next to the Hispanics, and the whites sat next to the whites. It literally looked like a pie chart. Every section of the circle could be clearly broken up and identified by a certain color and race.

The counselor said, "Look at what y'all just did! Y'all are so conditioned that you sat next to people of your own race without even noticing it." Truth was, we hadn't noticed it at all until he pointed this out. Prison was always very segregated. We were accustomed to sticking with our own for survival purposes. The counselor told us, "We're gonna mix all of this up!"

This initial exercise highlighted one of the main goals of the program, which was to break up ignorant ways of thinking, starting with racial division. They wanted to reprogram our minds to embrace diversity and interaction with all people, instead of succumbing to unhealthy thoughts and habits of racism. I thought to myself, "Wow, what a worthy cause; but man this is definitely not going to work, with all the racial divisions in the world and especially within the prison system."

My prison experience before then was by far the most racially divided environment I had ever lived in. We were always split into our own groups based on where we were from, gang affiliations, and most importantly race. Prison politics often reinforced this extreme segregation. The same racial groups would shower together, eat together, hang out on the rec yard together, work together, stay in the same cell together, and when it came down to it - fight together. One thing I clearly remember was the racial power shift in numbers during meal times.

Every race group would sit together at their own tables. As a particular race group grew, their space among the tables would increase. I remember at one point the Hispanics had a couple of tables just like the blacks and the whites, but the Hispanic group grew month after month, until they started overlapping into the black inmates' tables. Eventually, they ended up outnumbering the blacks at that table, so the blacks there had to move to another table alongside other blacks.

This represented part of the racial fight and the politics for gaining power and space in prison, something that is also very clear with the power struggles and politics within the real world. The mind-set in this world is that often there is not enough. So to get more, you must take from someone else. In a hostile environment such as federal prison, where most of your rights are taken away, this constant battle among racial groups was even more visible.

However, M.T.C. wanted to tackle this dilemma head-on. They continued to have us integrate and try to coexist in ways most of us were never accustomed to in prison or the real world. We were encouraged to do numerous things together, including staying in the same cell with someone outside of our race. But once word got around to the general prison population outside of the M.T.C. about our "co-racial mingling," many general population inmates had a huge problem with it.

Even in prison, where it would seem that everyone should want to change, there is extreme resistance to this type of change. Most wanted the racial prison politics to stay the same. Leaders of the Arian Brotherhood and the Mexican Mafia Gang on the prison yard said they did not want niggers in a cell with any of their own kind. The Black gang leaders on the prison yard responded by telling them to back off and let their brothers within the M.T.C. program do whatever was needed to complete the program and get out. From this, racial tensions began to grow on the prison yard as well as within the M.T.C. program.

I knew from past experiences in the pen that when things got racially intense like they had, you have to protect yourself and be on guard at all times. I had seen race riots break out before in prison. When they happen, anybody can get shanked up. So I began walking around with my own personally designed body armor on. I would wrap my stomach and waist up with several magazines, along with any other thick items I could use over my upper body. I would also layer up my clothing wearing multiple shirts and a jacket. I was ready.

One day during downtime, everyone within the program was watching TV. We had been trying to interact more with each other across racial lines; but things were intense, and we all began gravitating back towards our own racial comfort zones. So each racial group was at their own TV. In the area where I was, there was one Mexican Mafia gang member. He had his own TV, while several other blacks shared the same one. A black gangster disciple member, whom we called Squirrel, was heated about all the racial tension. Squirrel said "If he touches that TV, I'm gonna lay him out." The Mexican did, and Squirrel beat him down.

Race Riot

When this news got out to the general prison population outside of M.T.C., the Mexican Mafia gang members set up a plan to attack all the blacks in general population. One day they planned a setup where they brought out all the basketballs and other sports items to try and bait all the blacks to come on the rec yard. When many of the blacks came out to play, the Mexican Mafia gang stabbed them up. The blacks soon retaliated against all the Hispanics, and a huge race riot broke out. Dozens of inmates were seriously cut up and severely injured.

Due to this huge race riot, the warden locked down the entire prison, including M.T.C. for two weeks. During lockdown, no one is allowed to leave their cell. At the end of this two-week period, they made all the gang leaders "shot callers" come together to settle a truce. Because I was considered a vet from the penitentiary, I was called to represent the black Florida inmates during this meeting. All the leaders settled everything with a mutual truce, and the race riot ended.

It was obvious that the M.T.C. goal of correcting ignorant thinking as it related to racism had failed. The program began shifting more of its focus towards other therapeutic activities for reprogramming our minds. However, even this initial experience was a learning lesson for me. As intense as the racial riot and events leading up to it was, I discovered that I personally was not as impulsive to violently react. I would normally jump hard for my people. But here I was able to refrain from becoming physically or mentally consumed with reckless fighting for racial reasons that didn't benefit my goal of becoming free.

Roll Tide

Alabama University fanatics chant the rallying cry "Roll Tide." It's chanted to cheer their football team on to more touchdowns, defensive stops, and ultimately wins. The use of "roll tide" refers to the tidal waves in the ocean. They are very strong, and it's extremely difficult to go against the tide. A popular saying when sailing on the sea is to "roll with the tide." You can't control the powerful tide and waves, but you can properly adjust to them and make use of their momentum in going where you want to go.

I came to M.T.C. with the goal of changing how I think when avoiding trouble. So as the racial tensions escalated, I found that I gained an even stronger level of personal control over my mind and actions. It became very clear to me that I can't control other people. If others want to be racist and prevent others from peacefully existing, that's an ignorance all the way out of my control. I learned that I don't have to make others accept me. People are who they are, and if they choose to be racist, it's not the end of my world. The racist thoughts of others do not make me any less of a man. They have absolutely no effect on the man I am.

You can't make me jump on anybody as if I'm some predictable violent animal. You don't put the battery in my back to make me go. When it comes to Chris Freeman, I run the show. I determine with my own mind if I will or if I won't. I dictate everything that goes on in my own head and how I want to process it to live my life the way I want. I determined that not even the most racist Ku Klux Klan member could get me off my square in staying focused on controlling my own mind to go exactly where I want to go in life.

This newfound power over my mind to not allow outside circumstances to alter my own rallying "roll tide" really came in handy with my virgin hair business. The beauty supply industry that serves the black female market has been predominantly controlled by Koreans. I had never heard of other such ethnic groups allowing any blacks to have ownership in their hair business, and I knew they would never think of letting me in on their ownership, regardless of what I brought to the table.

As unfair and lopsided as this could be perceived, what other groups choose to do with what they own is their right. I have no control over it, and it would be foolish to try to control how they do business. However, I made sure that such a monopoly wouldn't stop my thought process on envisioning how I could enter the hair market and provide superior quality virgin hair. I had made up my mind that they couldn't stop me, and the successful results of the Beautiful Hair 4 U chain stores proves there was nothing they could do to stop my shine.

I learned by default through the M.T.C. race experiment that you must control the controllable, and adjust to the uncontrollable. Too often we do the reverse. We try to control the uncontrollable, and then adjust to what we do control, which is our own minds. Anything outside of you—whether that be a person, group, or event—is normally outside of your realm of full control. Yet we try to convince ourselves that we can control it. I can't control the bad weather, economic recessions, racist people fueling a riot, or anybody for that matter. I can only adjust to those situations and people the best way I can.

I'm not Superman, I'm not God, and neither are you. So when things happen, don't get all out of control by trying to control what's not in your power. Hitting your head against a stone wall or someone else's close-minded stone head will not make it move just because you want it to. This doesn't mean that you don't stand up and fight for what's right or pursue ways of gaining stronger influence; always do your best. But understand that it's not in your full control to make it go your way. So don't act erratic if it doesn't.

On the flipside, everything that goes on in your head should be totally controlled by you. Your thoughts, ambitions, and ability to process events are all on your mental home court. No one can stop you from dreaming about being a plastic surgeon, astronaut, President, or whatever you want to be. We have freedom of speech in our country, which means no one can stop you from talking about becoming whatever it is you want to be either. Once you convince yourself that your thoughts and visions can become a reality, no challenges in the world can stop you unless YOU let them. Never give away this power of thought to anybody. Always control your own mind at all times!

Self-Check

Before entering the M.T.C. program I had accepted responsibility for the crimes I had committed, but I hadn't clearly seen the wrong in the lifestyle I lived. I did want to change my life all the way around for the good, but I would keep in the back of my head the option of hitting the streets again if things didn't work out. If push came to shove in terms of providing for myself once I got out, I knew I could go back to hustling and selling drugs. It was my backup plan, until I had what I consider one of my greatest breakthroughs. It would change the way I thought for the rest of my life.

I will never forget one day at M.T.C. Everyone had to break out into groups, and each group was given pamphlets to perform a "self-check rational analysis" on eleven different scenarios that related to substance abuse. The purpose of the self-check exercises were to use our minds in evaluating a situation to weigh out the pros and cons. They wanted us to practice rationalizing what's best in situations for all parties versus acting out impulsively.

Part of the exercise involved each group playing out a skit for one of the scenarios. The skits were normally entertaining to see all these tough inmates, including myself, role playing and getting our fantasy Denzel Washington on. It was also a creative way to look at problematic situations to better determine the most rational way to solve things with everyone's best interest in mind.

This particular day I was watching as one group had to role play a scenario where the mom was on drugs and the kid was being neglected. There was a guy playing a junkie mom, and that was funny to see at first. But what made me see things in a total different light was the inmate who played the kid. He was a smaller guy with this innocent choir-boy-type face, so he made the role look very believable.

As the mom was walking around acting crazy because she was high on crack, the kid was trying to get the mom's attention and kept saying "I'm hungry! Momma, I'm hungry! Momma, Momma, Momma, I'm really, really, reeeeeallly HUNGRY!!!" I began to process what this meant for an innocent kid to be starving because his mom is too high to provide them the basics every kid deserves, like food. I, for the first time, began to see the horrible impact I had on so many kids and families as a drug dealer. Everybody requires food to live, especially young kids. If you don't eat, you'll die!

How many kids did I leave out to dry because I had their moms strung out on dope? I had cooked and distributed so much crack that I was well aware of the monstrous effect it had on adult addicts. However, I never thought about all the kids whose lives were ruined because of my role in selling crack. Drug dealers are only conditioned to see the mom with the money; we never thought about the kids at home suffering without proper food, clothing, or shelter because their mom is so high and messed up. Half the time she can't even remember she has kids dependent on her.

Yeah, I was making money; but it made me sick to my stomach to see how I literally was starving and killing thousands of innocent little kids. That consequence was far worse than my doing time in prison. I thought I was a high-profile d-boy, but I was something much worse than a drug dealer. I was a KILLER, a KID KILLER! I went around slangin something more poisonous than lead poisoning from an AK47 because I left holes in kids' stomachs from not eating for 2 weeks. Plus the holes I put in all those broken families were larger than the holes the most dangerous automatic firearm could leave.

I was a KID KILLER! I was killing their support system, dreams, and basic needs to live. The ongoing process of selling dope for years was worse than killing a kid. It was a slow torture because I was a part of a deeper process that had to be killing them inside. When considering everything at stake in hurting so many young lives, the cons heavily outweighed the pros. It would be ridiculous and evil to ever sell drugs again.

All the money in the world could never justify killing kids. By selling drugs, that's exactly what I was doing. Even in the movie *Scarface*, he had a code he wouldn't cross that ultimately led to his demise. As much killing and drug dealing as he did, when it came down to helping a man put a hit out on a person by bombing him with his kids in the car, Scarface murdered the hit man to prevent it from happening. I was being both Tony Montana and the Hitman. I no longer wanted any parts of either.

That skit and moment in M.T.C. changed my life and the way I would think forever. Forget the backup plan, it became so clear to me that selling drugs again would never be an option, NEVER! I will never again be in the business of ruining and killing kids' lives. Selling drugs consequentially does exactly this, and I was able to "self-check" my thinking to clearly see this. Ever since I was 14, I had been living a life of poisoning people to an unimaginable extent. No more. I told myself that day, "I'M NEVER GONNA POISON ANYBODY LIKE THAT AGAIN!"

I attribute 90 percent of the reprogramming of my mind to The M.T.C. program. Those 12 months were life-changing, helping me tremendously in correcting my thinking errors. I was able to clearly see what I was doing wrong and how it brought about harm to so many. I also knew I was creating horrible karma for myself, because I was doing way more bad than good.

When you do so much harm to others, I know bad has to come back with a vengeance towards you. That's why the ability to "self-check" and rationally analyze a situation is so critical. It allows you to avoid such destructive habits with deadly consequences. Through self-check, we're able to identify the root problem in any situation and come up with the best solution. I learned that our problems cannot be solved at the level in which they occur. You have to rise above the problem and create an almost "out-of-body experience" to look at the entire situation and all the factors involved to figure out the best thing to do.

That's why a coach is rarely ever a player on the field. That coach has to be able to see the entire game, removed from actively being in it. This way they can clearly see what's going on and determine the best way for their team to win. Phil Jackson is regarded as one of the greatest coaches in all of sports, winning eleven championships as a coach. To do this, Phil Jackson couldn't be out there throwing alley oops to Jordan and Pippen with the Bulls, or running the triangle offense at the point with Kobe and Shaq. To be the genius analytical coach that he was, Phil aka "The Zen Master" had to isolate his body and mind off the physical court, so that he could visually and mentally break down the game. In doing so, he was able to lead his teams with an analytical mind-powered approach to winning. We are the head coach of our own lives and must step away from a situation to truly evaluate the best winning moves to make.

Smartest vs. Fastest

Life is a game of the mind. The more you're able to do with your mind, the more you're able to achieve success in life. The body has its limitations just like the world we live in. But the mind can be unlimited, very similar to our infinite universe. The mind always controls the body, not the other way around. The most sophisticated computer artificial intelligence systems are designed based off the intelligence and power of the human brain. Because of this I tell my son constantly, "It's better to be the smartest versus the fastest!" This world is not controlled by the fastest, it's controlled and dominated by the smartest.

One of the worst myths slavery falsely projected about blacks was that we were incredible physical specimens, but inferior mentally. Centuries of ignorant slave conditioning sought out to paint black males as fast, strong, and physically gifted to the highest measures. However, we were purposely mis-educated, de-humanized, and reduced to perceived animals - lacking adequate thinking and mental qualities. We were historically conditioned to believe we were the fastest and the strongest, but never the smartest. Today the effects of this brainwashing are still evident as so many young black males aspire to be a ball player, rapper, or worse a dope boy. These young boys don't see any other way to be successful, because too often these are the only people they see who represent a level of success they can passionately connect to. They naively believe it's better to be the fastest versus the smartest.

It's quite natural in our society to admire people with special physical talents. That's why professional sports industries generate billions of dollars every year. Mainstream media glorifies athletes and entertainers for their remarkable physical gifts. Whether it's their elite athleticism, super good looks, amazing performing talent, or celebrity swag and possessions – we're infatuated with these mega superstars. However, the greatest idolization I see for such stars comes from young black boys in the hood. It feels like every other ethnic group of males is given the memo at some point in their maturation to manhood that it's better to be the smartest versus the fastest. But so often in the black community this memo is nowhere to be found.

Boys grow up being very physical by nature; so it's natural to idolize the fastest among peers. When I was young, we would have races out on the block all the time to see who was the fastest. If you were the fastest, you were king! You were the first one picked for all the football games on the block, and you were the most "jocked" because you were scoring the most touchdowns. Everyone strived to be fast. But I can't remember anyone striving just as hard to be smart.

The same props were given to the strongest boy. If you could pick up anyone and "flex" them on the concrete WWE style, or showcase that you could knock somebody out with a "one hitter quitter" or "2-piece combo," then you were that dude. If you had a reputation for being the strongest, nobody would bother you. Props were always given to the best at all the admired physical qualities like being the fastest, strongest, most "ups", best dressed, and best looking. But I can't remember anyone getting the same kind of props for being the smartest.

Just like when I was growing up, I hear the same occupations rattled off by the majority of young black boys. I ask, "What do you want to be when you grow up?" It's always either an NBA basketball player, NFL football player, or rapper. These are great careers, but they're only three out of thousands of great careers you can have. Plus, the probability of making it as a pro athlete or rapper are so risky and unfavorable in comparison to those thousands of other great careers.

For instance, let's look at making it to the NBA. First of all, the average height is 6'7". If you've ever been around a person this tall, it's almost scary; and that's just the "average." You can't teach tall, and the NBA is geared towards freakishly tall giants that reach a height most of us are just not genetically capable of. But you may be thinking, "So what, there are some average-sized guys in the league." You're right. But check out these stats:

- Only 0.03% of high school players make it to the NBA (3 out of every 10,000 players)
- 1.3% of high school players make it to a D1 college basketball team
- 1.2% of college players make it to the NBA
- 4,740 college freshmen positions are available each year out of 156,000 basketball graduates from high school[1]

So what if I told you, "Hey, if you can swim far out in the middle of the ocean, I'll pay you a lot of money. Oh, and by the way, there's a 1 percent chance you won't get eaten to death by a shark." Would you try your luck with this extremely low probability and go swimming? Heck no, unless you want shark teeth marks tattooed on your behind as your last life memory.

So why would you put all of your hopes and dreams behind this one career with such an improbable chance of making it. I'm all for beating the odds and pursuing being the next LeBron, but you need to be realistic. Take a serious "self-check" of your current basketball skills, height, and more importantly other fulfilling career options with a more favorable shot of success if you apply yourself.

The rap game is very similar. Millions of young brothas pick up a mic and drop their "hot sixteens." But very few successfully make it to the level of a Rich Homie Quan, Lil Wayne, Drake, or Jay-Z. Every year there are probably only twenty hot rappers you can name that are making serious noise in the music industry, and only about five new artists really break through nationally each year. So why limit yourself to just these nearly impossible careers?

Maybe you're thinking, "What's wrong with shooting for the stars? If I want to be rich and powerful, why are you hating on me?" Well, my response is, I don't believe you're shooting for the stars at all. For every LeBron James, Cam Newton, and 2 Chainz, there is a powerful person much richer than they are who is signing their checks. No, I'm pretty sure they're not faster. But if they own a business, making billions off the talent of these popular athletes and entertainers, many would argue that they're much smarter.

Forbes Magazine puts out an issue listing the 500 richest people in the world every year, all of whom are billionaires. In 2015 Microsoft founder Bill Gates was No. 1 at $79.2 billion, and *Facebook* Founder/CEO Mark Zuckerberg made it to No.16 at $33.4 billion.[2] Numerous other business owners in industries like computer technology, internet, investments, oil, retail, beauty products, food, and real estate were on it. Guess how many current pro athletes and rappers were on the list? None.

I personally like the Bill Gates model more than the LeBron James one. For me it's much better to be the smartest person over the fastest. Plus even LeBron leverages his athletic gifts into smart non-athletic related business opportunities. There are so many more long-term opportunities for finding success on so many levels when pursuing ambitions related more so to the use of your mind versus the body. You can make the fastest person work for you.

I don't have to be the smartest person. I just have to use my own mind smartly and strategically enough to be able to hire smart people. Through "self-check" I can recognize my own strengths and weaknesses. For example, with Beautiful Hair 4 U, I know as the CEO I am the best salesperson to talk about my product. Plus I'm charismatic and a natural leader who people like to follow. Now what I'm not good at or an expert at, I can hire or outsource others for. Heck, I could start up a hospital. I don't even have to be a doctor. I just have to know how to hire the best ones. This is called working smart.

Dunking a basketball, catching a football, and getting "turnt up" on the set of a rap video shoot are all cool and talented things to do. For those who are able to fulfill a dream while making a lot of money, that's an incredible blessing. But aspirations that involve using your creative mind to do great things in other areas of life can be just as incredible a blessing. Young black male, don't limit yourself or your mind. You're more than just a fast, strong, swagged-out person. You're smart and capable of putting in the mental work to be the smartest! You're a superior being with unlimited talents. Open your mind to exploring the endless boundaries and numerous outlets for making a mark on this world like no other.

Gifted IQ

When I entered the halfway house after successfully completing the M.T.C. program, I was tested for my IQ. This was a part of the standard evaluation process for being re-entered back into society. I scored a 131, which was considered gifted. My counselor looked at me and said, "Chris, this is a pretty high IQ! You're really smart!" I later found out that the average IQ score is normally around 100. Einstein's IQ was estimated to be 160, and Bobby Fisher the chess genius was 187.

My IQ score was a shock to my counselor, but it wasn't to me. Although my grades were horrible in school and I dropped out of high school, I always had a creative mind and a level of intelligence that enabled me to do well on tests even without studying. School was boring and irrelevant to me, so I rarely applied myself. But now, after all I had endured, I knew I was going to bounce back and make it. I had studied to show myself approved and earned my AA degree while in prison. I now had an even stronger urge to explore becoming the smartest during my next life venture.

After 2 months in the halfway house, I secured a job cleaning carpets with my cousin. I was released and placed on house arrest for 4 months. Although my curfew was at 7 p.m., I became the most responsible and timely person I had ever been, because I would not let my dreams and aspirations of making something out of my life be denied. I was filled with an intense mental focus that was relentlessly geared towards progress and positivity. I never missed curfew once or violated my probation. On April 28, 2011, I was taken off house arrest and officially became a FREEMAN!

There was an unstoppable drive that led me to breaking through the shackles of my ugly past. This drive got me through my prison sentence and gave me the mind power to overcome my alcoholism. It was my ambition and aspirations to go from the absolute bottom to the top in becoming the best person I could be. I think this sort of intense aspiration is directly linked to intelligence. My IQ test showed the counselor that I was logically gifted. But that test couldn't assess my aspirational IQ and drive, which was anchored by the power of my mind.

Just like me, I believe many troubled young blacks have a high IQ but are never tested. Plus young black males are tested in so many other ways that genius aspirational mind power is required just to survive. In the hood, we've been experts at putting together patterns from separated pieces for a long time.

The ability to dream and bring that dream into reality is a trait of a high aspirational IQ. That is the one thing I do like about young black kids aspiring to be ballplayers and rappers. Despite the humbling circumstances of poverty and a broken home, these kids are able to see through their immediate dark surroundings and internally shed light on a miraculous vision of becoming a superstar success. This inner aspirational intelligence leads them to connect with other perceived sources of greatness that they can model within their immediate surroundings. For those young black boys without a father or influential male in their life, they gain inspiration from a LeBron James, Cam Newton, or Lil Wayne - whom they can watch all the time on TV and the internet.

Unfortunately, many young blacks also gravitate towards the hustler on the block. So often these kids are not exposed to fun, empowering careers that can lead to happy and successful lives - such as doctors, dentists, computer engineers, and businessmen. They don't aspire to be that because they don't see enough relatable black men doing it. When they see nice material possessions and those who have it, they begin to idolize them—especially if they seem young and fly. In the hood and the media - it's the athletes, rappers, and drug dealers who have the material possessions they aspire to have.

This is all to say, young black male, "You are not crazy!" It's very understandable that you apply a high aspirational IQ to connect with what is most visual and tangible to you in breaking through your own struggle from the ugly bottom to the extraordinary top. But I challenge you to go a step further beyond a physically-driven aspiration, and expand your mental horizons to envision your greatest intellectual opportunities.

Don't limit yourself to just playing sports, rapping, or being the hottest hustler on the block. Commit yourself to developing your mind and brain muscle even more, so you can rely on the power of your own mind versus your body. There are countless opportunities to explore.

You know all the video games you like to play? Well someone learned how to make those games through software writing, and they got paid big money. Plus someone created a business to sell millions of those games to make even more money. You're intelligent enough to become one of those guys.

Look around at everything you love from your clothes, kicks, favorite foods, Snapchat, Instagram, your favorite commercials, your favorite cars, and that big beautiful building downtown. Each of those products were created and sold by some innovative person who got paid much more money than your favorite athlete, rapper, or trapper did this year.

Whenever you see a lovely woman rocking the best pure virgin hair in the nation...Beautiful Hair 4 U, it is a testament to a powerful vision that wouldn't be denied. Empower your mind with an aspiration so strong that you create a real version of what you want to become in your mind. Then bring it forcefully into the real world. Stay on course through your own "self-check" monitoring to make sure you're using strong rationale to make good decisions. Once you apply your genius to making this ambition a reality through the power of your OWN MIND, you become that real deal—100 percent thorough!

Chris turned a prison setback into a successful comeback…
by empowering his own mind

CHAPTER 3

Greatness, Dominance, & Killer Instinct: Stages 1-4 (PERSPECTIVE/PASSION/TALENT/WORK)

What did it feel like that day you hit the game winning shot on the playground? How did you feel that day in school when your teacher gave you back a test or project and you got a 100? How did you feel the very first time you received a paycheck you were proud of? How did it feel when your name was announced as the 1st Place Winner of a contest? How did you feel that time you were the absolute best at something and everyone in the room knew it? When did you feel most dominant, excelling in a zone that made you feel unstoppable? How did that feel, and what is it worth to feel that way again?

Normally, during these moments, we feel a thrill like no other. An exhilarating rush runs through our body, and time seems to stop. Even if you haven't achieved any of the following things mentioned, take a moment to imagine how you would feel if they did just happen. Imagine yourself being recognized as the best and No. 1 for something you love to do. If you visualize this kind of moment long enough, you could easily get goose bumps. This is the feeling of greatness, a feeling of being the absolute best at what it is you truly want to be!

Deep down I believe every human wants to be great! Every person identifies with a strong urge deep inside to be the undisputed champion at something. Being recognized by our family, peers, and the world as the best is an extraordinary feeling. Even more gratifying is the feeling we get deep within of knowing we're the best at something we have worked so hard and dreamed so long for. The journey and inner satisfaction accompanying life's rewards when we prove ourselves to be the best is what the drive to greatness is all about. I believe every breath of air and every pump of blood from our heart is designed to fill us with the life energy to pursue and achieve greatness.

7 Stages to Pursuing Greatness:

#1	Perspective:	"Your Stage" - understanding how you are set up for greatness
#2	Passion:	"Your Love" - discovering what you love to do
#3	Talent:	"Your Gift" - discovering what you are naturally gifted at
#4	Work:	"Your Will" - training yourself to WIN
#5	Mastery:	"Your Throne" - dominating and becoming the BEST
#6	Decision:	"Your Moment" - choosing to be the BEST, ALL THE TIME
#7	Impact:	"Your World" - leaving a legacy that changes lives and the world

In this chapter, we will discuss Stages 1-4, which are perspective, passion, talent, and work.

#1 PERSPECTIVE: "Your Stage" - *Understanding how you are set up for greatness*

The most inspirational stories are the comeback stories. In society we love to root for the underdog because we're able to witness the entire fascinating process of one overcoming insurmountable odds in making it from the bottom to the top. We see this especially in sports. The NCAA basketball tournament is one of the most exciting sporting events for this very reason. There are 64 teams competing in a single-game elimination. Regardless of what they did in the season, the game comes down to winning or going home. In this "survival of the fittest" competition, many upsets occur where a lower-ranked team upsets a higher-ranked team.

What we see during these upsets is a team that fights like they have nothing to lose. The perspective of these underdog teams that pull off epic wins is there's no pressure because no one expects them to win. They've already been counted out, so all they have to do is ball out. This was the case in the 2014 NCAA tournament when No. 14 Mercer beat the highly favored No. 3 Duke. The highlight many remember was the young white player for Mercer hitting the "Nae Nae" dance afterwards to celebrate the victory. For the record, Duke did manage to recruit a talented class of freshmen to lead them to an NCAA Championship the following year.

Point being, during these tournaments miraculous buzzer beater shots are often made because every team is fighting like it could be their last game. There's a sense of desperation these college athletes are playing with that makes them relentless and overachieving in many cases. We find that when our backs are against the wall, it's often the ultimate stage for a triumphant comeback towards achieving greatness.

I believe it was the legendary soul singer James Brown who said something like "You got to get down to get on up." Growing up in poverty feels about as down as you can get. However, the advantage to being from the hood is that you have nothing to lose. Because you have very little, you're forced to be creative in making the most of what you do have. This is a very valuable skill called ingenuity, which also reflects a high aspirational and creative IQ. Where many get stuck in not being able to see the logic with no 1s available to make 1+1=2, your aspirational and creative intelligence allows you to create as many 1s as you want to add towards the biggest sum you can imagine.

You learn how to work with practically nothing when you grow up without much and learn how to get by with less. I remember my friends and I would make basketball goals out of crates and hangers. To this day those were some of the most fun basketball games I ever played. We would make trampolines out of old mattresses and actually learned how to do backflips. My friends and I grew up learning how to flip and do gymnastics like we were training for the Olympics. We never took official classes but practiced with our own little resources we had available and used our imaginations.

I remember hearing in the news, while I was in prison, how the whole country was in such an uproar due to the recession the U.S. experienced in 2009. I thought it was ironic because now well off people experienced financial struggles that people in the hood have been experiencing all their lives. The hood is always in a recession. The advantage is you are used to having to make the most of a bad situation. You are used to being uncomfortable and operating in survival mode.

I remember talking with other cell mates like, "There's a Black President!?!? It's got to be on and poppin'! I don't care what they say about a recession, it's gotta be real sweet out there! There's no way you can't make money out there now!"

During a so-called recession, the stage is set for you to be strong during a time where most people are weak. In fact, the stage is set for you to become the strongest while so many others are becoming weaker. If you have survived the dangers and challenges of growing up in a disadvantaged environment, you're more strongly built with an inner toughness to progress beyond just surviving to thriving.

It's not as easy to be successful during tough times; so, many give up. Just like in the hood where we see so many giving up—succumbing to drugs, unemployment, abuse, violence, and crime. The world and every industry within it operate the same way. During a recession, many companies go out of business. Dreams are crushed and families are ruined all over. However, these harsh times are also where the most opportunity exists, because the competition and opportunity costs are lower. Most people are panicking trying to survive, so they sell things at a much lower cost and run away from the challenges at hand. The smart and mentally strong people take advantage of this in the streets as well as the business world.

Some of the most successful businesses started during a recession or tough economic time - like General Motors, General Electric, Disney, IBM, Microsoft, Apple, CNN, and Burger King.[1] The companies and people who are successful during the tough times are able to apply a perspective for winning at a high level by being more creative, resourceful, intelligent, and tough. During these "survival of the fittest" moments, they're able to see a triumphant way to win. Most others are blinded by challenges, believing they're doomed for failure and loss.

A popular business and life principle is "the bigger the risk, the bigger the reward." But when you have nothing and your back is against the wall, there is no risk. You can't lose much of anything because you have "nothing." So there's only an upside to gain and win. When I came home from prison the second time, I had absolutely NOTHING. No money, no hot rides sitting on rims, no clientele, no product, no nothing. I went from being the man who could pay all my ladies' cell phone bills to not even being able to afford a Metro PCS cell phone bill for myself. I had long, awkward-looking dreads because I couldn't afford to get a haircut on a consistent basis. To maintain a clean haircut would be too much of an expense for me, so I would put my hair in a ponytail just to style it in a way where I could avoid a haircut.

That was a very tough and uncomfortable time for me. But nothing was as uncomfortable as being cramped up in a tiny prison cell, where I had to do the No. 2 daily, right in front of another man cramped within 5 feet of me in the same funky cell. So I had a resilient mind-set and perspective on being able to still conquer the world, because I had been through hell and still could say I made it. I had reprogrammed my mind and had a newfound perspective that everything I went through was for a God-ordained purpose.

I did not die, and I was no longer a prisoner. I was, if nothing else, a FREEMAN. Everything I went through and lost was so I could rebuild myself the right way and attack the road to greatness. So that's what I did. I fought tooth and nail to learn everything I could about business, marketing, and the virgin hair beauty industry, to position myself as a successful and innovative entrepreneur who would turn this industry upside down.

I looked back at my life and saw that I was the man in the streets as a dope boy for a reason. I had certain qualities as a businessman and leader that brought me temporary success. But due to the life of crime I had chosen, it was short-lived. I had the right skills but was using them the wrong way. So this perspective became my unique edge in building my business, Beautiful Hair 4 U. In my mind, no other beauty supply owner in Jacksonville had been through what I had, so no other beauty supply owner would be equipped to stop my business success, regardless of what long-standing racial, economic, and competitive barriers were in place.

Now, as one of the leading virgin hair suppliers in Florida after only 3 years in business, I compete against beauty supply owners who have been in business for over 15 years. But guess what? They have more to lose than I do, and I use this to my advantage. I take calculated business risks that many of them are afraid to take because they feel they have too much to lose. Not me, I hustle like there is no tomorrow, because I know how it feels to be down and out with no tomorrow in sight.

Everything I have is a plus to me. Even with the current business success of Beautiful Hair 4 U, it wouldn't bother me one bit if everything crumbled and I had to go back to selling hair out the trunk. The most empowering perspective to this is I know I wouldn't go back to crime either. I made a permanent change in my life, and I know without a shadow of a doubt I can make it without reverting to a life of crime. I am clean, I am confident, I have truly made it from nothing to something, and simply stated I will not lose! I am built to win!

Young black male, what is perceived as our greatest weakness in our culture can in fact be used as our greatest strength. Regardless of the hardships you have faced in life and the crippling disadvantages that may have made you fall, you have the power to get up and place all your life experiences into proper perspective. They're all a part of your own unique, triumphant comeback story. It's all a movie script and screenplay for you to take the stage and perform to your highest abilities. This stage is set to pursue greatness in life and become everything you can imagine yourself to be. Let's Get It!

#2 PASSION: "Your Love" - discovering what you love to do

Everything we do in life is to ultimately make us happy. There is a popular quote that states "Life is made up of years that mean nothing and moments that mean everything." This is such a powerful quote to me because this speaks to life from a quality and not quantity perspective. A long life is nice, but it's the happy moments you create for yourself in life that makes longevity matter. The day-to-day requirements of life force so many of us to get a job we're not passionate about, go to school and attend classes we're not interested in, and spend countless hours doing stuff out of habit and boredom versus fulfilling activity that makes us truly happy.

Life becomes an amazing, purposeful adventure when you identify your passion. Your passion is what you would do if you never had to be concerned with money again in life. What purposeful and productive activity would you do if you never had to worry about money again? What activity makes you feel most alive and complete? What subject occupies your mind and curiosity more than anything else in the world? What craft would you be willing to wake up at 5 a.m. to practice because it gives you so much gratification? What's the one thing you enjoy so much that you lose track of time whenever you're doing it? If you could do one thing every day for the rest of your life, what would that be? What would you most want to do to best represent your love for God and humankind? That's your passion!

Passion is the energy that fuels your dreams into reality. It gives you the energy to want to work hard and get at it. To pursue greatness, you have to love what you do. You must have such a strong passion and love for your craft that you're willing to do whatever it takes to overcome any challenges in the way of making your mark.

Your passion shouldn't be confused with what you do strictly for pleasure. Your passion brings about long-term fulfilling happiness, whereas your pleasure satisfies short-term fleeting urges. A true passion doesn't come with regrets, but your desire to fulfill a pleasure can. Randomly having sex, eating chocolate cake, watching TV, and chatting on Facebook are pleasures. You may love to do those things, but there is a more productive and powerful desire you have that makes you completely happy. Our life experiences trigger various moments of real happiness where we encounter our life's passion.

When I was a young kid, I was always energetic and loved playing outside. We didn't get tired or stop playing until the dirt necklaces were on. We smelled like a herd of animals when we came back in the house from being outside all day. My friends and I used to play all kinds of games from "Hide-and-Go-Get It" (all the boys would seek out girls) to "Dat's Mine," (we would call out the names of cars that we liked as they passed, and then we'd claim fake ownership of them). We also played every sport imaginable, making use of whatever we had. We loved having fun, and that is an important part of being a kid, getting used to laughing and having a good time. It's also a very important part of life - maintaining your youthful and vibrant spirit, while continuously exploring outlets that make you happy.

Although I did not like school and found most subjects boring, I did like science. Science was always my favorite subject. I was always intrigued with how the world worked and how things were made. How could you mix water with so many other substances to create so many other different things like soda, beer, medicine, chemicals, and so much more? How can grapes be used to make wine? How could glass turn into sand?

I felt like a genius when I understood the speed of light is faster than the speed of sound, because when it's raining you see lightning strike before you hear thunder? I was intrigued that even though all we see is land for the most part, 70 percent of the earth is covered with water. I would look at a map and notice that the continents were like a puzzle that was separated - and then excited to find out that there's a continental drift theory stating all the continents were once together as one land mass. The Big Bang Theory and Theory of Evolution were all intriguing to me. Man evolving from apes over the course of millions of years? That's wild!

I really loved space, astronauts, and the solar system, too. It was so fascinating to me that the universe had no end. Like you could go a gazillion miles in space, and you weren't even close to traveling all the way through it. That was mind-blowing. I was intrigued by the fact that humans could fly in space shuttles and go to the moon, and satellites could be sent to other planets. The stars, the sun, and how the planets within our own solar system functioned was fascinating to me.

As an adult I learned that because of the speed in which light travels, when we look at the stars we're really looking at the past. Yes, what we see as stars in the sky is really the light that has traveled in light years from where that star was. So for stars that existed 10 million years ago that we see, we are really seeing the light from the star that took 10 million years to finally get to us. Meaning that star we see is really the past and what that star's light looked like 10 million years ago! That star may no longer exist, but we can still see the light that came from it 10 million years ago. So when we look into the stars at night, we are looking at past pictures of how the light from galaxies looked millions and billions of years ago.

The sun is 92,960,000 miles away from earth. So it takes light about 8 minutes to reach us from the sun. Meaning that when we see the sun, that's what it looked like 8 minutes ago. To this day science and space is amazing to me. Is there life on other planets? Are their aliens? I could ask questions about science and space all day long. As a kid, language arts and math were boring to me, but science was the stuff.

I also enjoyed social studies. I was always curious about how powerful governments and regimes were created. How were wars fought and won? How did Africa allow the slave trade to take place, and why did the whole world conspire to mistreat Africans in that way? I also really enjoyed learning about the greats in history and what they did to become great—People like Benjamin Franklin, Thomas Edison, Abraham Lincoln, Frederick Douglas, Harriet Tubman, Marcus Garvey, Albert Einstein, Martin Luther King, and many more.

Although I did not recognize it then as a child, science and history were passions of mine. If I had not clowned around and if I had learned to channel my energy more productively - I could've been placed on an early track to becoming a scientist, anthropologist, or even an astronaut. Ironically, today social studies and science are my son Chris's favorite subjects. I stay on him to read up on them as much as possible. I push him to study hard, especially in those subjects, because he has a natural passion for it. With the proper work, he can be much better than I am and become the best in those fields if he chooses.

Unfortunately, I believe I discovered my true passion the wrong way. The day I sold my first rock that I was supposed to be holding for my cousin, I was introduced to my passion for business. Although crack was the product, I became infatuated with selling. It wasn't my love for drugs, but more so my strong thirst for building an enterprise within a marketplace. I was in love with the science of business and providing goods in exchange for money. But it wasn't just making money that I loved, I was passionate about the entrepreneurial way in which I was able to make money and profit.

Here was this free market known as the Canterbury Court Apartments, with numerous buying customers in the form of crack addicts. There were dope boys supplying the crack product left and right. There was such a high demand for this product that when I showed up with it, I was able to sell it in under a minute. Plus I made enough money to pay my cousin back and keep $10 for myself. When I got my product to sell, I was able to make more profit and reinvest to buy more supply to continue flipping and growing my money stash. Then I could use that money to buy what I wanted without having to rely on my grandparents. This was what life was all about to me in my mind at the time. I saw a way to be unlimited in my hustler's ambition to making money.

Nine times out of ten, if you love hustling, you love business too. If I could've been introduced to another way of flipping sales legally—whether that was electronics, clothes, stocks, or real estate—I believe I would've been on the cover of *Forbes Magazine* by now. However, I was misguided and had to learn the hard way that there is a right way to pursue a passion, and an illegally wrong way that can jeopardize your life and freedom.

As wrong as my illegal dope boy hustle was, there is no denying that it represented a genuine passion that I had for operating a business and maximizing profit within a marketplace while grinding my behind off. I love absolutely everything about strategizing on how I can become the best business man I can. I am passionate about every marketing step of business from getting the product, setting the right price, promoting the product, distributing the product, and making a profit, while supplying a demand for my customer base. I love business and marketing, these are my passions. I eat it, I breath it, and I live it 24/7.

Young, black talented male, you too have a legitimate passion. Don't allow your passion to be misguided by a lifestyle that can lead to trouble and unnecessary danger. There is no such thing as being passionate about selling illegal drugs. That's a distorted pleasure for pursuing death, imprisonment, and the destruction of people.

You may find that you have a passion for debating subjects; that's great for becoming a lawyer. You may have a passion for helping people when they're hurt; that's great for becoming a doctor. You may have a passion for animals; that's great for becoming a veterinarian. You may have a passion for babies; that's great for starting up your own day care. You may have a passion for fashion, which is great for becoming a clothing designer.

You may have a passion for evaluating athletic talent or playing fantasy sports online, which is great for becoming an NBA or NFL general manager. You may have a passion for telling incredible stories, which is great for becoming a book writer or film director. You may have a passion for creating rules and leading people in a charismatic way, which is great for becoming a mayor or President of the United States. There is no limit to how far your passion can take you in life. Following your passion is a great way to ensure you're doing things that make you happy and fulfilled, which gives you powerful energy for pursuing greatness.

#3 TALENT: "Your Gift" - discovering what you are naturally gifted at
Talent is that natural gift you possess and do better than most other people. In many cases your talent is that thing you're able to do that others simply can't. It's a spark of genius that allows you to uniquely stand out through your performance of that activity. Talent enables you to connect and move people in a special way. Whatever you received top recognition for as a kid is often a talent at that time. Where your passion

may be what you like to do best, your talent is often what others recognize you do best. Your talent can be something you do so well that you may not even be aware of it because you do it so effortlessly. Talent is exclusive because it is your God-given gift to offer the world.

At a young age, my family and teachers recognized that I had a talent for getting people to follow me. In the mix of getting into a lot of mischief, I would always have a crew with me following my lead. My grandparents and teachers often referred to me as the "ring leader." I would get my friends together and start up some adventure for us to do. I would get friends together to build a treehouse or set up dirt bike tournament courses, where we would put all types of ramps and obstacles in place to go ham on.

In addition to being a natural leader, I was an adrenaline junky. I would be the lead daredevil doing all the craziest tricks and stunts. I loved taking risks; it gave me a serious rush. Whether it was doing 360s on the bike, getting on top of roofs to do flips off houses, or playing football on the block and trying to hurdle over anyone trying to tackle me, I was a wild, risk-taking energetic dude.

When I was young, I actually wanted to be a stuntman. I wanted to go to Hollywood and be the guy who would play double doing all the crazy flips and stunts like falling off buildings and motorcycles. I also was very aggressive as an athlete. I was always one of the fastest on the block, with a tough running-back style, and was naturally athletic. I enjoyed physicality and wasn't afraid to take a hit.

The charismatic, cocky go-getter energy I had about myself attracted people to me and contributed to my natural talent for being a leader. I was very confident in myself and felt like I could creatively pull off whatever I put my mind to. I think people also gravitated towards me because I had a talent for putting together next-level hustle ideas and could actually follow through on them, where most couldn't.

In the 6th grade, I decided that I wanted to organize a crew to sell candy at school. One day I went to the candy store and bought a load of candy to sell, mostly blow pops. I then went to Woolworths, a store that is no longer in business, to buy three walkie-talkies. I got my homeboys Jeremiah and Josh to sell with me. We were the crew.

During school, I would dispatch the walkie- talkies and communicate with them. I would take orders in between classes and talk to them through the walkie-talkies to deliver the blow pops where they were needed. I'd grab my walkie-talkie and hit the crew up saying things like, "Hey, Jeremiah, hit the 2nd floor and meet Tameka and her girls. They want some of that sour apple." "Hey, Josh, come in Josh! Hide the stash because we got a code red, the principal is coming your way."

We had a trump-tight communication system for moving those blow pops. Even to this day, ladies who buy virgin hair from my store joke around and tell me how they remember me hustling those blow pops in middle school. They remembered how I was the leader of the crew and had created a cool system with walkie-talkies and all for conducting my candy business.

I also coordinated gambling circles in the bathroom as well. We would skip 6th period and roll dice in the bathroom, where I would take bets. I enjoyed gambling because I felt an extra rush to perform when money was on the line. There was a clutch factor I would tap into to compete even harder when the stakes were high. My gambling obsession went hand in hand with my obsession for doing stunts as well. Part of the reason I think I was bored with school was because I felt like there were no real life stakes on the line. Money to me became the motivating factor, and unless money was involved, it wasn't worth it.

My personality and talents allowed me to conduct all these different activities effortlessly. I was able to create an aura and culture around me for getting things poppin'. I was naturally creative in coming up with money-making ideas, and I had the ability to follow through. During these times, I learned that I had something going on for myself that attracted people to me. My peers liked being on my squad and felt they could benefit anytime I had something going on that included them. This was because in their eyes I was winning.

I knew how to lead situations where we all could make money and be fly. I noticed that everyone wasn't able to come up with ideas quite like I could. Plus there were others that talked the talk but could not walk the walk. They would have great ideas but would never come through. My talent was being able to create structure and put things in place where I could make an innovative idea a reality real quick. There's a special magic to executing things and being successful at it. It's magnetic because people love success and want to follow that in being a part of a winning team. I had proven to my peers that I was about my business as a transformational go-getter who knew how to make things happen and win!

People also respected me as a leader because I would not back down from people. If someone bothered me, I would act out and often fight to make an example out of them. People admired this trait in me and followed me because they knew I had their back and would fight for them. I was known for stepping up to people and giving them the business if they crossed somebody close to me. I felt respect for me and my peeps was mandatory, and I would go to great lengths to make sure people got checked hard for getting out of line.

My knack for being a leader and organizing people was also what I used to work my way up in the drug game. When I started seriously selling crack, cell phones weren't out yet, so I had a beeper. When I reached a certain level where I had a lot of clientele stored in my beeper, I gave it to my older cousins that wanted to work under me. I put them on under me and began selling them crack at a wholesale price. This meant I didn't have to deal hand-to-hand with crackheads any longer. I began putting together teams of dope boys who would sell under me. This included my good friend Jeremiah, whom I put on to sell blow pops with me in the 6th grade. I had already dropped out of high school by the time he had dropped out of the 10th grade, and he wanted me to put him on.

When I was 17 years old, I bought my first ¼ kilo for $6,000. I was just a kid and didn't even have hair on my face, but I was cocky and knew I could put together teams to move weight throughout the city. At the time I believed in working hard, but even more so working smart, by coordinating my own system with more people to make more money. By 19 I bought my first kilo and grew to a level with my team where I was moving 20 kilos a month. I grew to a level where I sold to over 20 dope boys all around Jacksonville extending up to Georgia.

Great talent applied in the wrong way can be catastrophic. This careless way in which I was applying my talents of leadership, people skills, and development of business systems was a means to short-term gains and catching long-term losses. I became so confident in my dope boy enterprising tactics that I began to think I was invincible. I became such a cocky hothead and was so naive to the dead-end lifestyle I was living, that I often looked for trouble.

I would look for reasons to make an example out of people just to prove that I was powerful enough to do it. I could care less about jail being a repercussion for my idiotic actions, because with my dope boy grind I felt I could always buy myself out of jail. But all the talent in the world is worthless if you're applying it the wrong way. Too often that talent blinds you to the harsh realities of your self-destructive ways.

You know the statistic that stands out most regarding my awesome charismatic leadership and team building talents as an illegal hot boy drug dealer? It led to me getting arrested 32 times. My mind-set whenever I got arrested was, "my money is long enough to pay my way out of this." So I would lean on my talent to be resourceful in finding good lawyers I could pay to beat my cases.

When I was 18, one week I was out on five felony bonds at the same time: two crack cocaine charges, assault, attempt to allude, and something else ridiculous. I had two lawyers at one time fighting my cases, and I was paying them serious money. I'd go in a courtroom and sit my arrogant behind in the back. When my case came up, I'd sit in-between the lawyers chilling and let them do all the talking for me.

They found ways of getting me off every time: sometimes proving there was an illegal seizure, or sometimes paying off the witnesses who were supposed to testify against me. I thought I was above the law, because of my talents and their short-term rewards. I never was sentenced to the county or state prison. I would tell myself, "the only way I could go down is if they send the Feds to come get me." Guess what? They did! All the money and street credibility gained from my talents went right down the drain when I was eventually taken away by the DEA and sent to prison.

However, after being broken down to a point of knowing I had to completely change my life once incarcerated for the second time, I was able to shift my mind towards applying my God-given talents and passion towards an entrepreneurial venture that would be legit and a million times more rewarding. I used the same talents that got my blow pop candy business poppin', as well as my dope boy business network, to create one of the largest chains of quality pure virgin hair in Florida—Beautiful Hair 4 U.

One of the keys to greatness is synchronizing your passion with your talent. This is combining what you love to do with what you're really good at. I loved engaging in profitable business, and I was very talented at organizing networks of people. For me the two always went hand in hand seamlessly.

Young black male, you have a talent and God-given gift that effortlessly shines in everything you do. There is something special that only YOU can do. Despite the wrong or misguided roads you may have traveled, you have a talent that can be used for your highest good. Don't just waste your talent on meaningless activities that take away from your life. Find the best outlet to blaze your light, because your invaluable talent can very well make a superstar mark on this world.

#4 WORK: "Your Will" - *training yourself to WIN*

As the author John Maxwell states in the title of one of his bestsellers, *Talent Is Never Enough*. No great person just wakes up and starts winning championships, winning Oscars, winning Nobel Peace Prizes, generating billions of dollars, or impacting millions of people. It's a long process in which the common denominator is work. It takes putting in serious work to be the best!

The greats become great by doing what others won't do. It takes incredible sacrifice, discipline, and will power. Nothing worth having comes easy. Success is a process that takes time. Great work is the invisible engine of human progress. Talent is a special ability you are born with, but skill on the other hand is something you acquire after putting in a lot of work refining your talent. Entertainer Will Smith said, "The separation of talent and skill is one of the greatest misunderstood concepts for people who are trying to excel, who have dreams, who want to do things. Talent you have naturally. Skill is only developed by hours and hours of beating on your craft."

No matter how talented you are, a great work ethic is imperative to honing your craft and becoming a master expert in consistently delivering extraordinary results. Great talent with no work ethic will eventually be dominated by no talent with a great work ethic. Everything you need to be great is already inside you, but you have to work your behind off to make your dream a proven reality. When you witness greatness taking place in any field, it is often the refined result of hard-core practice and work.

Michael Jordan's personal trainer Tim Grover wrote the book *Relentless*. In it he breaks down how Michael Jordan went above and beyond with a relentless mind-set and work ethic to turn his great basketball talent into an unstoppable skill. When Jordan decided to take his game to an even higher level in pursuit of his first championship, he started a workout regimen with Tim Grover called the "Breakfast Club."[2]

Jordan wanted to go above and beyond to improve his stamina and conditioning, because he felt that was required for peak performance to break through the grueling course of the season and playoffs in pursuit of a championship. So he created the "Breakfast Club." A couple of teammates, including Scottie Pippen, would come over to his house at the crack of dawn to do serious weight lifting and conditioning with his trainer Tim Grover. After a hard workout, they would have Jordan's chef cook breakfast for them and they would all chat, before going to team practice and putting in more hours where most players were just starting their day. This is just one example of how the greatest basketball player didn't just rely on his amazing talent, but a relentless lifestyle of working harder than everyone else to achieve greatness.

A story hit the net of an athletic trainer who worked with Kobe Bryant during the 2012 Olympics. He got a dose of Kobe's tremendous work ethic first hand. The trainer met Kobe for the first time earlier in the day. He told Kobe if he needed anything to give him a call. The trainer heard his phone ring early that next morning at 4:15am. It was Kobe asking if it was ok for them to meet at the gym for a workout. The trainer agreed, and when he arrived at the gym at 5am Kobe was already drenched in sweat.[3]

For the next 2 hours, they worked on conditioning and a series of strength training exercises in the weight room. Afterwards, Kobe went to the court to shoot around, and the trainer went back to his hotel to crash. When the trainer went to the Olympic Team practice that afternoon he greeted Kobe and said, "Good work this morning." Kobe said thanks and the trainer then asked, "When did you leave the workout facility?" Kobe said, "Oh, just now. I wanted 800 makes, so yeah, just now." The trainer's jaw dropped as he said to himself, "Mother of Holy God!" Kobe had never left and had been working out for over 6 hours...before practice even started.[4]

It was then that he realized why Kobe was well into his 30s and still wrecking shop in the league as one of the greats. Talent even at Kobe Bryant's level is not enough. Greatness requires tireless hard work!

Michael Phelps is a professional swimmer and the most decorated Olympian of all time with a total of 22 medals. Phelps' swim trainer Bob Bowman said, leading up to the 2004 Athens Olympics, Phelps trained every day for 6 years straight—not one day off.

When a reporter asked Bowman, "You all trained on Christmas too?" Bowman replied, "Yes, we trained twice on Christmas day." When everybody else was off on vacation sleeping in late and celebrating the Christmas holidays with their family, they made sure Phelps didn't divert at all from his workout. In fact, while everyone else took off, he went twice as hard. Christmas can wait, but greatness can't. That is definitely the unyielding mind-set and work ethic of a true champion.

An incredible work ethic is also the common thread for the great business leaders of our time. When the richest man in the world Bill Gates started Microsoft with friend Paul Allen, they would work on software programming every day until 3 or 4 a.m. When Microsoft first opened its offices, Bill Gates would stay in his office for days. One day his wife and receptionist at the time came into work and was so alarmed she wanted to call the cops. She saw a man sleeping under his desk, and figured he was homeless and had snuck in. It was Bill Gates, taking a quick nap after a series of all-nighters. Even today, the cafeteria at Microsoft Headquarters in Redmond, Washington, is open until midnight to allow for people to work late.

When launching Apple, Steve Jobs gained a reputation for being unkempt and having bad hygiene. Jobs would go days without showering, deadlocked on constant computer programming. Mark Cuban, billionaire and owner of several successful businesses including the Dallas Mavericks, said when he started his first company he routinely stayed up until 2 a.m. in the morning reading about new software and went 7 years without a vacation. General Electric CEO Jeffrey Immelt spent 24 years putting in 100-hour weeks. Pepsi CEO Indra Nooyi worked the graveyard shift from midnight to 5 a.m. as a receptionist to put herself through school for her master's degree at Yale.

Even our most celebrated entertainers put in endless hours of work that we couldn't imagine. At one point in rap icon Lil Wayne's career, he decided to go from a cliché hot boy rapper to one of the best lyrical rappers of our generation. Many see his swag and seemingly carefree lifestyle and think his music success comes easy to him. No, to achieve his iconic status in the rap game, Lil Wayne had to do way more than just smoke weed and lay up with chicks. Lil Wayne put in that work.

Lil Wayne began putting in countless hours of work in the studio and made a commitment to out-rap the entire industry by outworking everyone in it. Around 2004, Lil Wayne went on a lyrical barrage, releasing numerous hot mixtapes one after the other, creating a buzz that elevated Lil Wayne to No. 1 status on MTVs popular "Hottest MCs in the Game" Top 10 list in 2007. Every time you jumped on the internet, turned the radio on, or stopped at a red light, you heard a new hot Lil Wayne verse that he was killing. All leading up to one of the most anticipated albums in rap history.

In 2008, despite the decline of rap sales from the internet and his album being leaked early, Lil Wayne released "Tha Carter III" and sold over 1 million copies in the first week. One rapper observed Lil Wayne's work ethic and said "he puts in work at the studio like he doesn't have a dollar in his pocket. He's always recording!" This means he's always putting in that work.

Every Day I'm Hustling

I've always had it in my mind that "you're not going to outwork me." Even when I was hustling crack on the streets, I used to get up early before all the other d-boys to hit the spots. I would hit all my areas up to sell, so by the time all the other d-boys were just waking up from sleeping in late, I had already gotten all the morning and daytime traffic. By the time they got out of the bed to hit the streets and really hustle around 5 p.m., I had already hit my quota for the day. I always made it a point to make my work ethic stronger than yours.

Actor and comedian Terry Crews once said, "The road to greatness is always under construction." And I would add to it that there are no detours. So once I learned the hard way that putting in work as a drug dealer is the epitome of "hustling backwards" all the way to a prison or cemetery, I took that same work ethic and applied it to my business - Beautiful Hair 4 U.

To this day, I wake up early at 5 a.m. I tell my employees while they're asleep, I'm up working. While they are turning over in their bed, I'm in my home office putting in that mental and entrepreneurial work. Every day I'm still hustling. I wake up early and stay up late working. I'm strategizing on ways to make my business better, faster, leaner, and bigger.

As I'm writing this now, payroll is tomorrow. I have to know how much money should be in each bank account to pay my entire staff for four stores. In addition, I have a couple of new competitors arising in the market. So I have to strategize on how I maintain my edge as the leading virgin hair supplier. I must make sure I do even more things to ensure my brand stays at the top of every lady's mind, so when they think of the best virgin hair, they think of Beautiful Hair 4 U. My brain and my business must be ready to work 24/7.

Many people have big goals and visions, but the drop-off comes when it's time to put in that work. Their work ethic isn't strong enough, and that's where it always comes back to bite them. They can never get a great business idea off the ground. Or they do and can't stay in business long, because they don't have the work ethic to consistently deliver a quality product or service. Or they can't grow their business, because they don't work hard at the management aspect of generating resources, manpower, technology, and capital to adequately expand.

Even when you become the best, there is a whole new ballgame of relentless work to stay at the top. When you're making your run to the top of the mountain, it can feel new and fun. But once you conquer that mountain and have to do it again and again with a target on your back, it gets real tough. As other competitors are using your success as a blueprint for theirs, you have to work even harder to go from good to great, and from great to the greatest.

I entered the Jacksonville market as the only pure virgin hair supplier. A couple of years later, many other virgin hair businesses have now popped up. Plus, my target market is constantly changing and introducing new dynamics I must consider. I have to stay on top of my game, so I have to work even harder to continue capturing the lion's share as the market leader. Point being—the work never stops, never! You will always have to put in that work to be the best. It's an ongoing infinite process.

It takes work to get what you want out of life. The shortcuts are short-lived because you have a weak foundation. Despite the hard grind that I put into the streets as a dope-boy, it was a losing cause because there was no longevity. It was a "renter's" lifestyle, where I was getting everything illegally, meaning I couldn't "own" anything. I couldn't own the drugs, which were the lifeline products or the expensive possessions I bought with the drug money. In fact, I didn't even own my life.

My life and freedom was for rent, with no guarantee, because at any time I could be evicted from life by getting killed or sent to prison. My freedom could be taken away from me at any time, along with everything else. Once I did get arrested and sent to prison for the second time, I knew I had to grind and put in work the right way. This was the only way I could out-right own my life and truly be a FREEMAN.

There is no logical reason for living a life of crime. It's a short-term fantasy to a long-term hell. Good legitimate hard work is fulfilling, because it's gratifying knowing you're building up your own incredible stairway to greatness. Bad shortcuts ultimately take your life and do exactly that—cut it short.

As a dope boy, you're putting in work to make more money selling drugs. This gets you more hot cars, hot chicks, and nice homes. However, at some point the IRS is going to want to know how you're accumulating all this nice stuff. Now you have to set up a business that is illegitimate because you're constantly funding it with illegal dope money.

You're also more of a target in the streets, which means you're at way more risk of jack boys, other envious drug dealers, and of course the cops. The more money you make, the more luxury items you get, the more you're setting yourself up for a bigger fall. You won't be able to get full credit for the work you're putting in because you're mastering the wrong outlets for doing it, which can only expose you.

A goal without work is just a dream, but work without a legitimate goal is a nightmare. A life of crime is pretending to live a dream when you're really creating a nightmare that will come to haunt you. It's not worth it. Put in the right work and get the right unlimited results.

Start Somewhere

Instead of going out and taking other people's property or selling drugs, look for a job. You have to start somewhere. Once you put in the right work that gets the right results, you "earn" the right to get whatever it is you feel you deserve. But giving up or resorting to crime after filling out a couple of applications and saying "nobody is hiring" is BS. In most cases, I've found somebody saying "nobody is hiring" means "I haven't really been looking." If you can't get a job, make one! Heck, collect cans if that's what it takes to legally provide for your family and secure a starting place for going wherever you want to go in life.

In life you will not always be able to start off as a top manager in a nice office with a downtown 45th floor lakefront view. Wanting all this while not having any idea of how to manage payroll, taxes, lawsuits, and so many other things that come with the responsibilities of those titles is delusional and unrealistic. But finding a starting place, even with an entry-level position, is a great place to begin.

I'm proud when I run across young brothers who tell me they just started working at McDonald's as a bus boy, or at Winn Dixie as a grocery bagger. I tell them to be on time and put in the work it takes to develop a skill they can build on, to one day own their own McDonald's franchise, restaurant, or grocery store with their name on it. You have to start somewhere and you have to attack the process of putting in work to succeed in life.

Young black male, we're built to grind! Our entire urban culture celebrates the dedication it takes to become successful by getting it out the mud. The bottom of the earth is very muddy and dirty, but it's the start to where everything naturally grows. You reap what you sow, so begin planting those seeds and putting in that work to grow the desirable fruit of a good life. As men, we are built to work. As black men, we are natural born leaders gifted enough to show the world the "right" way to work a dream into reality.

Our minds, bodies, and souls yearn to create the fabrics of our own greatness by grinding our way to that top spot on the mountain we know has our name written all over it. Develop that drive and energy to outwork anybody around you. That's what it takes to be No. 1. Embrace work as a constant process that we must do as long as we live. There's plenty of time for that body to rest once everything in life is all said and done, but for now we are living to the fullest. Live it up by going extra hard in putting in the work to continuously develop those skills that will prepare you for that long road to glory and greatness. Go Get It!

CHAPTER 4

Greatness, Dominance, & Killer Instinct: Stage 5 (MASTERY)

Once you develop the proper perspective and put in the necessary work to create a skill out of the passion and talent you have identified for yourself, it's WINNING time. It's time to hone in on that skill so intensely that you become a master expert at your craft and learn to dominate at a supreme level. It's time to make a blatant reality of everything you know you deserve to be the BEST at! The first four stages of exemplifying greatness were the following discussed in the previous chapter:

#1	Perspective:	"Your Stage" - understanding how you are set up for greatness
#2	Passion:	"Your Love" - discovering what you love to do
#3	Talent:	"Your Gift" - discovering what you are naturally gifted at
#4	Work:	"Your Will" - training yourself to WIN.

In this chapter and the next, we will discuss these final three stages to achieving greatness:

#5	Mastery:	"Your Throne" - dominating and becoming the BEST
#6	Decision:	"Your Moment" - choosing to be the BEST, ALL THE TIME
#7	Impact:	"Your World" - leaving a legacy that changes lives and the world.

The stages of mastery, decision, and impact solidify the platform you consistently use in your life cycle of evolving greatness to show and prove to the world. You learn how to use your gifts, to drive greatness beyond yourself in making significant contributions that inspire the betterment of mankind.

#5 MASTERY: "Your Throne" – dominating and becoming the BEST

Life itself is a fight. Life is war. We're not all engaging in hand-to-hand combat or planning to drop military bombs on others, but at the root of every person's life is the desire to self-assert ourselves within a competitive landscape. We recognize that we're not the only ones who want the same ideal outcomes for ourselves. Others are competing for the same. This is the case among bums in the street competing for loose change, kids in a classroom competing in a spelling bee, adults competing for jobs, athletes competing for championships, or businesses competing for the greatest amount of market share. We learn real quickly in life that everyone doesn't get 1st place. There's only one 1st place per event. Mastery is about conquering and re-conquering a master program to consistently be No. 1.

The pursuit of mastery is a process of becoming the best competitor in your field. This is the initial surface level of mastery. The highest level of mastery is consistently competing against yourself. You're ultimately in a fight and war against yourself. Everything and everyone you compete against are all a part of a process leading to that ultimate duo against yourself. You're always fighting to become better than the old self you were yesterday. A true master is constantly looking for ways to "outdo" what he has done, because he recognizes that mastery is not a final destination but a life-long evolving process of self-discovery.

Who's the Master?

The Last Dragon, with Bruce Leroy, is a cult classic urban movie. Bruce Leroy was a martial arts expert in the hood, awkwardly out of place within a family, where his cool little brother was ashamed of him and his loving parents just recognized him as being very different. One day Bruce Leroy's karate instructor told him he could no longer train him. His trainer felt that Bruce Leroy should go out on his own journey to find "the real master," who could give him the final level of karate expertise that would be demonstrated by acquiring "the glow." The glow would be a bright light surrounding his body, representing karate mastery.[1]

Bruce Leroy went out on his quest. It led to an encounter with his soon-to-be karate nemesis, "Shonuff," who ended up working in cahoots with a shady businessman to take over the city. Shonuff went to extreme ends to humiliate Bruce Leroy. He even tore up Bruce Leroy's karate school in front of the students, while constantly asking him, "Who's the Master?" Shonuff continued his onslaught by tearing down the Leroy family's pizzeria and kidnapping Bruce Leroy's lady love interest and his younger brother. This all led to a vicious karate match showdown in the streets between Bruce Leroy and Shonuff. During the match, Shonuff began beating Bruce Leroy so badly that it appeared Shonuff had taken on "the glow" and had become "The Master."[2]

During the grueling battle, Shonuff is drowning Bruce Leroy in water and bringing him up just to ask "Who's the Master?" Bruce Leroy begins to reflect on all the moments of his journey, and he reaches a deep, self-reflecting revelation that he himself is "The Master." He answers Shonuff's last question, "Who's the Master," by saying "I AM." He then proceeds to receive "the glow" all around his body and goes on to beat down Shonuff in triumphant fashion. Afterwards, in a desperate attempt by the shady businessman to kill Bruce Leroy by shooting him, Bruce Leroy miraculously catches the bullet with his teeth and saves the day. Bruce Leroy ultimately proves to everyone and most importantly to himself that he is "The Master."[3]

The great lesson in this cult classic is that Bruce Leroy had to go on a rigorous journey, overcoming all types of life obstacles and competitive forces to reach a place of self-actualization, finally recognizing that there is no one on this planet better at being a martial arts master than he is. Bruce Leroy was "The Master" all along, but had to go through hell and back to refine his mental and physical powers as the true master.

Many other great stories, such as the popular book *The Alchemist*, use this same theme of having to explore a whole other world while on a journey of self-discovery and self-assertion. One recognizes the very gifts they're looking outward for are ultimately within themselves. You are "The Master," but you must go so far above and beyond your comfort zone to prove it!

Mastery is creating a highly refined life skill program of supreme technique, discipline, focus, self-motivation, and clutch performance to reach this self-actualization place of knowing you are the BEST. Then you must be willing to chase this fleeting position to re-create being the BEST in every moment. There is a common misconception that being dominant and possessing killer instinct involves being physically aggressive and malicious in walking over people to get to the top. I disagree. You do not have to be an "a-hole" to be great. There is a cutthroat factor to being the BEST, but it's grounded on the premise of not being discouraged by anyone or anything in pursuit of being the BEST.

Mastery is a very calculated art and science. Mastery and dominance of your craft is 90 percent mental. This means that every move you make is calculated with accurate precision. Thus, every action you take is backed by a very calculated thought process that is refined to an instantaneous level of conquering whatever is in your path to greatness.

The Art of War

One of my favorite books is *The Art of War* by Sun Tzu. There are several principles this book discusses, which are valuable in mastering the art of war in life. One of the key principles that stands out to me is "always be calculated." War must be fought and won from a standpoint of mental superiority. Meaning you should do as much research as possible on your craft, opponent, and the terrain in which you're competing. Become a master of all the information important to having a superior knowledge of your competing arena and how to best execute depending on various situations. This way you can be efficient and accurate at using the right resources at the right times to conquer as effortlessly as possible.

Sun Tzu states, "The skillful leader subdues the enemy's troops without any fighting."[4] To me this means that the most powerful characteristic of a master warrior is not necessarily being super powerful in physically overcoming an opponent, but being strategically powerful enough to win without even having to fight. If you create a superior enough position and advantage at the point of attack, there is no logical way for the opponent to counter. Masterful timing and even-kill energy are essential. Never being emotionally distracted or off balance are critical to "out-thinking" your opponent. Once this is done, 90 percent of the battle is already won.

It's not about being an aggressive hothead, but more so a supremely calculated competitor. This requires a great commitment to mental and skill-based conditioning. Acquiring the experience-based knowledge to gain the proper "know-how" to build a mental, physical, and instinctive ability for achieving dominance against all odds is what mastery is all about in any area of life.

10,000 Hours

To dominate as the best, it takes a tremendous amount of practice time. It never happens overnight. The greats get great by doing what most others won't do. The type of conditioning that is required for true mastery must consume a great portion of your life. In the book *Outliers*, by Malcolm Gladwell, he states that studies show it takes 10,000 hours of practice to achieve a level of mastery as a world-class expert.[5] Bill Gates and Steve Jobs had been a part of elite programs in which they put in over 10,000 hours of computer programming before they reached their early twenties. The greats transcend to the "unconscious competence" mastery level not by accident or mere talent, but by unconditional and unrelenting skill-driven work.

Ten thousand hours of studying Japanese can make you a master communicator of the Japanese language. Ten thousand hours of brain surgery tests can make you a neurologist like Ben Carson. Ten thousand hours of shooting jump shots can make you a master sharpshooter like Kevin Durant. Ten thousand hours of investing in the stock market can make you a master stock investor like Warren Buffet. What does it take to get in 10,000 hours of work to reach this elite level of mastery? Let's look at the math calculated by writer and blogger Paul Welch:[6]

- 10,000 hours/365 days (1 year) = 27.5 hours/day   (Impossible)
- 10,000 hours/1,095 days (3 years) = 9.1 hours/day   (Possible, but exhausting)
- 10,000 hours/2,190 days (6 years) = 4.6 hours/day   (More likely)
- 10,000 hours/3,650 days (10 years) = 2.7 hours/day   (Most realistic)

This shows that even with a conservative effort of almost 3 hours a day of practice, it can take up to 10 years to achieve mastery. This breakdown shows the importance of starting while young. If you can identify a skill by the age of 13, with a master program regimen in place you can become a world-class expert by the age of 23. For others who are older, there is always a chance to become a master as well, but you have to relentlessly commit to sacrificing the necessary time to hone your craft. If you're 25, what can you become a master at by 35? When you turn 35, what can you reach world-class status at by 45? 55, 65, 75, 85? For me it has to be the same question. How can I become a master of my craft, and then master another one?

Boxing

In my younger days, I definitely put in a lot of hours at fighting. Boxing, scrapping, wrestling, illegitimate mixed martial arts—you name anything in the fighting category and I did it. I was always fighting to prove myself among those I felt were disrespecting me or someone I cared for. However, as a mature adult now, I only box as a hobby.

I don't want to try and win the heavyweight title, because I'm too old to invest that type of energy into it. I don't want to go 12 rounds with professionals who have a goal of making me brain dead. However, I do use the sport of boxing as a recreational means of staying sharp to benefit other areas of my life, such as my physical health, mental sharpness, business success, and solution-building for causes dear to my heart. This includes black economic and social empowerment. These segments of life are no game, which is why boxing makes such an excellent metaphor. You play basketball, you play baseball, you play soccer, but you don't play boxing.

In whatever I do, hobby or not, I want to be the best. This is the mind-set that I want to have all the time, so I can constantly sharpen my senses for always doing my best. I take a boxing class that I go to a couple times a week where we do conditioning some days and sparring on others. Most other boxers in the class only do their conditioning during class time, since they're not professionals training for a title belt or anything. Not me. Outside of class, I get on the Stairmaster for 5 minutes, jump rope for three sets of 3 minutes each, burpies, ab work, push-ups, bench work, and then pull-ups. For me to master the art of the jab, right cross, left hook, uppercut, and combination of all, I must be in good condition and strong enough to execute.

In my spare time, I also look at boxing clips of the greats - like Joe Louis, Muhammad Ali, Sugar Ray Leonard, Floyd Mayweather, and several others to see how they maneuvered in "out-thinking" their opponents. So guess what happens when we go back to class? I'm usually the standout boxer and much ahead of the class. I've put in so much more work that I've become pretty good with several boxing techniques and styles. I am able to slip in jabs from angles that are hard to counter in getting an upper hand on my opponent. I'm also able to apply various boxing techniques that enable me to move my body to punch with force without getting hit. I'm getting stronger and sharper mentally at the sport, which drives my physical strength and sharpness as well.

Chris "getting it in" training in the gym

Like I said, boxing is not my career, but I believe in being the best at whatever I do. Even with a hobby, there's no place for slacking. I view slacking off as a mental illness that could seep into other areas of my life and weaken me. So whether it's a card game of spades, carpet cleaning, or a boxing class—I want to master the skills it takes to be the best I can be. Life has taught me that once I do what it takes to become the BEST I can be, I should have a great shot at being the BEST.

Ali - The Greatest

The boxer I idolize the most is by far Muhammad Ali. I consume myself with Muhammad Ali clips all the time when studying boxing. It's easy to look at boxing and think the strongest, most powerful puncher will be the best. Ali was far from the strongest and didn't' have that knockout power most boxing fans want to see. Yet his footwork, speed, mental strength, and will to win were beyond masterful. Ali was brilliant inside and outside the ring.

The brain controls everything and has to send a message to our body for us to do anything physical. So when a person possesses great physical skill, I attribute it to having a great physical IQ. Even in a brutal sport like boxing, a boxer's brain is controlling how they punch, in what sequence they should punch, when to duck, and how to maintain while getting hit. The brain will even send a message to shut down the body if you get hit hard enough. That's the science behind a knockout. Just like a computer hit with too many viruses, it will shut down because the message sent is "something is wrong and we need to chill out and reboot."

In boxing, and any other "fight activity" in life, your brain and ability to think is the most important asset. As a three-time heavyweight champion, Ali was a masterful fighter because he was a master thinker and strategist. Ali was a student of the sport and did his research on what made certain boxers champions. Ali had been training to be "the greatest" ever since he was a young boy and watched endless footage of various champion boxers, to formulate his own unique champion style.

At a very early point in Ali's career, he discovered that most heavyweights were flat-footed and relatively slow in comparison to faster fighters in lighter weight divisions. So Ali chose to perfect a fighting style based on tremendous hand speed and lightning foot speed. "Float like a butterfly and sting like a bee" was a famous quote Ali would say with his trainer. Ali perfected the craft of being able to move all around the entire ring constantly, sticking and moving at will, while being able to avoid punches. He was also able to punch with a serious rhythm that landed painfully on his adversaries.

This made it extremely difficult for the stronger boxers to catch him, all while taking irritating punishment from a lightning quick jab that was constantly tagging them in the face. Eventually, this style wore down his opponents, and Ali would often win by knockout or TKO. This fighting style shocked the world, as he won his 1st heavyweight championship by TKO, "out-boxing" the much stronger and feared Sonny Liston. In the rematch fight, he knocked out Liston with what is known as the "phantom punch," a punch Ali threw so fast that many viewers in attendance didn't even see it.

One of Ali's most notable wins was against hard-hitting young heavyweight champion George Foreman. At the time, Ali was much older than Foreman and was a huge underdog. In what is known as the "rope-a-dope" strategy, Ali posted up on the ropes, allowing Foreman to punch himself out for the entire fight. The strategy was to make this hard-hitting, ferocious boxer, who was used to knocking people out in the early rounds, fight much deeper into later rounds for which he was not well conditioned.

By the 8th round, Foreman was out of gas. Ali then chose to shift the tide and become relentless, hitting Foreman with a series of left-right combinations to maneuver off the ropes and knock Foreman out. This fight is still regarded as one of the biggest upsets in boxing history. Ali was not the stronger boxer, but he was definitely more strategic and prepared.

In an interview, Mike Tyson was discussing his opinion of Ali's boxing prowess. Tyson admitted that there was no way he could've beat him. "He's an animal! He looks more like a model than a fighter, but he's like a tyrannosaurus rex with a pretty face. He'll take you into deep waters and drown you! He's very special, the best in the world."[7]

Deep waters and heavy drowning is in fact where Ali took Foreman and most of his opponents...mentally! Tyson, arguably the most ferocious fighter ever, was referring to Ali's mental mastery of strategizing a fight scheme so treacherous that very few opponents could prepare for it. Constant movement, constant punching, constant speed, and non-stop 1-2 - 1-2 combo action! All of the strongest and hardest-hitting punchers in that era knew they didn't have close to the mental nor emotional strength of Ali.

Boxing strategies, such as the "rope-a-dope," were not strategies he just came up with overnight. Ali was special because such strategies were a part of his arsenal of masterful skill-sets that he had perfected all his life. All of his training and conditioning, mentally as well as physically, were for preparing him to make the most of those fighting moments.

Ali had a relentless work ethic, training 8 hours a day. He was known to run 10 miles in combat boots. He also practiced hours of shadowboxing and sparring, to perfect his stick-and-move style. With the speed and sting of Ali's jab, he became recognized for having one of the most lethal punching weapons in all of boxing. This acclaim came despite a jab being traditionally regarded as a boxers' weakest punch. The jab was the ultimate setup tool for Ali's master fight strategy.

I once heard a Navy Seal say that the three keys to their expert military success are speed, surprise, and overwhelming force. Speed used in every action towards the enemy, surprise used in attacking the enemy when they least expect it, and overwhelming force applied where the enemy gets demolished. Ali displayed all three of these tactics in his upset of Foreman. Ali also mastered each of these tactics in making his entire life a rigorous regiment of perfecting these traits.

His speed was not only shown in the ring, but also with his uncanny wittiness that made him popular in the media. On the fly, Ali was always prepared to say witty, poetic, catchy lines like "If you want to lose your money, then bet on Sonny!" He would constantly say things to his opponents before the fight and during the fight, to give himself a psychological edge. Often he would give his opponents insulting nicknames that the media would run wild with.

Ali was a master of Jedi mind tricks, which made his opponents more emotional and distracted; while he remained the more focused boxer, who never got emotionally rattled or thrown off. Ali would literally set up shop in his opponent's head and take control of their own thinking before the fight had even begun. He did this normally with a smile and joking demeanor, all while channeling a killer instinct that propelled him to becoming the Greatest of All Time!

Ali was a gallant fighter in every area of life, going toe to toe with credentialed journalists and broadcasters any chance he could. He was able to do this because he had a brilliant verbal IQ as well. His most popular debates were with broadcaster Howard Cosell, who had a hard time competing with Ali's clever arguments, despite having a law background. One time Cosell was telling Ali how old and washed up he was getting, stating "You aren't the man you used to be!"

Ali quickly responded, "Well I saw your wife the other day, and she said you aren't the man you used to be either!"

Ali had a master character for being entertaining and was brilliant at articulating his thoughts in a creative way. In addition, Ali was the most charismatic and generous to his fans. Ali recalled a devastating moment as a teen where he waited hours outside of a restaurant to meet his boxing hero Sugar Ray Robinson, only to be blown off by him when asking for an autograph.[8]

Ali told himself that when he became boxing champion he would never forget where he came from or how that felt. So Ali always treated his fans with the utmost respect and gratitude. He spent hours signing autographs and allowing fans to capture life-cherishing moments with him. Ali was "the people's champ," with a warm heart and spirit that captivated the world.

"The Champ" Muhammad Ali with Marcellus (3 years old) and his Dad

Ali single-handedly took boxing to new levels of popularity and prosperity, because he was such a magnificent figure who transcended the sport. This transcending quality is most recognized in his decision to not enlist in the U.S. military to fight in the Vietnam War. It made no sense to Ali to kill others in a far-off country and fight for a nation that would not even treat people of his own race fairly. Ali had embarked upon a quest for spiritual mastery in embracing his Islamic faith. He wanted to be more empowered as a black leader and spiritual being than as a boxer.

Ali was arrested, stripped of his heavyweight title, and not allowed to box for over 3 years, because he had the heart to stand up to the U.S. government in defending his beliefs against war. The greatest fighter of all times was willing to lace up his gloves of heart and character in taking on his biggest fight...by choosing not to fight or support the killing of other humans through war.

Ali is one of the only fighters who was never knocked out—knocked down, but never knocked out. This shows how Ali empowered himself with a dominant, unstoppable master mind-set and heart that would never allow him to stay down. He was built to stand up for what he represented...greatness. Greatness always comes back and is never overcome with any fear that stops it from showcasing its character as the BEST.

This is why Muhammad Ali is regarded as not only the greatest boxer of all time, but also one of the greatest human beings ever. He not only displayed an awesome mastery of his boxing skills as a master boxing strategist, but he also showed that boxing was merely a platform for him to pursue mastery of the real meaning of life and greatness. He was willing to go to jail, be banned from boxing, and even die, all for his religious beliefs. This was most important to him as a man and leader.

He fought against injustices upon blacks and humans across the globe, even in the face of losing absolutely everything. There are not many, if any people we consider great today who are willing to do this. In the relentless program Ali embraced for achieving boxing mastery, he was ultimately sharpening his mind and spirit for fighting not with his fists, but with his heart for mankind. That is the powerful soul fabric of a true champion, one who has mastered the true meaning of life.

When society speaks of dominance and killer instinct, these great attributes of character exhibited in a powerful yet peaceful way are too often underrated. Ali's greatness shows that the highest levels of dominance and killer instinct are never about how you can kill somebody literally or dominate a person physically. We have no records of Martin Luther King, Gandhi, or Jesus knocking someone out. Their power, greatness, and everlasting legacies lie within mastering a mentality and set of thinking skills that fueled their greater purposes for life itself. In mastering our chosen crafts, we too begin to build mastery character and skill sets for larger life purposes, which can help change the world for the better.

Dope Boy MBA, Rich Man PhD

Unfortunately, I dropped out of the 9th grade and did not have the foresight to get my 10,000 hours in as a computer programmer, like Bill Gates, when I was 14 years old. I quickly fell into the traps of the streets as a distributor of crack cocaine. As detrimental and life altering as this decision was for me, I look back and recognize that there were several business skill sets I managed to cultivate in the streets. These very same business skill sets were legitimately fine-tuned after re-programming my mind for mastery of the Beautiful Hair 4 U business.

When I became serious about selling dope, I committed myself to learning everything that I could about crack cocaine. I retained as much info as I could from the respected OGs in the game and numerous other sources, regarding where it came from, who the major players were, how it worked, and how it's processed. I studied everything about crack cocaine and spent countless hours daily in the kitchen mastering the process for cooking it. I learned all the ins and outs for how to cut it, compress it, re-process it, and every other means to creating the desired potent reaction. I wanted to become the best d-boy possible, by having the best quality product that reacted exactly as it was supposed to.

I was also good at putting together a game plan. As a street hustler, I would start every day by putting together a to-do list and schedule for what needed to get done. Cook my product by 10 a.m.; hit the streets and the various spots between 10 and 12 noon; meet this connect or such and such at 2 p.m.; put in more sales work on the block from 3-5 p.m. By 5 p.m. I would be done, while most guys were just getting started.

Looking back, I would leave the house sometimes committing 10 felonies at once without even knowing it. As blinded as I was, I did have intentions and a plan. Beyond the daily schedule, I also became good at setting big goals for myself, while following through to accomplish them. I never wanted to just hustle on the same level forever. I was never content and wanted to be the man on every level of the game I could. My goals were a combination of the next level of weight I wanted to sell and the rewards I would joyfully splurge on myself after selling at that next level. I learned early that the key to making moves was saving my money. You can't take on an opportunity without having the money to fund it.

I knew there was no real way to elevate in the game by continuously buying 2 ounces every day. So I decided to stop spending money carelessly and go into grind mode. I stopped spending money on kicks, clothes, and everything else to save more money so I could buy dope in bulk. I became great at saving money, while most other dope boys around me were blowing theirs, never getting to the next level of hustling. By the time I was 17, I had put away $6,000, which was my target goal needed to buy a ¼ kilo. From there I grew my clientele even more and sold it all hand-to-hand, making over $18,000.

I continued to re-up and flip for a while. Whenever I got off most of the weight I had bought in bulk, I would get to ballin'! I was spending money on women, fixing up cars, and partying every night. But afterwards, I would settle down and go right back into grind mode.

When I went into grind mode, my rule was I would only eat peanut butter and jelly sandwiches or bologna sandwiches. No fast food, no restaurants, no splurging, none of that. I would catch every serve, and then stack to hit the next level. I eventually saved enough to by a ½ kilo. After the flip, I would celebrate by showing my behind off again and ballin' out something serious. I'd get a new car, a bigger house, a couple more chicks plus their expenses, and then go straight back into grind mode to hit that next lick.

Today, I am in grind mode right now with Beautiful Hair 4 U. I just ate a peanut butter and jelly sandwich for dinner to remind myself of the hunger and hustle it took to get me here. It's always necessary to recommit a greater focus in going to the next level of business. No longer am I confined to the dead-end, self-destructive path of drug dealing; but I have the same hustle and hunger within me to continue mastering my craft to succeed in the marketplace. I received my illegitimate MBA in business on the streets the hard and ignorant way, but I feel I was able to legitimize myself in pursuing a higher mastery of business through an unofficial honorary doctorate used to build a virgin hair empire.

When I first became interested in selling hair after recognizing the huge opportunity with so many ladies desiring it, I learned everything I could about virgin hair the exact same way that I did dope. I literally took the same fundamental business blueprint and skillsets applied to selling kilos of dope, and appropriately retooled it for selling kilos of virgin "Beautiful Hair" by the bundle.

I gained tons of knowledge talking to hair professionals and surfing the internet for hours daily. I learned about where the hair originally comes from, where it's processed, and how it works. I learned all about the science of hair - how it gets tangled from the cuticle standing up, how water content affects hair fibers, how it should be washed, how it should be maintained, what styles are the most popular among black women, and what accounts for superior quality extensions that last for months versus inferior weaves that don't even last 3 weeks. Now I can tell a hair stylist how to treat and color it. Most hair stylists are experts at doing hair, but I have now become a master expert many stylists rely on to educate them on the science behind how hair extensions work.

I applied the same entrepreneurial grind for being a dope boy in the streets to mastering the art and science of winning at business with Beautiful Hair 4 U. By placing a strong focus on superior quality, low-cost international sourcing, creative social media promotions, mass media advertising, and exceptional customer service - I was able to grow sales from 10 bundles a week to 1,000 bundles a week, becoming one of the leading distributors of virgin hair in Florida.

At five storefronts and still expanding, Beautiful Hair 4 U has generated well over a million dollars annually. This can be significantly attributed to the 10,000-plus hours of experience I have accumulated during my misguided earlier hustling days to now channeling the right redeemable qualities of business to make a mark in my respective industry.

Chris literally transitioned his exact skills for selling kilograms of dope to kilograms of "Beautiful Hair"

Chess Master

I first learned how to play chess in prison. I would see these inmates playing with intense concentration and wonder to myself "Why do they waste their time with that boring game." I became more curious and finally asked an OG what was all the hoopla about with chess. He told me it was a supreme game of strategy. I asked him to teach me. He told me he could teach me how to move the chess pieces, but he couldn't teach me how to play chess. That had to be learned on my own. He sat me down and taught me the rules to chess and how to move the pieces. I became addicted to the game and soon learned that chess is truly a process of self-discovery and personal mastery.

Chess is by far the best mentally stimulating game I have ever played. It's a one-on-one competitive thinking game, with an infinite number of possibilities that could happen during the course of any game. No game is ever the same. There are offensive and defensive strategies. Some chess players are more offensive minded while others are mostly defensive. I've become a semi-expert at both. Some will sacrifice their queen aggressively to make their ultimate move, while others will be overly conservative even with their pawns. Various skilled chess players can think 1, 2, and 3 moves ahead or even more.

Chess for me is a great tool for mastering strategy and discipline. Playing an intense game of chess with a worthy opponent helps train my mind to look at competitive problems from a totally unique perspective. Playing chess allows me to think creatively and strategically, helping my mind become sharper at adapting to complex circumstances where I have to be calculated in weighing out all my options. For me it helps reinforce the mind re-programming analytical skills that helped me change my life around. Fully analyzing a situation is always beneficial in mastering your craft, competitive landscape, and ultimately your own self.

I highly encourage everyone, especially young black males, to learn the game of chess. We need all the training we can get in making the best decisions, given the complex traps society strategically places all around us. Chess totally develops skills that can transfer to mastery of the game of life.

Young black male, you're a dominant force to forever be reckoned with. Your power for achieving greatness lies within your ability to master your mind, body, and soul. Make your 10,000 hours count for achieving a world-class mastery of a craft that you can confidently build and make your unique mark with in the world. Don't feel compelled or stuck to honing your skills of greatness in the streets, losing precious time the way I did. You're much smarter and greater than that. I am beyond lucky to still be living, and I still had to do time in prison before being given the chance to turn my life around. Most other dope boys who were stuck in the game had to face much deadlier consequences.

Seize your rightful throne the "right way," and properly channel your dominant skill sets to "out-think" the world in becoming the absolute BEST! Instead of being dominated in a world where you never find your way, put in the right work to dominate at a level of elite mastery. Nobody can stop YOU but YOU. So don't ever stop evolving as the ultimate master of yourself. Relentlessly prepare yourself, so that when anyone asks you "Who's the Master?" you can confidently respond "I AM!"

CHAPTER 5

Greatness, Dominance, & Killer Instinct: Stages 6-7 (DECISION/IMPACT)

#6 DECISION: "Your Moment" – choosing to be the BEST, ALL THE TIME

Achieving a level of expert mastery does make you elite. However, it does not automatically certify your name in history as a G.O.A.T. There are many master professional athletes who do not want the ball in the clutch moments when everything is on the line. There are many master lawyers who do not want to take on a high-profile national case with extreme media scrutiny. There are many master social activists that do not want to stand for a worthy cause that might jeopardize their current lifestyle and place in mainstream America.

Upon this next level of greatness, only the BEST of the BEST make the critical decision to step up and claim their moment of truth, knowing their life will forever change. Within this moment is huge risk, but also the opportunity to become the BEST. This also comes with the responsibility of being the BEST, ALL THE TIME.

This moment of decision can be referred to as an "aha moment," where one has a revelation that they're solely dedicated to consistently performing as the absolute BEST. It can also be referred to as the "tipping point," where one makes the world stop by executing unparalleled exponential change that forever transforms the course of history.

Glimpses of such decision point moments include Michael Jordan hitting a buzzer-beater shot over Craig Ehlo, to win a playoff series and showcase his unbelievable trajectory for athletic greatness; or Michael Jackson's debut of the moonwalk during his performance of "Billie Jean," catapulting his artistic greatness to unforeseeable heights. Even more historical decision point moments include Abraham Lincoln delivering the Emancipation Proclamation to free the slaves, and Martin Luther King Jr. delivering the "I Have a Dream Speech," to bring about better laws of justice for equality and civil rights. These moments set the stage for greatness on unprecedented levels.

These epic decisions reflect an internal commitment for achieving greatness and create an instantaneous platform for incredible external results. These moments of clarity and decisive action prove such individuals are ready to fulfill their destiny for becoming the BEST at whatever they have chosen to be GREAT at, to whatever maximum capacity possible. This level I call "Greatness Critical Mass" is the crucial point when the source achieves a self-sustaining trajectory for uninhibited greatness which can lead to G.O.A.T status. At this stage, killer instinct is totally embodied within the individual pursuing legendary greatness. They have made the decision to exist as the epitome of unstoppable, time and time again.

President Barack Obama

I believe the amazing journey of Barack Obama becoming the 1st black president of the United States is the greatest historical event that has happened during my lifetime. Seeing him giving the State of the Union address on TV, I would sometimes have to pinch myself like "Wow, we have our very own black president of the most powerful nation on the planet."

All his incredible gifts and skills, such as his heart-warming charisma, state-of-the-union swag, oratorical intelligence, world-class debate skills, resolved temperament, political acumen, and inspirational motor, are all attributes I've never seen so greatly embodied within one man. Under the most intense scrutiny and malicious attacks ever for a president, President Obama has shown an unprecedented level of resolved determination to inspire and lead the United States during turbulent times of crises. He is definitely "The Man."

As good as I am at chess, President Obama is one man whom I think might give me the business on the chess board. As calm and peaceful as he is, I know deep down within him is an unyielding killer strategist who sees nothing but optimized visions of dominance and greatness. Of all the many things you can become in life, you don't just stumble upon becoming President of the United States. To date, only 44 men in history have ever achieved this title. To be in that position, endure all that he's endured, and achieve victory for what could be regarded as the greatest title on earth as U.S. President - I believe it all speaks volumes about his determination to be a real

Commander in Chief. The Art of War from a political campaign, national policy, and global authority standpoint are all activities he has reached world-class mastery of... intentionally.

Just like the Navy Seal skill sets discussed earlier, our Commander in Chief has displayed relentless speed, surprise, and overwhelming force with a pursuit of greatness in becoming President. To many it seemed as if he came out of nowhere. The impact with which he won over the hearts of mainstream America to be elected the 44th President of the United States was historically groundbreaking. I believe this was all masterfully devised.

I believe Barack Obama knew he was going to be President of the United States before his college professors could even pronounce his name. At some point early in life, Obama intellectually and intuitively recognized that he could align himself with the changing tides of the world and gain the necessary experiences and exposure to achieve presidential greatness. The positions that he held, including community organizer on the south side of Chicago, President of the Harvard Law Review, State Senator, U.S. Senator, and eventually U.S. President, were all intentional decisions made to create his own blueprint for achieving greatness.

Obama's predisposition for being the absolute BEST man for the job of U.S. President became clear to many all across the world in 2004, when he delivered an electrifying keynote speech at the Democratic National Convention, while also running for the U.S. Senate. Watching his speech again on YouTube, it's clear to me that the stars were aligned for Obama to become the brightest rising star of all in modern-day politics. Obama seized this moment by delivering a speech that, till this day, can immediately resonate with the hearts of millions all over the world. His poise, vibrancy, stature, and refined demeanor were all visuals of a natural "chosen one" for world leadership.

Obama masterfully articulated a vision of what America is supposed to be. He powerfully stated, "There is not a liberal America or conservative America, there is the UNITED STATES OF AMERICA! There is not a Black America, and White America, and Latina America, and Asian America, there is the UNITED STATES OF AMERICA. We are all ONE people."[1]

In front of a cheering crowd, Obama captured the pulse and hearts of the nation by sharing America's greatest God-given gift and responsibility—"the audacity to hope." At a moment of emphatic patriotic cheers and a seemingly everlasting standing ovation, Obama stated the audacity to hope reflects "The hope of slaves singing freedom songs, immigrants setting out for distant shore, and even a skinny kid with a funny name who believed America had a place for him too."[2]

Every experience he had from growing up without his father, to being of mixed racial background, to losing in a previous political campaign, all led to this defining moment. He was prepared and positioned to be the BEST leader of the free world. Very few moments in political history invoke such a feeling of genuine patriotic oneness and unity in America like the moment created with that speech.

Although John Kerry was at that time the democratic nominee, the writing was paramount on the wall that this country would soon be Barack Obama's to lead. A couple of years later, Barack Obama announced his candidacy for U.S. President and spearheaded a dominant team that engaged in one of the most brilliant grassroots, guerilla marketing political campaigns in history.

Record breaking voter registration drives, door-to-door groundwork, ingenious social media engagement, compelling national advertisements, cunning debate tactics, inspirational speeches televised globally, and supreme resourcefulness all led to Barack Obama making history as the first black President of the United States. As miraculous as this achievement seemed to be, winning a second term in 2012 solidified President Obama's pursuit to greatness.

Get Rich or Die Tryin'

The dope game was my way of becoming a Commander In Chief in my head. My version of sitting in the oval office was sitting in a candy-painted old school whip, tricked out with oval-shaped 26-inch rims. I made an illogical decision to ride a derailing "get-rich-quick" money train until the wheels fell off. I told myself in order to end my reign in the streets, I would either have to die or "The Feds would have to catch me."

My passion for balling was still fueled by a killer instinct mentality to be the best dope boy. So I would never forget the grind that was funding my stunt game. Whenever I would get back into grind mode, my mind-set was "I'm gonna beat you every way I can." Stunting was a marketing tool I used to show everybody that "I'm the man you want to buy product from or serve under. I'm that dude making all my wildest dreams happen. If you're on my squad, I can get your dreams jumping too. So get like me. Get behind me, or literally get behind me!"

With the drug hustle, I was ultra-competitive. I wanted to outdo every other dope boy with a better quality product. I would research to find out all the other sellers' prices and then find a way to beat them with a more superior cut of dope. In my mind, quality always wins and drives superiority, whereas competing on price can quickly make your product inferior.

So if I had a smaller rock than a competitor, I would make sure it was a rawer cut of coke that was more potent. In a 1,000-mg beaker, a competitor might put in 10 grams of coke, stretch it out, and beat it. So I would put in 14 grams of coke, stretch it out, and beat it to give it more kick. I became an expert at just being able to look at what other d-boys were selling to determine how diluted and how much it was cut. This was all a part of my game plan for staying ahead of the competition and growing as a more dominant force in the dope game.

Unfortunately, the more you grow and surpass others in the dope game, the more envy and hate you attract. All the stunting and balling out eventually makes others "feel some kinda way". This is one of the main dangers in the street hustle. Part of your power is in being able to protect yourself and maintain respect, so that few ever have the guts to test you. But the reality is, in such a dirty game there are no golden rules and somebody hating on you eventually does test you.

Death Around the Corner

I will never forget the near fatal turning point in my outlandish pursuit to greatness as a dope boy. I recognized that a smaller-level dealer I sold to started falling off and was now smoking dope. He was becoming unreliable and wasn't buying as much, so I had to remove him from my direct down line because I was on another level. I began having one of my other workers sell to him. Due to this downgrade, and his growing envy of me as I got bigger in the game, he decided to plot against me. One day my close homey Jeremiah, who served for me, came over to my crib with dude. The dude noticed that I had just gotten back in town from picking up a shipment in Miami. From there, dude made up his mind that he was going to have me set up and killed.

I wasn't aware of this at the time, but I received a call from Geechy, a drug dealer turned crack head. I still had respect for him and would holla at him whenever we crossed paths. Geechy called me to let me know that he had received a call from the dude. Geechy told me the dude said, "Chris just got a big shipment of coke from Miami; we need to get him! I got this Iranian dude in on it too."

I recalled, before getting that call from Geechy, an Iranian showing up to my crib. I had a fierce pit bull with me at the time. When the Iranian rang my doorbell, the pit started barking ferociously and I had to hold him back. I went to the door, but I didn't open it. I yelled, "Who is it?"

The Iranian asked, "Did you need a cab?"

I said, "Hell naw, I ain't call for no cab!"

I was now able to put it all together. The conversation with Geechy had let me know dude had contracted the Iranian to rob and kill me. Luckily, I had my pit bull with me, barking so loud that I didn't open the door. So the Iranian just asked if I needed a cab and left. But if I had opened that door, I probably wouldn't be here right now.

I was furious and knew I had to make a real example out of dude. I was boiling hot and ready to get all the way gangsta. I paid Geechy $500 to get him over my boy Jeremiah's house by tricking him into thinking we were going to have some strippers coming through to party. Meanwhile, I was in the basement getting ready. I was taking some drugs called android stacks that turn into a steroid when metabolized in the body. They have an effect of making you crazy strong and real mean. Both Jeremiah and I were poppin' andro stacks, while lifting weights getting "geeked up!"

I was ready to kill dude. I had put on weight-lifting gloves and chilled in the back waiting for dude to show up. He arrived and started shooting pool with Jeremiah. I came around, cocked my fist all the way back, and knocked dude out cold. I then pistol-whipped him, hammered his feet, and duck-taped his whole body. When he woke up, I cocked a pistol right to his head. I saw the fear of death in his eyes, and I'm sure he saw a deathly vengeance right in mine.

I was ready to shoot and kill this dude, but Jeremiah convinced me to stop. Jeremiah was so afraid that I began to fear that, after shooting dude, Jeremiah would be so messed up by it that it could become a problem for our friendship. We ended up putting dude in the car and throwing him out on the road while the car was in motion.

My whole erratic purpose of that episode was to make an example out of dude, but that was a turning point for me because I had never felt so violent and out of control. I was ready to do anything at that point to make an example out of him. Dude was so messed up that I think he believed I did even worse things to him than what actually happened.

By the time the streets got a hold of the story, they added so much more exaggeration to it that it made me a street legend. It grew to mythical levels. I supposedly held him captive and locked him in a closet for days, while doing all types of torturous stuff to him. I hadn't done any of that, but the streets took it and ran with it. I'm sure that back on the block someone is still bringing it up as one of the wildest street stories around the way.

Dude never retaliated, because he knew I had every intention of doing away with him. He saw something in me that day, which evoked a fear that had him too frozen to even remotely think retaliation. My reputation as a ruthless d-boy, who didn't play one bit, grew from that incident. I never had a problem like that again. However, knowing I could go to such malicious killer levels really messed me up.

Although I wanted to be the greatest dope boy ever, I was more so into selling drugs for the money, grind, and ballin' rewards. I knew how to cook killer product, come up with killer power moves for making money, and enjoyed killing 'em when I stepped out to floss in the nicest things. But I had never intended on becoming a real killer.

Although I had experienced other dangerous situations before, knowing that I had just dealt with a real "kill or be killed" scenario did not make me feel the best. For the first time, I felt slightly stuck in a mode where I had to forever live up to a huge reputation I had now earned for being literally "killer" about mine. Despite this newfound discomfort, I wasn't willing to trade in my lifestyle, regardless of how consciously shackling it had become. I was in it to win it now. There was only one way in and one way out. It was never going to stop until I took my last breath. The Feds were literally gonna have to catch me.

Killer Instinct & Fearlessness…As a Freeman

Looking back, it was a blessing from God that the Feds caught up with me and I got incarcerated when I did, because I was headed towards a path of self-destruction. I was in a dark space in the streets. My killer instinct for achieving my version of dope boy greatness was going to get me killed. In fact it almost did. I was in prison long before I got sentenced, because my mind was incarcerated in the streets. Being money hungry with drug dealing is the same as being blood hungry, because in the streets blood is the only sign of retribution when protecting your reputation and life.

We all have the desire to protect ourselves. One of the main rules of life that we always adhere to is self-preservation. There is a killer instinct within us all. It's yearning to dominate by any means, in pursuit of our unique form of greatness. But we're not primitive naked animals running around a jungle, exercising our dominance by killing and eating each other. The drug game had me turning into an uncontrollable animal, self-destructing in a cage that I was too delusional to see.

I became just as much the pit bull barking out of control, ready to bite any opposition in sight. I was constantly in a mode of violent defensive paranoia, where I felt I had to always be strapped and ready to kill. I thought I was a FREEMAN, but I was far from it. My mind was trapped, my lifestyle was trapped, and my intentions on becoming great would always be trapped in a self-imprisoning cage. This cage could turn into a coffin box carried by six at any moment. Every temporary success I achieved would lead to a more permanent path to failure and destruction.

So my ultimate decision for pursuing greatness and becoming the BEST CHRIS FREEMAN I could be came when I decided to turn my life all the way around after serving my time in prison. It required being fearless, to start from scratch and never turn to a life of crime or drug selling again. The killer instinct I honed in the streets never disappeared. In fact, it was amplified even more through a more sophisticated mental and emotionally stable approach. I channeled every bit of this killer instinct edge in the right direction, to reinforce my will to win and reach success...the right way. The only person I had to maliciously kill was my old self, so that the new Chris could prevail.

I adopted a fearless approach to attacking the virgin hair industry. As a street hustler, my desire was to be the best and biggest. So with even more legitimized opportunity in front of me, I was not going to settle with my newfound ambition as a business owner. My mentality was "I can shoot for the stars of the biggest businessmen in this field, and even if I miss I'm still up there. So let's get it. Whatever it's got to be...I WILL NOT LOSE!"

You can't be scared to lose. Sometimes you have to take a short-term "L" to learn how to win. The beauty is, you'll learn what to do versus what not to do. As Thomas Edison stated after his initial invention struggles, "I have not failed. I've just found 10,000 ways that won't work." After making that ultimate decision in your life to be the BEST, you must be fearless! That is the only way to think and fully liberate that killer winner within. Even if it appears like I will lose, I am never scared. I've been through too much, I work too hard, I have too much of a mastery over my lane, and I know without a shadow of a doubt, God is on my side.

Below is a great quote Will Smith said about fear in the movie *After Earth*:

"Fear is not real. The only place that fear can exist is in our thoughts of the future. It is a product of our imagination, causing us to fear things that do not exist at present and may not ever exist. That is near insanity. Do not misunderstand me, danger is very real, but fear is a choice."[3]

Hunger Games

I could've been content with the couple of stacks I was making selling hair out the back of my trunk. I had reason to be proud of myself for getting back on my feet in society, learning the hair industry, finding a low-cost international source, and sufficiently providing for myself and mine. But one of my mottos is "I Don't Get Tired, I Get Money!"

I had created my own niche business and was beginning to hear the rumblings of other beauty supply owners asking, "Who is this Chris? Why are so many girls talking about this special kind of hair he's selling? Why are my sales so low and declining for the third month in a row? I knew I had created a demand that meant I had to work 24/7 to adequately supply. I couldn't stop selling out of hair every week. When I realized how I had actually occupied a mean corner of the market, which had huge potential for even more growth, I made a decision to put on a show!

This was not the beginning of my desire for being great at business. My hunger to excel in this hair game goes deep. Do you know how long I had to watch my mom and every other black woman I knew shop at beauty supply stores where the owners were never black, but only sold to blacks in our community without ever contributing to it? Do you know how many times I went into one of those stores as a kid with my mom, and one of the owners followed us up and down the aisles like we were trying to steal something?

Do you know how disturbing it was to see the one black-owned beauty supply store, Bernard's Beauty Supply, which was thriving in the black community in Jacksonville decades ago - fight tirelessly to stay in business against emerging foreign-owned beauty supply chains? Those foreign shops were able to leverage upon international loans and a unified front, to eat away at the black customer base year after year with no other black beauty supply businesses in position to help? These are all prime examples of the deterioration of black economic empowerment that I no longer wanted to tolerate.

So I had been starving for this opportunity right here! Now that I found a strong competitive position, as a black entrepreneur, to distribute a highly demanded new superior product with better service to my people - why wouldn't I go all out to pursue creating a new business landscape that best serves our people. These are some of the very things Marcus Garvey, Elijah Muhammad, Martin Luther King Jr., Malcolm X, and so many others fought and died for. So in my heart this too was a driving force behind what I made a conscious decision to capitalistically kill for. As a people, our stomachs had been growling and empty for far too long in this hunger game, it was definitely time to eat!

The growth and success of a black-owned beauty supply business was now my calling and my fight. I read the *Art of War* constantly during my start-up, to gain a masterful understanding of the principles to being calculated, strategic, and competitively superior. These were all tools I needed to properly devise a game plan. I needed to know I could win this hair war before I began. And after all my strategizing, I felt I could. Like TuPac said "I got my mind right, money right, ready for war!"

No Mas

As I've mentioned, life and business are very much like boxing to me, and I planned for this war to go down like the rematch fight between Sugar Ray Leonard and Roberto Duran. It was a classic known as "No Mas." In their first fight, Sugar Ray tried to go toe-to-toe with the expert brawler Duran and ended up losing by decision in a brave yet unwise attempt. The brawling style was the wrong way for Sugar Ray to fight the slugger Duran. Sugar Ray paid the price with a respectful yet devastating loss. Duran had a mega ego and made sure Sugar Ray felt bad about the loss as well.

During their rematch, Sugar Ray came out with an entirely different approach. He was much more mobile and danced around on his toes, versus being a stationary target like in the first fight. After a couple of rounds of masterfully using the entire ring to stick-and-move against Duran at will, Sugar Ray began to put on a world-class boxing clinic. Sugar Ray psychologically and physically mutilated Duran.

Sugar Ray had proven in the earlier rounds that Duran couldn't catch him on the move, so Sugar Ray began pulling out all the tricks. He was throwing crazy circus punches from all different angles, while shuffling his feet like he was Salsa dancing. Sugar Ray then started sticking his head right in front of Duran in a peek-a-boo manner that made Duran look stupid. Duran would try to swing at Sugar Ray, miss, and then get clobbered with a right cross. Sugar Ray would wind his right hand around like a windmill, and then throw a sharp jab out of nowhere with his left.

After a series of embarrassing sequences for Duran, it became apparent that he was being "out-classed." Sugar Ray was hitting him with faster, more painful punches, while making a mockery of Duran's slowness and inability to hit Sugar Ray back, even when he was being playful. Sugar Ray was not only attacking Duran's body with vicious blows, but the theatrics was killing his ego. Being too prideful a person, Duran took one more combination of punches and then waived his hand to tell the referee "No Mas!" Duran quit, in what has become known as one of the most embarrassing and masterful boxing clinics ever.

No mas means "no more" in Spanish. During my street hustling days as a dope boy, I was using the wrong style of fighting in the game of life, similar to Sugar Ray during his first fight versus Duran. No matter how I made moves by moving dope in the streets, I was always a sitting duck, bound to get hit much harder than I was hitting. However, after I said "No Mas" to a self-destructive style of hustling, which caused me to take unwise life risks and suffer huge losses, I began to execute my hustler ambitions more intelligently with a free-spirited, winning entrepreneurial style. I used this style while fighting my way up in the business boxing ring called Beautiful Hair 4 U.

No Mas became my theme in virgin hair combat. No Mas/No More would I be denied a free opportunity to maximize on all of my entrepreneurial talent and greatness. No Mas/No More would I tolerate how the hair game was monopolized in our community by non-blacks. "No Mas/No More" were the words I wanted my competitors to say after being outclassed by the business domination of Beautiful Hair 4 U.

I engaged in highly unconventional guerrilla marketing tactics to eat away at more and more market share. I began having fun hitting the market upside the head with numerous types of promotions to brand my business. Once I had the streets buzzing I worked with the best up-and-coming stylists in the market to help them grow their salon businesses. They began purchasing their virgin hair exclusively from me. I then targeted all the popular female socialites in the city, from models, entrepreneurs, radio personalities, music artists, and more. This created a word-of-mouth frenzy all over the city. Whether it was the club, the salon, or the job – all the ladies were talking about Beautiful Hair 4 U.

I was highly underestimated by my competitors, which was exactly what I wanted, because I could surprise them with a monstrous attack that they couldn't prepare for. They had no idea how hungry I was to succeed at their expense. They had no clue that I was studying Machiavelli's *The Prince,* day in and day out. Mastering how to be a king, how to rule a kingdom, how to apply strategy, and how to gain the love of the people. They had no clue what kind of black capitalist warrior was upon them.

As the buzz and love from my people grew, I took the show online as well. Instead of a generic website, like most other beauty supply stores had at the time, I created a home page gallery on my website. It was flooded with pictures and videos of hundreds of girls all over the city co-signing Beautiful Hair 4 U. I also became one of the first beauty companies locally to aggressively engage on social media via Facebook, YouTube, Twitter, and Instagram. I built thousands of followers, when it was unheard of for local businesses to have that many, by seriously connecting and entertaining my customer base.

I posted pics of stylists and popular models wearing Beautiful Hair 4 U extensions in Jacksonville, as well as other markets, such as Miami, Atlanta, and other cities across the country. This showed that, unlike most beauty supply stores, my brand extended beyond the local market. Through my social media presence, it was quickly understood that women all over the country were co-signing Beautiful Hair 4 U and exclusively buying from us because we had the best virgin hair on the market.

I also used social media as my witty platform for throwing comedic Sugar Ray bolo windmill punches at my shabby-product-carrying counterparts. I would have realistic and exaggerated comedic picture comparisons between our virgin hair and other beauty supply store hair, to exploit how much of a difference there is in the quality and time the hair lasts. This not only became entertaining for the growing customer base viewing my marketing antics online, but it also creatively got the message across that "Beautiful Hair 4 U virgin hair is what's poppin', while that normal beauty supply store hair is wack and played out."

Once I evolved to a point where I was using mass media to run creative television and radio ads, other beauty supply stores knew they were in trouble. I was hitting them and now hurting them from every angle possible. The ferocious guerrilla-marketing fight style was throwing them all the way off and beginning to embarrass them, like Sugar Ray Leonard did Duran. I know they were like "How is this black dude with no international bank funding or traditional hair conglomerate connections whuppin our butts?"

I continued doing my thing, talking my "ish" on social media, and strategically maneuvering the market in ways that were making my competitors say my name without me having to say theirs. I would make sure I never mentioned a competing beauty supply store's name when throwing my combo punches at them on my pages. Ladies began telling me that other store owners were saying, "We can get the same kind of quality Chris has too" or "Beautiful Hair 4 U gets their hair from the same company we do." That was totally untrue. Competing stores had to recognize that Beautiful Hair 4 U now carried the hottest hair on the market and they had to justify their sales by saying they were "just as good." But the more they saw those customers leaving their stores without a hair purchase and never coming back, many were forced to waive their hands to the virgin hair ref and say "No Mas!"

Let me get loose for a few moments and speak candidly about domination in business and this thing I'm possessed with called killer instinct. If we're competing, it's war. It's World War I, World War II, and World War III at the same time. Even though I've evolved into becoming a leader within the virgin hair market in Florida, I will not take my right foot off the pedal, unless I must smash the brakes on my competitor's neck. That goes for newcomers as well. Once you start doing what I'm doing, we are in serious competition.

We can be friends or associates outside of business, but once you step in my competitive ring, I hope you're ready to dance! I am Commander in Chief, and I have my special forces of business watching you around the clock. I will be drinking cappuccino, while rocking a white tee and camouflage cargo shorts with some old vintage timberlands on, reading my reports about your tactics— all before I plan my move to counter-attack with earth-shifting force.

Trust, you won't be able to keep up with me. My mentality is that you aren't willing to do what I'm willing to do, so you're not going to beat me. I will begin embarrassing you in the ring, "Sugar Ray Chris style," while doing a little Ali trash talking with extra flamboyance. Even your closest friends will start laughing at you. I make people quit! No Mas! Straight up, no chaser. That's how it has to be in pursuit of being No. 1 of ALL TIME, ALL THE TIME!

I Don't Want No Mediocre

Call me TI or better yet "Hair King of The South" (please excuse the overdose of "cocky" for the time being), because like he says in his song, "I Don't Want No Mediocre." I can't stand mediocre! There's no room for it. My style of winning at business and life is to "Do What It Takes To Be The Best That Ever Did It!" I always want to shoot for the stars and the greats in my field. Even if I miss, I'm still up there. I never just want to be out there. I want to be the best that ever did it.

That's what I wake up for! How can I "out-think" my competition? How do I find a way to gain more customers? What new product can I offer to stand out and get further ahead of my competition? I always want to make my business better than what it was yesterday.

BE THE BEST at whatever it is you do. Whether it's writing books, rapping, sports, cooking, blogging, selling phones, making graphics, selling lemonade, or picking up garbage. If your job is to clean the bathroom at a gas station, stand out by making that bathroom spotless. If you work at McDonald's, stand out by being the best French fry maker there is. Drop them fries with perfection and make them the crispiest. That kind of relentless work ethic to perfect your craft, regardless of what it is, will take you very far in life. There's always a demand and higher calling for anyone who can stand out in any capacity as the best.

One of the most important times to scrap mediocrity is as a student in school. Scrap mediocrity and stand out in your class for the right reasons. Class clowns think they stand out, but when award ceremonies are conducted at the end of the year for awards like A/B honor roll, perfect attendance, best reader, and science fair winner—there is nothing ever given out for being a Grade A fool. When you're a class clown the entire year and aren't rewarded whatsoever it shows you really didn't stand out.

In fact, you're really regular. The ones who weren't being a distraction to the class, while paying attention, doing homework, and acing tests, were the real standouts! Your work ethic should speak for itself with the ways in which your field must reward you for excellent performance.

Young black male, you know you want to be great. So do it! BE THE BEST! Fulfill that desire you have deep down to be great, by making that decision to do everything it takes to stand out the right way. This involves putting in the work to master a skill, craft, or subject and choosing to never stop escalating from better to BEST. Instead of getting Bs and Cs, why not get all As?

Become a master of whatever subject most interests you. In going the extra mile and allowing your work to speak for itself, you will attract all kinds of life-changing opportunities and rewards. I go above and beyond, so my work speaks for itself. I have a successful business that affords me a lifestyle far more luxurious than when I was selling drugs in the streets. I'm just one example of the good fortune you can create for yourself at a "balla' status," when you make the right life decisions to use all your energy to LIVE HARD rather than DIE HARD. Make a concrete decision to get the most out of this great opportunity we're blessed with called life, and watch how much fun you have while doing it.

#7 IMPACT "Your World" – leaving a legacy that changes lives and the world

I've read that since the beginning of time man's greatest fascination has been with immortality. Man is still trying to figure out "How Do I Physically Live Forever?" As a young wild d-boy, I definitely lived as if nothing could hurt me, let alone take me out. Regardless of where you're at in life, we all realize that our time here in physical form is not forever. However, the next closest thing to living forever is having such a strong impact in life that, even after you're gone, you're remembered a long time afterwards by others.

This is why heirlooms are valuable in our society. They're possessions of significance, which are passed down to symbolize the presence and generosity of someone who lived generations or even millenniums before. On a larger scale, greatness can also be defined by what impact you're able to leave on this earth that will live forever through humanity.

The typical life cycle takes us from a phase of childhood learning, to a young adulthood phase of surviving, to a mature adulthood phase of succeeding, to the golden age phase of defining our legacy that we will leave behind. Our ability to go beyond, to transfer the energy of greatness that we've established from our own personal lives to the lives of others, is how we truly contribute to the world with everlasting impact.

Nelson Mandela - "Madiba"

Nelson Mandela, also referred to as "Madiba" (the tribe he was from), initially blazed the path to his calling for greatness as a South African anti-apartheid revolutionary. Mandela fought against the cruel system of white minority rule, institutionalized racism, poverty, and inequality in South Africa. Mandela rose to prominence as a lawyer and a leader within the South African National Party, who promoted fighting systematically, aggressively, and even violently to overthrow the injustices against his people. In 1964, Mandela was convicted of conspiracy to overthrow the state and sentenced to a life in prison.

Mandela was incarcerated for 27 years and confined to a small prison cell. In his deep solitude of dehumanizing suffering, Mandela's turning point was when he "made the decision to forgive his jailors and display compassion for the horrific acts of those in power, who had caused great pain to him and his people."[4] Mandela developed the capacity to transcend his feelings, in order to set the right example for achieving justice and pursuing higher causes of humanity.

Mandela was an incredible visionary, who mastered the skill of being able to see beyond the current struggles and pain of his life and his country, to create a plan for peaceful resolution. Mandela was characterized as a man of quiet dignity and immense humility, as he sought out an even greater purpose while being incarcerated. Mandela stated, "One of the most difficult things is not to change society, but to change yourself."[5]

Mandela became committed to reprogramming his own mind and perspective, to lead South Africa into a new direction by processing every action, good and bad, as an "indispensable part of a purposeful whole." Mandela once said, "It is better to lead from behind and to put others in front, especially when you celebrate victory. But you take the front line when there is danger."[6] Mandela made the conscious decision to become the absolute best leader he could in healing the racially conflicted hearts of his country. Mandela became a mindful leader who became superior at managing his emotions.

Mandela was released from prison in 1990, during a time of escalated civil tensions. He then played a monumental role in uniting South Africa and abolishing apartheid. Mandela was elected as the first black President of South Africa, and instituted numerous initiatives for progressively moving the country forward. He also won many honors, including the Nobel Peace Prize. After his presidency, Mandela remained an elder statesman and focused on charitable initiatives to combat poverty and HIV/AIDS through his foundation.

Nelson Mandela was a relentless fighter in every sense of the word, but channeled his killer instinct for justice through a loving form of leadership, which enabled him to passionately connect with people all across the world in sparking a legendary movement towards equality and unity. Despite being stripped of his freedom for what was supposed to be a lifetime, Mandela displayed the unstoppable inner strength of elite greatness by making a permanent decision to "out-think," "out-vision," "out-lead," and out-love" any forces of oppression standing in the way of freedom for people in his homeland for generations to come. This sparked an eternal light of freedom all across the world.

Greatness in itself is impactful. Great athletes, entertainers, businessmen, inventors, writers, and all the other fields often impress us to such a large extent that their talent alone can make a huge impact. However, in our dominant pursuit to catapulting ourselves to our highest levels of individual accomplishment—the greater opportunity for good is magnifying that effect on others, which requires a selfless sacrifice for a higher cause.

At some point in life, even after achieving great success, you have to come to the realization that it's not all about you and what you can get. Everything done in life is to help set up the best means of evolution for the next era to successfully come after you. When you master the art of giving from the heart, you add a whole new exciting dimension to life. You're investing in the most awesome creation ever, mankind. I strongly agree with the African proverb, "It takes a village to raise a child"; and I believe our youth are the most underrated asset in today's culture. Truly great men at heart understand it's a personal responsibility and amazing feeling of fulfillment to take part in giving back to your people when you have been blessed with the ability to create value for others.

Fatherhood

Living a life of great impact as a man starts with your family. A man's role of leadership is at home. Every life born has the potential for greatness, and our very own children are the most amazing representations of greatness we could ever create. They're how we truly leave our mark. They're the source for carrying our most treasured legacy.

That God-given responsibility of being a father is an awesome task. That's where all our love, strength, passion, will to dominate, killer instinct, and desire for greatness most matters. How can we magnify the fabric within our kids to give them the happiest opportunity to explore their own unique greatness in life? A father protects, provides, and demonstrates the most important values in life for his heirs to build on in creating an even greater world for generations after them.

Kids spell love T-I-M-E. Despite all the financial and worldly priorities men see as important, kids most value from their father the quality and quantity of time they are able to spend with them. They often could care less about how much money you have, how hard you grind, or how admired you are in the world. What matters most is that, as a father, you're there for them and with them. The absence of that father's time, which equates to love in so many ways, can leave a kid in a very vulnerable state, feeling all alone in a cold world where they have to fend for self.

The Fatherless Generation website provides the following stats from various research studies about fatherless homes:[7]

- 85% of youths in prison come from fatherless homes
- 71% of all high school dropouts come from fatherless homes
- 90% of homeless and runaway children are from fatherless homes
- 71% of pregnant teenage girls lack a father
- 63% of youth suicides are from fatherless homes
- 80% of rapists with anger problems come from fatherless homes
- 75% of adolescent patients in chemical abuse centers are from fatherless homes

One of the tragic goals of slavery was to remove the black man from the family structure. The effects of this removal, which includes higher incarceration rates of black men and other debilitating societal factors, are clearly evident in our communities. A father is the rock to a child's life and the family structure. You remove that rock, and that family loses the strong ground on which it is able to firmly stand. That family loses a primary provider and protector, who makes all the difference in the world. The presence of a father can literally be the difference between freedom or imprisonment, happiness or depression, success or failure, and life or death.

Super Hero

Young black male, it's vitally important to prepare yourself to become the greatest father you can be, when that time comes. You have the opportunity to fulfill the greatest life purpose by successfully raising your own flesh and blood. You literally become a SUPER HERO. A real man is a real father, and a real father is a real super hero. Superman, Batman, nor Spiderman can compare to the super hero qualities of a Super Dad. The most talented NBA player, hottest rap star, and most street-certified trap star in the hood doesn't come close to the heroic impact of an extraordinary father who is present to constantly and unconditionally uplift his family.

My pride and joy are my three children: My prince is my son Chris Jr., and my princess baby girls are Kismet and Chrislynn. Every day, I get to put on my Super Daddy cape and be their hero. I can't put into words how much I love them and how fulfilling it is to be their father. Although Chris Jr. and Kismet have two different mothers, as Chrislynn's mother is my current beautiful wife Sherrina—I unconditionally love them all equally, and I make sure no Baby Momma Drama ever stands in the way of fulfilling my cherished responsibilities as a father.

Christopher's kids: Chrislynn (left), Chris Jr. (center), & Kismet (right)

Like Terrance Howard's role as "Luscious Lion," I'm building my own Empire (just without all the drama). As a father you get to build your own castle of love and strength to give your kids the greatest opportunities and experiences in life. I love my son Chris Jr., but I stay on him like white on rice and black on Maybach. I do all I can to teach my son the value of hard work, so that he knows, regardless of how much I have, you must learn how to go out in this world and "Get It." Nothing comes free. I let him know that everything worth having, you're going to have to work hard to get it.

I lost so much time with Chris Jr. being locked up in prison for the first years of his life. I missed being there for his birth, first steps, first words, first day in daycare, and so much more. That's why now I don't take any time I have with him for granted. Every day that I'm blessed with, I seek to instill within him strong values. This includes a hard work ethic, manly character, discipline, education, and mind-over-body power, so that he can avoid the traps I got caught up in.

These tools are helping him carve his own unique lane for fulfilling a valuable life purpose. I enjoy the fatherly process of recognizing his talents and championing him to excel by building him up to achieve greatness in life. Every young boy gravitates towards an older male in learning how to be a man. It's my God-given job and greatest pleasure to be the best personal example I can be for my son to use as a model for coming into his own manhood.

Chris and son Chris Jr. after Pop Warner football game

I let my son know however we need to get it, let's get it...and I'm a show you! "You want to go hard at football, throw that ball deep over Dad's head so I can catch it and show you how to ride out." "You're having problems in math, son sit down at the table and pull out your homework so we can break down this pre-algebra and isolate these x and y variables one problem at a time." "Oh, you wanna make a little money selling gym shoes with your friends. Boy, let me put you on to game. Here's how you need to price them and how you sell them in the hood, without somebody moving in on your lil crew and jackin' y'all." My son knows whatever he needs, I got him, and I will do everything possible to show him how to "Get It!"

Now my style of fathering my little baby girls is much different. In addition to my daughters being much younger than my son, girls in general are delicate and deserve 1,000 percent affection. I can be hard as nails with my son, but with my precious girls I can be softer than a pillow. It's nothing but hugs and kisses with them. I don't care how old they get, I won't stop kissing them. They'll always be Daddy's little girls to me.

It's like little girls live for their daddy's love. So for my daughters, I am the best man on this planet, most committed and able to give them this love. Both of my daughters have amazing personalities, too; you can see the little ladies in them already. Kismet is doing so much talking now at 2 years old, and she totally lets everybody know that I am her Super Dad. When anything happens, she is quick to say "I'm a call my Daddy!" I love it, and I'm going to always let my girls know they can call on me for anything.

How a father treats his daughter is how she will allow a man to treat her. When a father abandons or abuses his daughter, she is sadly vulnerable to allowing men to abandon and abuse her all through life. Unfortunately, I've seen so many girls grow up without a father and become victims to men in the streets.

They don't get that healthy love from a real daddy, so they go wherever they can to seek that love and protection from a "Big Daddy," even when it's unhealthy or abusive. Unfortunately, daddy to them is a sexual term. They have no concept of what a real daddy means. A real daddy loves his girl in every healthy way except sexual. A real daddy values her mind over her body. A real daddy always considers her well-being as an absolute priority over his. He will die for her in a heartbeat. I will do anything for my girls and have no problem going back to prison or leaving this earth to protect them. I'm their Super Hero Dad.

Motivation & Mentoring

An excellent way to fine tune your blueprint for achieving excellence is through the guidance of a mentor. Ideally, a responsible man in one's life - such as a father, brother, coach, or teacher can be that ultimate mentoring source for a young male. It's also important to seek out a mentor who is an expert in the career field in which you want to become great.

Unfortunately, my only mentors growing up were the major dope boys I looked up to. I aspired to be like them and could easily relate to them. However, after being released from prison and starting up my own business, I felt the need to have a business mentor who could give me guidance on being successful. I found a mentor by the name of Dr. Laster "Bernard" Walker, who has enhanced my personal and business life in ways I could never repay.

One day Dr. Bernard's lovely wife Semone came into my first Beautiful Hair 4 U business office to buy hair for her salon. I was out of stock and told her I would give her a call as soon as the next shipment arrived. It took a little over a week before I received the delayed shipment for the hair she wanted. Because she struck me as a very professional salon owner within the beauty industry, I thought it would be best to give her the hair for free to show my commitment to building a value-adding customer relationship with her for the long term.

Little did I know that she would be the golden angel who would add the most valuable mentoring relationship I could've ever imagined. Impressed with my up-start success and buzz with Beautiful Hair 4 U, Semone set up a meeting for me to meet her husband. When I met Dr. Bernard, he took a liking to me. He put a blessing hand on me and my business that would change my life.

Dr. Bernard took me under his wing and began schooling me on taking my business to another level. Dr. Bernard is a successful business owner with a doctorate degree and an IQ of 160. He's not merely a jack of all trades, he's a master. Dr. Bernard is brilliant at business financials, investments, economics, management, distribution, and much more. Dr. Bernard has taught business courses online and began teaching me everything I needed to know about business. He taught me how to manage my financials and payroll, increase my revenue streams, and much more.

As my mentor, I feel like I have practically received a doctorate's degree for free. His wife Semone also began mentoring me as well. She shares priceless business and life insight for professionally managing conflict and channeling every experience into a positive one. After every bank turned me down for a loan, Dr. Bernard and Semone went the extra step in believing in me, by investing heavily in my company to help take it to the next level. They're both the kind of life-changing blessings you only run across once in a lifetime. I was very lucky to have them come into my life.

To this day I meet up or talk over the phone with Dr. Bernard as often as three to four times a week. I come by and sit with him in his office, drinking coffee while talking about business strategies for hours. I go with him to exclusive cigar clubs and network with other millionaires while they play poker in the back room. Dr. Bernard has polished my business sense and taught me how to do profit and loss statements for my business, the most valuable skill set I have to manage my business financials today.

Dr. Bernard constantly shows me the importance of hard work by example. I thought I worked around the clock non-stop, but he wakes up at 4 a.m. every single day. Sometimes I think he never sleeps. He has a motor to dominate and excel that won't stop for anything. He's also the one person I am close to who stunts harder than I do. He has a movie theater, bowling alley, and full court basketball court— all in his house! When I first came to their crib, I was like WTH! It was better than Disney World. I thought I used to do it big in the streets, but when I saw his quality of life, I was like "Man, this dude is BALLIN'!"

When I went into his garage and saw the meanest Lamborghini sitting on Forgiatos, I was done. I almost passed out right in his garage! In every way possible, I knew I could rock with Dr. Bernard and learn from his ways, because he had the glorious fruits of his labor to back it. He knows how to work hard and play hard by rewarding himself with the finest things this world has to offer. That is totally my style.

Dr. Bernard is such a phenomenal mentor to me not only because of his business brilliance and investment in Beautiful Hair 4 U, but also because he is a relevant and touchable example to me. He exemplifies that greatness is attainable for a black man cut from the same cloth as I am. He was a country southern brotha that came up literally from nothing. He can talk as intellectually as any Ivy League professor, and then turn around and chop it up about street politics like he's from the meanest country backwoods. Thanks to our mentorship, I continue to grow by leaps and bounds, both as a business owner and as a man.

Young black male, find someone special in your ideal line of work to be your mentor. Stay on your grind, and be open and receptive to soaking in the knowledge of a professional OG who is a positive and productive force in this world. In addition, you can also use mentors that you may not know personally for mentoring guidance as well.

I've gained invaluable knowledge from reading everything I can about Steve Jobs. I believe Apple is the most revolutionary brand during our lifetime; and I constantly gain insight from the gems he shared regarding leadership, branding, innovation, and being a cutthroat winner! You too can connect with extraordinary leaders you admire, through books, articles, YouTube interviews, and any other resource you can get your hands on.

Chris the Mentor

Now as a successful businessman myself, I feel it's my responsibility to help mentor others coming up. That's how the cycle works, give as you have received. So I mentor several up-and-coming stylists in the beauty industry as well as other young black entrepreneurs. Whenever I can inspire and motivate others to be the best they can be with their entrepreneurial endeavors, I'm a very happy and satisfied man. I'm all about creating networks of like minds who want to master the art of being a "go-getter" in pursuit of accomplishing their life goals.

I mentor many and take pride in motivating them to pursue their dreams, while educating them on how to win at this game of business. I often start with giving them insight on how to recognize the unique value in themselves. I also give them invaluable knowledge on how to successfully manage their brand, promote themselves, and surround their business with the right teams. I emphasize how important it is to create a winning culture. Just recently I began setting up engagements for business seminars, where I teach business and marketing lessons.

It's very important to me to give back to the community, because it's best when we all elevate together. My individual success as a business owner in the community should produce goodwill and forward gains for the community. That's the reason why my business is successful. The root of future progress is in building up our youth. So I sponsor numerous youth organizations, including several Pop Warner Football teams in Jacksonville, FL. I also make it a point to frequently go to alternative schools and programs for at-risk youth to speak. This is very important to me because I was once them.

Chris with award for sponsoring a Jacksonville Pop Warner Football team

I know all about the path many of them are trying to take, and I'm committed to helping save as many lives as possible. Many of the kids I speak to are labeled with behavioral problems or ADHD. Many have already committed felony crimes before even entering high school. Often when I ask the kids what they want to be, they say a ball player or rapper. So I pull up to the school in my Beamer, walk in the class with my jewelry on, and show them, up close, how I can floss and look like their favorite rappers or athletes. But I happen to run my own business, and I'm my own boss.

**At Bronner Bros. Show booth Chris is in Business & Biggie
mode - "I stay Coogi down to the socks"**

Many of the kids are shocked to find out that I can be a successful business owner and still dress like the guys in the streets that they idolize. They don't know it's possible to have swag and money without doing anything related to athletics, entertainment, or street crime. Many of the kids have heard stories of when I ran the block with their older family members. From the jump, my street cred as a major dope boy gets their respect. But I tell them, in all my experience, the only way the street hustle drug game ends is getting killed or going to prison.

When speaking to extremely troubled hostile groups, I ask them to look around the room and cherish that mental picture, because "50 percent of you won't make it!" You won't be around a couple of years from now, because you're on a path that only leads to death or imprisonment. As harsh as I have to give it to these youngsters, I also let them know that it's only out of love, and the strong commitment that I have to help them turn their lives around for the better, that I give them the real. I let them know that, just like I did, you can make it out of your immediate environment into a world where you can be great!

I'm also a motivational speaker for the Federal Re-entry program. This is a program to help ex-inmates reintegrate back into society with strong life skills, after serving time in prison. It means a lot for me to speak with them, because many of them have heard about me and know that I was locked up and reduced to nothing, just like they have been.

We would often call the word-of-mouth communication within the federal prison system "Inmate.com." In the communication flow, word gets back to the inmates all the time about how well or bad you're doing once you get out. They cheer me on in the prisons and see me in a heroic light, because they hear of my success with Beautiful Hair 4 U and how I have the lady consumers all across the state going wild over this great virgin hair.

To them, I'm proof that you're able to turn your life around and find success after prison. I reiterate to them that I've been where they are and, at times, had the same doubts; but I also teach them how I overcame everything by staying focused and not relapsing to a life of crime or drug use. I let them know you have to STAY AWAY FROM THE DRUGS! Selling or using them, it's all a trap and not worth it. I tell them my success is their success, because we're all from the same place and destined for the same type of comeback story in tackling this thing in life called greatness.

Young black male – we're all a part of the same village, the same family, and the same squad, built to win and make extraordinary life achievements happen. It's our role to be the BEST fathers and the best men. Be the best husband, brother, son, cousin, neighbor, classmate, teacher, mentor, and any other role we can find where we can contribute to the success of another person within our own culture.

Build a relentless appetite for achieving greatness. But in achieving your own personal success, never forget that our true greatness lies within leaving an impact that will make life greater for the awesome generations to follow. This is how we truly carry out our own legacy.

CHAPTER 6

Education

With our intellect being our greatest luxury asset, education is the most empowering activity we can immerse ourselves in. The mastery of anything in life is attained and sustained by the mind. Formal education through schooling must be a gateway to self-empowering education through our own personal curriculum to achieve success in life. Education is the most powerful weapon we can use to change our world and the world around us. Learning in itself is so powerful because it creates the building blocks for whatever it is we desire to create for ourselves in life. It's also something that can forever be protected because it's the one thing no one can ever take away.

Underachiever to Valedictorian

As I've mentioned earlier in this book, I was not a good student at all as a kid. When I wasn't cutting class or getting kicked out of school, I would be in the classroom bored out of my mind. Mostly everything I was being taught by my teachers was extremely boring. All the lecturing was unbearable.

I wouldn't pay attention because I'd either heard what they said the first time and had no interest in hearing the same thing over and over again, or they were teaching something I felt was totally irrelevant. Writing the main idea to a boring book passage, coming up with a hypothesis and conclusion to a stupid science experiment, or doing long division for 20 similar math problems all seemed like a complete waste of my time. There was no creativity or usefulness to any of this for me. So I was very lazy and rarely did any homework or classwork.

Despite my serious disinterest in school and never doing my work, I would always seem to pass my tests. While goofing off in class, I was still able to understand the gist of whatever was taught. I would listen to the teacher, watch the teacher do a couple of problems, and I could remember it and be able to pass the tests. I was always a C student because I would get a bunch of zeroes on homework and class assignments for not turning them in, but I would get 90-100s on the exams. I was bucking the homework but was forced to take the tests, which I normally did quite well on.

I thought school was a waste of time. But I found out what real boredom and irrelevance was the hard way when I was sent to the Jesup, Georgia, medium security prison for my first bid. They call it "doing time" for a reason! That's all you have when locked up. Hours, days, weeks, and years of dreadful incarcerated time on your hands. I would much rather be in school listening to a boring teacher instructing me for a few hours than in a prison where I was stripped of all my civil liberties 24/7.

There are only so many sets of push-ups and crunches you can do to fight the boredom and depression that settles in when realizing how much precious time is being wasted in a prison cell. The mind becomes your main weapon, sanctuary, entertainment, and primary outlet for experiencing freedom. Whatever you want to do in life outside of the confinement of a prison cell must be done within your mind. So for the first time in my life, I felt like I could be most productive with all this time in prison by reading a book.

Other inmates I respected told me about the author Donald Goines, an ex-con who wrote hood classics about ghetto life in the streets. I thought that would be interesting to read, so I got his book *Crime Partners* out of the prison library. After reading the first chapter, I was hooked. I read the entire book in about a week. I would look forward to the hours I could spend reading this wild street adventure about two small-time hustlers linking up with a black activist ghetto lord, who led a heroic gang movement to take back the streets from drug dealers and crooked cops.

What amazed me about reading this book was that I could visualize everything going down just like it was a movie. It was even better in a way, because everything that happened in the book could be brought to life through my own perspective and imagination. I was thinking to myself, "man this book is the truth!" When I finished it I felt like a part of me had been in those same streets getting it in with those dudes as well. I didn't know books could pull off those kinds of gangster plots and twists to draw in somebody like me. It was such a rush that I was like, "man I gotta read all of this dude's books." My addiction for reading had begun.

My first year in prison, I read his entire series and also read most of the hood novels. I then began reading books by Iceberg Slim, after finding out that he was the street pimp author who inspired Donald Goines to begin writing. Their books were always fast-paced with non-stop action and drama I could get into. Their stories were not only entertaining, but they also reinforced the experiences and street code principles that were so familiar to me. Iceberg was dropping some real-life gems on how the world really works through the eyes of a street hustler. Finally, there was something within a book RELEVANT to me! After reading so many of their books, I got inspired to write my own first urban street fiction novel while in prison, titled *From Crumbs to Bricks* (available on Amazon.com).

Gaining a passion for reading literally changed my life. I always thought reading was for nerds and cornballs. But once I discovered you could travel through any place in the world, or any hood for that matter, through the journey of reading a book, I became more open to becoming an avid book reader.

Because I was going to the library so much now to check out books, I decided to take the G.E.D. test on a whim, without taking a class or studying at all. I scored well on the reading part, mostly because I had learned proper grammar and reading comprehension from reading the books by Donald Goines and Iceberg Slim. However, I failed the math section because I had no idea how to do math problems with fractions and percentages. This was all due to dropping out of school in the 9th grade. Of course I knew how to add large amounts of money and break down kilos into grams, but I found there was a lot more to math than that.

In prison they were offering a G.E.D. class for free. I told myself since I have nothing but time on my hands, why not take it. I enrolled in the class and began taking school seriously for the first time in my life. I began to understand the importance of learning all the academic fundamentals. I then became curious as to how smart I could become academically, if I applied myself.

I had already developed a skill for being a relentless reader, so I was able to dig into the reading material and comprehend it with ease. I did all the assignments and started actually studying for the first time. I was focused and gained confidence more and more, as I received As and Bs on my assignments and tests. After putting in the most time I ever had with school work, I was confident that I would pass the G.E.D. test next go round.

Not only did I pass the G.E.D. test with a very high score, but I was the top student in the class and was awarded valedictorian for the prison G.E.D. program. I was just as proud of this accomplishment as I was when I made enough money hustling to buy my first car. This academic accomplishment proved that I was built to succeed at anything. After receiving the valedictorian award, I told myself, "Hey, I'm not dumb at all!"

I feel like the majority of everything academically I know I learned in prison. Don't get me wrong, prison was the worst time of my life. It's nothing I would recommend for any free thinking human. But in hindsight it was the isolation I needed to get my life right. When I was young I missed out on so much in school because I could care less about it. But being isolated to such a humbling extent in prison forced me to find alternative ways to stimulate my mind.

I learned that education can be as enjoyable and practical as you make it. The whole school process finally made sense to me. I was always driven to win, and now academics became a new platform for me to empower myself and stunt...intellectually with my mind! Any form of stunting for me must always go hand in hand with getting that paper! So I embraced going from Crumbs to Bricks, Bricks to Books, and Books to the Bank through education.

Since I received the honor of valedictorian for the prison G.E.D. program, I was given a Pell grant that paid for me to enroll in a junior college program for my AA Degree. I took this opportunity very seriously because I knew that was a significant program that could really help change my life. I always wanted to have my own business; and by majoring in marketing, I knew I could gain a learning experience that would give me the necessary skill sets to be a successful boss within the business world.

I knew I was not built for waking up and working for other people. I knew it would be very hard to get out of prison and work on the clock with my boss mentality. I didn't even want to work in prison. So just like a hood basketball star looks at the NBA as his golden ticket out the hood, I saw this college AA degree as my very own platinum ticket to escape mediocre existence and become a wealthy respected businessman. I wanted to learn all I could for the purpose of becoming the best businessman I could be!

I remember getting my economics and accounting books and wondering "what the heck is this?" The business terminology, financial documents, and statistical charts were just a few of the things that intimidated the crap out of me. However, I told myself "I'm All In" and forced myself to make it happen. I set goals for myself and wouldn't stop until they were accomplished. Whether it was outlining an entire complex chapter by breaking down the content into notes I could totally understand, or striving to maintain at least a B average, I worked hard to get the job done.

I also knew that in order to be a successful business person I would have to go beyond just what I was learning in the classroom. I had to immerse myself in as much knowledge about business as possible. This was also necessary to customize my learning experience to what I wanted to learn and what interested me the most. So I read other complementary resources for learning business. I read *The Art of The Deal* by Donald Trump, which taught me tactics for winning high-powered negotiations and making power moves. I also read *Rich Dad Poor Dad* by Robert Kiyosaki, which taught me the value of financial literacy and a true business owner's mind-set.

Plus, I would stay on top of current business events through the *Forbes Magazine*, *Entrepreneur Magazine*, and *The Wall Street Journal*. My mentality was, I could never learn too much or be too intelligent. I graduated and received my AA degree in marketing with a 3.0 G.P.A. From that point on my whole demeanor said "Warning, Highly Educated Black Man in the Building!"

Chris Jr. with book "Rich Dad Poor Dad" given to him by his Dad

A Reading Rainbow

Reading exercises your brain muscles. They are the free weights for the mind. Reading also makes you think in ways that allow you to expand limited perceived boundaries of the mind to being unlimited. It gives you the confidence to do all types of things because you have empowered yourself with the knowledge and "know how" to do it.

Sylus Green is a computer technology trainer and owner of "myT," a company that stands for "Mentoring Youth in Technology." At myT they specialize in creating computer technology programs for inner-city youth, in an effort to "bridge the digital divide one mind at a time." They have created amazing curriculums that have taught young middle school students how to build their own computers and hardware from the ground up.

Green is also developing Code Kid Academy which is a curriculum for teaching young people how to learn coding. Coding is the digital language required for creating computer software, apps, and websites. Over the next 10 years, it's estimated that there will be thousands of more jobs in computer sciences than the graduates qualified to do them. Coders are the highly demand architects and builders of our future; and myT is empowering young black minds with the ability to create the next digital frontier to create products beyond Microsoft Office, iPads, and Facebook.

When Green hosts discussions about digital age education, he talks about the *Reading Rainbow*. Back in the 80s there was an educational TV show called *Reading Rainbow* that inspired kids to read books as much as possible. Green starts many of his sessions by reciting the words to the jingle that was played at the beginning of every *Reading Rainbow* episode:

Butterfly in the sky
I can go twice as high
Take a look
It's in a book
A Reading Rainbow

I can go anywhere
Friends to know
And ways to grow
A Reading Rainbow

I can be anything
Take a look
It's in a book
A Reading Rainbow
A Reading Rainbow

You think Derrick Rose and LeBron James can get up high? You think smoking weed can get you high? Man, nothing can take you higher than reading a great book! You literally can go anywhere. Reading allows you to travel the world and beyond in exploring limitless creations of the imagination. A rainbow is that colorful array in the sky that can symbolize supernatural promise and enlightenment. Reading can create infinite rainbows of supernatural promise and enlightenment, to awaken your greatness and means to happiness in your life. Wherever you want to go right now, you can go. Whatever you want to do right now, you can do...now!

Want to be an astronaut and explore what it feels like to walk on the moon after a wild space shuttle ride? Read *First On The Moon* by Neil Armstrong and Michael Collins. Want to learn all about the lifestyles of the rich and famous, including the most luxurious hotels in the world, the fastest cars to drive, and the most exotic islands for sale? Read the *Robb Report* magazine. Want to learn how to become a millionaire with multiple streams of income? Read *The One Minute Millionaire* by Mark Victor Hansen and Robert Allen.

Want more insight into the plight of the black man and an empowering life story of overcoming a life of crime while, breaking socio-cultural shackles as a black leader? Read *The Autobiography of Malcolm X*. Are you curious about the life of a pimp in the streets? Read Iceberg Slim's *Pimp: The Story of My Life*. Want to get a head start on building your own record label? Read *All You Need to Know About the Music Business* by Donald Passman. Want to go on an adventurous journey overcoming monsters in a quest for precious treasures? Begin reading the first book in the Percy Jackson Series called *The Lightning Thief*. However high you want to fly or far you want to go, it's all possible through the "Reading Rainbow." What's even more incredible now is that anything you ever want to read and learn is available ...on the INTERNET!

Google & Youtube University

Young black male, you have the world at your fingertips. You can literally just hop on your computer or stay lying in the bed with your phone and learn whatever it is you want to know. There's no excuse for not educating yourself or finding out more about what it is you're most passionate about.

When I was young you know what I had, *Encyclopedia Britannica*. Those big ole heavy books, broken down by alphabetical order, was what I had to go through. Plus, they were in the library, a place I never cared to go. But now you have Google. You can learn about anything in the world, just by typing it in a Google search.

Instead of going to the library, you can stay right at home eating a sandwich with your socks off, or handling your business in the bathroom while learning about anything you want—in one CLICK. Wikipedia will pop up to tell you about any subject or popular person you want to search, along with thousands of other links you can click on for more insight. Research that used to take hours now takes just a couple of seconds to access.

Plus, you have YouTube University. Sometimes we need visual excitement to comprehend a subject. So if the topic is too boring or complicated to understand through reading, you can get the visual for it on YouTube. You can learn how to tie a tie, dissect frogs, cook tacos, do a crossover between the legs, make a rap beat on Fruity Loops music software, make money in the stock market, learn a foreign language, and learn how to do the Rich Homie Quan dance (something I'll definitely take a pass on). Point is, you can go to YouTube and there will be hundreds of videos on how to do all of these things, for free!

With this type of fast online access, it's easy to take it for granted and be distracted by the entertainment gossip sites and Vine videos of foolishness. It's cool to be entertained by some of this content, but why not use the internet primarily as a high-powered vehicle for learning and empowering yourself with everything you need to know to achieve greatness.

In addition to downloading thousands of songs, customize your own educational program by taking time out each day to perfect your craft through learning more about it. Click on tutorials, links, autobiographical clips, historical footage, and any other valuable resources online to become a master of your craft. Plus, use your social media feeds to stay on top of the latest events and network with other like minds. Get started with your own personal curriculum, based on your top learning interests, and watch how far you go!

20 Hours

In the earlier chapter on greatness and mastery, we discussed the 10,000-hour rule, which is the amount of time it takes to become an expert at a skill. This can take years and may seem a bit discouraging. However, during a TED Talks presentation author Josh Kaufman shared a newfound philosophy for effective learning from his book *The First 20 Hours*. Kaufman states that studies show it only takes 20 hours to become very knowledgeable about a new subject.[1] In 20 hours, you can tackle the learning curve of knowing nothing about a skill to being reasonably good at it and knowing more than most people about that subject. If you put 20 hours of deliberate focus and practice into learning a skill, which is about 45 minutes a day for a month, you can acquire the fundamentals required to thoroughly perform a skill.

In 1 month, you can become knowledgeable about the core fundamentals to playing the drums, buying real estate, designing clothes, learning geometry, designing graphics in photo shop, learning how to play golf, or whatever it is you desire. However, you can't jerk around during this initial 20 hours, randomly surfing the net or lazily reading over subject matter. You have to put in some serious, deliberate work.

According to Kaufman, these are the four steps to learning a skill in 20 hours:

1. Break down the fundamentals of the skill, and identify what is most relevant to you.
2. Learn enough to be able to put together your own learning program on the subject
   (i.e., clicking on YouTube/Online link after link, to gain a base for what it is you need to practice and improve upon).
3. Remove distraction barriers so you can focus on practicing (i.e., unnecessary texting, TV watching, chill time with chicks, or social media chatting).
4. Put in the actual 20 hours of practice time.

Young black male, what is it you want to get good at? What subject in school are you tired of struggling in, that you want to become the smartest at, and shock everyone in the class? What career are you curious about that you would love to start understanding? In what sports activity do you want to go from being the last pick on a team to the first pick?

What current events are you constantly hearing about in the news that you want to be able to better debate in the barbershop? What new technology do you think is fascinating and worth getting an advantage on? Maybe you want to learn about all the different college scholarships you can apply for and find out which ones best fit you.

Whatever skill or subject matter it is, you have the entire world at your fingertips. You literally have an infinite amount of resources to get at it. YouTube, Google, Wikipedia, Barnes and Noble, Amazon.com, they're just a few of the millions of resources that have all been created to work for YOU! No excuses and no time to waste. Figure out what it is you want to become the man at, put in those 20 hours of work, and go get it!

The Power of a Degree

Below are a couple of statistics from DoSomething.org regarding high school dropouts:[2]

- Every year, over 1.2 million students drop out of high school in the U.S. (7,000 students a day).
- A high school dropout will earn $200,000 less than a high school graduate over his lifetime, and almost a million dollars less than a college graduate.
- In the U.S., high school dropouts are charged with committing about 75 percent of all crimes.

Knowing what I know now, I would've never dropped out of high school in the 9th grade. I was setting myself up for failure! Our society favors and rewards those with a degree much more than those without. In fact, our society prepares to incarcerate people based on early projections of not being capable of doing well in school.

Students begin taking standardized tests in the 3rd grade. These test results are used to project the number of new prisons that will be built in the near future. The government is basically predicting to what extent an 8-year-old will become a criminal in 8 years or so, based on how bad they do on these tests. There is an unfair correlation made between a bad test result and a kid's likelihood of dropping out of school. Once a dropout their banking on that kid resorting to a life of crime because they don't have the skills to make an honest living. There is a brutal system in place that is evaluating the chances of an 8-year-old kid going to prison.

Who does this mostly affect? Young black male...YOU! In many unfortunate ways, the school system is set up to push young black males into the prison system. This is called the "School-to-Prison Pipeline." The African-American male has been labeled as the group with the lowest test scores, highest dropout rate, and highest rate of incarceration, more so than any other race or gender.

This may hurt to hear, but there is an entire world betting on you to fail. In some twisted way, your failure contributes to the financial and political power of the No. 1 country in the world. I allowed myself to fall right into the hands of this trap, by neglecting the vital need for an education. However, I was fortunate enough to right my wrongs and make a comeback like no other, all through education.

You might look at Bill Gates, LeBron James, or Lil Wayne and say they didn't get a college degree and look how successful they are. Know what? You BETTER be every bit of an once-in-a-lifetime innovator like Bill Gates; a 6'8', 250-lb. absolute freak of nature like LeBron; or a 1 in a million multi-platinum phenom rapper like Lil Wayne to successfully make it in this world, which is stacked against you without a college degree. They're like 1/1 millionth of 1 percent of the population. Even with all of their mega wealth and success, you can bet your bottom dollar that they will do everything in their power to make sure their children go to college and get a degree.

In prison, I discovered that an education was the turning point for changing the trajectory of my entire life. I jumped on the opportunity to get my G.E.D. as well as my AA degree in marketing as a top student. Afterwards, I was fortunate enough to start up a successful business with Beautiful Hair 4 U and find alternative ways of educating myself beyond enrolling in college for a 4-year degree. However, if I come across any business or life challenges requiring an additional degree in order for me to grow, please believe I will get my bachelor's degree, master's, doctorate, or whatever additional professional degree is needed to continue achieving success. I will also do everything in my power to make sure my kids get a college degree as well.

College Degree 5-Cs

While striving to get all A's in school, here are the only Cs I want you to embrace in understanding the importance of a college degree.

1. Civil Right

One of the main tactics used to oppress blacks during slavery was to prohibit us from getting an education. All of the controlling powers knew that an education was the main source for empowering one's mind to an unlimited extent. Our ancestors fought relentlessly for the right to an equal education. Knowledge is power, and education is a civil right. America promises us the civil human rights to life, liberty, and the pursuit of happiness. The quality of a life worth living, the liberty of being free, and the opportunity to pursue what makes us happy are all based on gaining the proper knowledge to make good decisions.

Going to school and gaining the proper reading, math, science, and history knowledge to be productive citizens in this country is our right. This country owes us an education and got away with not honoring this civil right for far too long. Mastering everything the education system has to offer is not only empowering for realistically pursuing a happy and successful life, but it is a civil right owed to absolutely every black child in this country. It's the process of getting a degree and not dropping out that holds this country accountable for providing us adequate means to a higher education.

2. Choice

You may have heard the quote "Knowledge is the key to success." Well, knowledge, education, and a degree is exactly that...a key. A key is a tool that can open a locked door for you to be able to go through. Certain keys can open doors to an Accord, Grand Am, Escalade, Benz, or Bugatti. Just like certain keys can open doors to a shack, project unit, studio apartment, 3-bedroom townhome, 20-bedroom mansion, Governor's Mansion, or the White House. When you get an academic degree, society values this as a key received, which allows you to go through a door to "pursue happiness" at various levels or "degrees."

An 8th grade certificate of completion is a key to accessing some things, a high school degree is a key to accessing more, and a college degree is a key to accessing even more life opportunities at a higher level and "degree." Degrees beyond a bachelor's, such as a masters and doctorates are keys that provide access to even more doors. Point being, there are certain life opportunities, such as the high-paying careers of a doctor, lawyer, aeronautics engineer, and many more that won't even give you the choice to pursue them if you don't have a degree. Most job applications ask "what's your highest degree attained?" If you don't have a certain level degree, you will not be offered the choice to work there, and someone else who has that degree will.

In life, you want to have the choice of going through as many doors as you can to pursue what will make you happy and successful. The gatekeepers of so many jobs, pay increases, and many other life opportunities require that you have a certain level degree. If not, they won't let you in the doors to next-level opportunities. So if society is playing this game of thrones through acquiring degrees, why not empower yourself with the keys of a college degree, which has become the standard qualification for most professional high-paying careers.

After getting this degree, if you decide that you want to be an entrepreneur, car mechanic, youth activity counselor, or something else where a degree isn't required, it is YOUR choice and not the world dictating what YOU can or cannot do. Get that key to a Beamer, Benz, or Bugatti figuratively and literally through a college degree. Afterwards, if you want to ride your bicycle or skateboard around town, you can do so as YOU please, because it's YOUR choice and ultimately what YOU want to do. Empower yourself with an education and a college degree that gives you the keys to unlocking doors to happiness in making your OWN choice with your OWN life.

3. Career

A college education gives you an excellent opportunity to carve out your niche role and career in society. However, a major part to fulfilling this opportunity is completing the studies required to graduate with a degree before being rewarded a promising career track. Suzanne Manzagol, an executive recruiter for jobs at law firms in Atlanta stated that, "When 800 resumes are sent for every job ad, companies have a need to weed them out somehow."[3] Even for entry-level positions, such as receptionists, assistants, file clerks, or even in-house mail runners, a bachelor's degree is often required.

The college degree is the first filter for cutting off job applicants with many jobs in professional fields. No longer is it the high school degree, but the college degree that has become a minimum requirement for applying for many companies' lowest-level jobs. This more stringent academic requirement is partly why the unemployment rate for workers with just a high school diploma is more than twice that for workers with a bachelor's degree.

Unfortunately, those who do not graduate from college are often assumed to be less ambitious and less capable. When you buck the higher-learning education system by forgoing college, society will actively seek to punish you by placing limits on your career advancement opportunities and earning potential. A college degree shows that you learned the fundamental skills for that career and can behave and perform in a way that reflects that—by being able to add professional value in a manner conducive to being paid for it. Your college graduation is considered a rite of passage for pursuing the career you want.

Even professional sports, such as the NBA and NFL, require a high school degree and typically some experience in college. Before franchises invest millions in a player, they want to make sure they have matured through the education process. I don't care how athletically gifted you are, if you drop out of high school or fail to achieve the minimum requirements for getting into college, you will not have a career in the NBA or NFL. The education system is the most trusted and widely used filter for selecting professionals in most industries. Your college degree is your American Express card providing the best chance at a promising well-paying career. So don't leave the education system without it.

4. Confidence

Knowledge is power, and getting a degree helps validate that you have acquired a level of expertise that is harder for society to refute. I pull up to meetings in a BMW with Gucci sneakers on, to meet all types of business owners, financial analysts, lawyers, accountants, marketing experts, and even professors. There is a respect given, because they know these are luxury items; but it could be real easy for them to mistake me for a street hustler, who is not legitimately running one of the fastest growing virgin hair distribution chains in the entire state of Florida.

However, when they begin fast-talking me, and I counter with intelligent points reflecting that I have an AA degree in marketing, serious respect is shown. They know, at that point, they can't just say anything to me, because I am certified and understand business. In some cases, they even begin to fear my position, not because of any street credibility but because of my impressive level of knowledge backed by academic credibility.

In prison, I was fortunate enough to pick up my schooling again. The completion of fundamental academics, as well as accelerated knowledge, contributed to my increased confidence, despite my hardships. I sometimes run across old partners of mine, or people in general, who dropped out of high school and have a problem doing basic reading.

Life is very uncomfortable for them, because it's way harder to survive in this world without the basic academic fundamentals. They always have to overcompensate in other areas just to get by and avoid being exposed for lacking certain skills that they should've learned as kids. The lack of confidence and fear constantly plaguing their minds is a tragedy no one should have to deal with.

Too often, people without a college degree are at the mercy of society looking down upon them. The world unfairly makes non-college graduates feel limited and inadequate. They have to work two and three times as hard as their college graduate counterparts to prove to the world that they are worthy of just as many opportunities. When you have an education, you don't have to prove you are worthy; but when you don't have an education, you always do.

The first means of breaking us is by attacking our confidence through failure: failure to get good grades, failure to get a degree, failure to look non-threatening in the presence of cops, failure to stay out of prison, failure to keep a job, failure to pay our bills and keep the lights from getting cut off, failure to provide for our kids. There is a trail of failures that society sets up for young black males, specifically once we fail within the education system.

These failures can eat away at our ambition to succeed in life the right way. However, we're successful black men in the making at all times. We must showcase that, by confidently matching this opposing force with our educational excellence. With each successful completion of a grade level and each successful graduation, all the way through college, we triumphantly beat the odds stacked so high against us and channel an even greater inner confidence that positively resonates throughout our entire culture.

5. Culture

The college experience can be a fun, life-fulfilling scholastic journey, which puts you around other young scholars from various walks of life that can be added to your grand network. Major power moves in business, entertainment, and other industries are often based on the relationships of mutual college alumni. A college education can bring about an enriched culture of diversity that can expand your mind so much farther than your neighborhood block.

You can meet people from all over the country and in some cases from all over the world. Late nights studying in groups, combined with late nights celebrating at a frat party, can all contribute to incredible moments based on education and fun experiences that many college students regard as the best time of their lives.

Having a college degree also helps broaden your access to other social circles. In some social circles, certain types of advanced college or professional degrees are respected just as much as a Benz or platinum Rolex watch. The ability to make moves while "playing the game" in this world is so often tied to gaining access to the power circles that are making things happen. A college degree is not the only gatekeeping criteria for making power moves, but it significantly helps in many scenarios. Even in the case of many of your favorite rappers who were high school dropouts, when the cameras are off, they try to conform to the most elite standards of education. They send their children to the same upscale private schools as their wealthy professional counterparts to get social access to elite circles.

Greatness Beyond a Degree

A college degree is very important in being able to go hard and compete in this world. However, as valuable as a college degree is, it's not the end all be all. A degree doesn't guarantee greatness and success in life, especially in this fast-changing 21st century. Some are naive enough to believe that if they coast through school and get a degree, a secure well-paying job is going to drop in their lap. Then that job will promote them to higher levels of success. The harsh reality is, this is not true. Another harsh reality is, some may unfortunately find themselves in a situation where, for whatever reasons, college is not a feasible option.

School, as well as any other mass learning environment, is designed to teach the masses the fundamentals and deliver skills for a sufficient level of productivity in society. That's it! Conditioning you to operate "within a box" is one of its primary effects. They're not designed at all to make you great. Greatness is all about shattering the rules of normality and performing "outside the box."

As a self-made entrepreneur, I find myself in a much greater life position than most college graduates I meet who have professional degrees and credentials far surpassing mine. This is due to my ability to think "outside the box" in a dominant manner far superior to theirs. My will to win, entrepreneurial spirit, fearlessness to take risks, and reality-based approach to applying knowledge for achieving unlimited results puts me at an advantage. I can create my own platform for success and wealth versus relying on anyone else. I learned how to get everything I ever wanted on my own, whereas many other college graduates are hindered by a crippling dependence on the conditioning done by the education system.

A degree alone is not going to get it in today's world, and my advantage is that at an early age I discovered this for myself and learned how to not be dependent on it. Many college graduates fail to get this memo and are hit with a brutal real world lesson, when the degree they worked so hard for is obsolete and unable to get them what they desire out of life. The school of hard knocks groomed me to be in a stronger position, where I'm capable of displaying the initiative to creatively maneuver through the challenges of life and the business world, in order to create my own wealth and standards for how I want to live. I am often in a position to hire college graduates and those with advanced degrees to work for me versus the other way around.

You can't rely on academic institutions alone, because they will never customize a superior plan for your ultimate success and happiness in life. No school can make you an Albert Einstein, Mark Zuckerberg, or Martin Luther King Jr.. A class of 20-50 students won't ever really accomplish this. The same applies with other mass group learning environments. No basketball camp will turn you into a LeBron James. No golf camp will make you a Tiger Woods. No political science curriculum will develop you into a President Barack Obama. You have to dig deep within yourself and create your own blueprint for greatness.

There will always be a disconnect, especially in school. This is shown more and more by the alarming, growing rates of college graduates having problems finding quality forms of employment relevant to their degree. They are being taught a brutal lesson that what works in the classroom does not always equate to success in real life. The conditioning that goes on in school does not prepare you for the conditions you most encounter in life.

For example, it doesn't take long to look at the real world and see how important the role of money plays. I'd like to say money alone accounts for at least 50 percent of what you focus on as an adult. Everything done in some way equates to money. The world we live in is heavily driven by it. However, I was never taught one personal finance class in all of my traditional schooling. I'm sure you weren't either. School never teaches us how to balance a checkbook, establish good credit, save up money for retirement, or how to balance a budget for personal expenses in class.

Of all the things taught, these important personal finance life skills are nowhere to be found within the standard curriculum. I had to learn all these skills on my own through life's school of hard knocks. I know people who have spent over 20 years in school getting a master's and doctorate, who were never taught basic personal finance skills in school at any level. That's beyond absurd to me. But it totally shows why I would never trust the school system alone.

School will often seem boring and highly irrelevant. It may feel like a mean trick set up against you, designed to watch you fail versus succeed. You will have to always go above and beyond to connect the dots to ensure the content you're being instruct-ed on makes sense to you. This does not mean you drop out of school because it's irrelevant. It means go the extra mile to master the content and make it relevant to you.

The interesting thing about the education system is that it will continuously provide you information. You will constantly be bombarded with information in the form of homework, research projects, exams, and other various assignments for as long as you're in school. But you must take that information and appropriately sort it out, so that it becomes knowledge. Take that information you're presented in class, and then do your own work outside of class to really break it down as to what's most applicable to pursuing greatness and making it big within the real world. Your success in life will be determined by the work you put in outside of school in combination with the work given in school, as opposed to just doing the work provided in school alone.

Mastery in the Classroom

There are three levels of learning that students fall into while progressing through the school system, if they don't fail. The first level is "Passing." Some students are just content with getting a passing grade on the course work and passing the class, even if it's a C or D. Just doing the minimal activity needed to "get by." Getting by will not cut it in today's society.

The second level is "Achieving." At this level, students are content with achieving whatever standard it takes to receive an A or B grade status in the class. Once they meet this standard, they feel their job is done. But the requirements for excelling in the professional workforce are not just limited to the theoretical minimum standards of excellence in the classroom. Many are finding way too often that just a good G.P.A. and degree doesn't cut it as well.

The third and highest level is "Mastery." At this level, a student prepares far beyond the point of grade status and excellence for the standards set for the class. The student is all about incorporating any learning regimens inside and outside of the class that they feel are necessary to "master" the subject. They do this not just for getting the highest grade. With the work they're putting in, good grades are a given. They're going above and beyond the 20 hours to get in the 10,000 hours of expertise it takes to successfully apply this knowledge in life. This third level is like getting the Bruce Leroy "Glow" when you're in an intellectual zone and your ability to learn and apply is unlimited.

Young black male, get your degree! You have a much greater advantage in life when you do versus dropping out or not going to college. But don't let your degree of learning be confined to the limits of the degree you get. You're gifted beyond measure. The educational system has always failed at accurately calculating your intellectual talents that are off the chart. Become the master of your own customized educational regimen for whatever drives you towards becoming the best at whatever career you're committed to dominating with your mind. Even in the scenario where getting a college degree is not possible, build your own personal continuous education program; and push yourself to acquire the knowledge to achieve to the best of your ability.

Secret Treasures of Life

There's an old fable about a ruler of the world who wanted to hide the secret treasures of eternal life from man. At first he wanted to put it at the bottom of the oceans, but then figured man would one day be able to build submarines that could get there. Then he decided to place it high in the sky, but figured man would one day build planes that could fly there as well. He finally said, "I'll put it where man will never think to look, a book." Over time this fable has been twisted and condensed to "if you want to hide something from a black man, put it in a book."

I'm counting on every young black male who reads this book to make this statement just as much of a fallacy as every other statistic highly undervaluing our intellectual capacity for greatness. We were built to win, with the power of our minds. No systematic weapon formed against us shall prosper anymore.

We must value the keys to unlocking any shackles of the mind. Knowledge and education are indeed the keys. Some of the most valuable treasures and secrets for achieving success in life are hidden right in a book. A lifelong commitment to education and knowledge through reading is vital to success. The gems are all there, within an infinite amount of books and resources that we can now access. There is no excuse for not empowering ourselves through the highest forms of learning we can achieve. This always starts with self-taught knowledge and expands by using the educational resources around you.

Young black male, acquiring knowledge is the only way to beat the system betting against you. Your mind and brain power is the ultimate tool to overcoming any obstacles placed in your way. The system is flawed because it can never calculate your will to succeed or your drive to empower yourself. Only you control this factor.

Regardless of what the world tells you, it's never too late to learn. I'm living proof! By passionately attacking the learning process through schooling and acquiring a degree, you're able to master the rules and parameters society has created for the game of life. Then by going beyond your degree and furthering your own quest for true knowledge through self-education, you gain the power to create your own rules for continuous success.

CHAPTER 7

Million $ Transition: How Dope Boy Skills Translate to a Successful Entrepreneur

B Gizzle

B Gizzle was one of the biggest dope boy legends in trap history. At one point, he was making over $350,000 a day. He made so much money every second of the day, from the drug empire he built up around the nation, that the saying in the hood was, "If B Gizzle dropped a $20 bill on the ground, he would make more money just walking past it than taking the time to pick it up." B Gizzle was not only a household name, but a verb synonymous with "Hustling," in the same way that Google became a verb synonymous with online "Search." In record-breaking time, B Gizzle rose up the ranks as the hottest d-boy on the scene.

B Gizzle grew up in a single-parent household with two sisters in a small city right outside of Jacksonville, Florida. His father was a heroine dealer during the early 80s, who was murdered in the streets when B Gizzle was only 2 years old. His mother worked two part-time jobs at a local cleaners and diner. She always aspired to be a science teacher but never finished high school. However, her biggest commitment to B Gizzle was to get him a pair of Jordans and a new chemistry set for his birthday every year.

As a jit, B Gizzle kept his hands in all types of scientific experiments. He was a natural chemist and a little business man as well. His favorite TV shows were Nickelodeon's *Don't Do That On Television* and *Family Double Dare*, where people got "slimed" with sticky thick green goo. At 10 years old, he learned how to make the slime from borax powder and glue. He would set up his own slime wars among everybody on the block. He made all types of slime guns; and he sold them to the kids and teens, starting at $3 all the way up to $30 for a super-soaker slimer. During the summers, B Gizzle would make over $1,000 profit in the hood with his toy military slime products.

B Gizzle would also evaporate a solution of Epsom salts in the sun and then mix it with water colors to make "bling bling" crystal spikes that resembled diamonds. He made a killing with those as well – selling them as accessories on necklaces, bracelets, shoes, clothes, and fitted caps for everyone who wanted to add some bling to their wardrobe. His favorite chemistry experiment was the baking soda volcano. He won the 6th grade science fair with his baking soda volcano that mesmerized the entire class when he set off a chemical reaction to make it erupt.

However, by the time B Gizzle got to high school, he was tired of school and thought it was a waste of time. Some of his other friends started dropping out and making money by selling weed. Since he couldn't take his favorite subject chemistry until the 11th grade and everything else about school was lame to him except gym, B Gizzle dropped out at 15 years old.

B Gizzle noticed that the major stunt boys in the hood were moving real weight, so he wanted to bypass selling weed and began serving dope. He latched on to an up-and-coming flashy dope boy they called Diezel. Diezel showed him the game. Diezel told him the key to moving weight was finding a good untouchable connect (like his plug in LA) at the lowest price to buy low and sell high, in addition to being able to cook and distribute that 5-star quality crack.

Below is Diezel's 5-Step Dope Boy Plan:

#1 - Hit That Lick	(Plug)
#2 – Flick That Wrist	(Cook & Whip It Real Good)
#3 – Grind Till Every Pheen Get Dat Hit	(Work Hard & Catch Every Serve)
#4 – Stunt Till Every Hater Get Sick	(BALL OUT & STUNT!!!)
#5 – Re Up & Flip	(Stack & Keep Growing)

"Hit That Lick, Flick That Wrist, Grind Till Every Pheen Get Dat Hit...Stunt Till Every Hater Is Sick...Then Re Up & Flip" is what Diezel would often say again and again. B Gizzle initially took an extreme interest in cooking crack because of his natural fascination with chemistry. Diezel put B Gizzle on to his first nickel rocks to sell.

Diezel had a secret formula to re-rocking his product to make it potent and still stretch from 1 ounce of powder cocaine to 2 ounces of crack rock cocaine. Diezel only let two females he had on his squad in on the formula, and they were responsible for cooking up his product. Because B Gizzle grinded hard and absorbed everything

Diezel did like a sponge, Diezel allowed him to hang tight at the bando spot, where he didn't allow many to come. B Gizzle got in real good with the two females who were a couple of years older than he was. He would strategically hit the spot when Diezel wasn't there, and secretly "back-doored" Diezel, by working over his ladies to eventually learn everything there was to know about his formula for stretching crack.

In a year, B Gizzle worked his way up to selling a quarter key. Diezel loved B Gizzle and took him all the way under his wing as if he were his own little brother. B Gizzle admired Diezel and his whole swag. Diezel would grind from 12-7 p.m. every day, outworking a lot of other dope boys. Diezel also made sure he was the biggest dope boy in his area by outdoing everybody around the way. He would cop the latest whips, from Escalades to BMWs to Range Rovers and trick them all out—painting each one indigo blue as his trademark. He kept at least five to six fine women with him whenever he was at the local clubs, and made sure he out-did every other d-boy in the spot to keep his name hot in the streets as a means of promo. B Gizzle soaked everything in, learned everything about Diezel's blueprint for success in the dope game, and was plotting for his own time to rise as the man soon.

Diezel was eventually indicted by the Feds and sentenced to 10 years in prison for intent to sell. When that happened, B Gizzle took over. B Gizzle had studied and eventually mastered everything Diezel did. So he swagger-jacked Diezel's entire style. He stole his entire dope boy swag and way of doing things. He took his exact same blueprint for moving weight and perfected it on a whole other level, always keeping in mind that 5-Step Dope Boy Plan.

B Gizzle had created a favorable positioning with Diezel's two female cooks, his team, and his clientele to begin a takeover. In watching Diezel's every move, B Gizzle had often wondered, "How can I do it bigger than Diezel? Why does he settle for copping a Charger and a Lexus versus a Bentley and a Lambo? Why doesn't he grind earlier than noon or later than 7pm? Why doesn't he take over more cities across the nation? Why is his main plug somebody on the West Coast versus a more direct plug in Mexico, where the price has to be much cheaper?"

B Gizzle used this heightened sense of curiosity and ambition to find his own solutions to these questions.

B Gizzle knew that to build a more powerful empire, he had to start with Rule #1 - Hit That Lick. B Gizzle went to LA and developed a relationship with Diezel's plug that had the "lick." The plug sold cocaine to B Gizzle at the same rate he gave Diezel, $17K a key. From there he discovered that the LA plug bought from a "higher-up" in Mexico. B Gizzle took a trip to Mexico and worked his way through to a major Mexican cartel connect.

He got in good and was able to get keys at $15K a pop. B Gizzle built upon this incredible price to build a squad of dope boys to move weight all across the state of Florida.

B Gizzle built off Diezel's Dope Boy Rule #2 - "Flick That Wrist" upgrading his entire process for cooking dope. Instead of two females from the hood, B Gizzle courted two recent college graduates from pharmacy school to enhance the chemistry behind his dope recipe. They perfected the method with baking soda at a 3:1 ratio and an even more potent freebase process with intricate compound solutions and isotones while still being able to stretch from 28 to 42 grams with a quick drying time. B Gizzle's product was so potent that his crack was branded and known in the streets as "that Megahard."

B Gizzle also made it a point to grind hard all day, every day. Forget the 12-7 grind, he wanted to catch every serve from 12 a.m.-12 a.m. non-stop. B Gizzle inspired his d-boy squad with the same sort of tireless work ethic. He would only allow the hardest rap songs about "Hustlin" to be played in his whips for constant motivation. B Gizzle flooded the streets with a 24/7 grind and built up a trump-tight distribution network for outworking the competition and serving the most potent product on the market, staying true to Rule #3 - "Grind Till Every Pheen Get Dat Hit."

When it came to Dope Boy Rule #4 – "Stunt Till Every Hater Get Sick," B Gizzle would break the knob off and get all the way "Turnt Up!" B Gizzle stole Diezel's entire swag and then multiplied it by 100! When dope boys and rappers were all on the trend of wearing platinum and white gold, B Gizzle brought it back to the yellow gold. He copped some of the most luxurious cars, including a Bentley, Maserati, and Lamborghini, which were all painted black and yellow. Everything was souped-up and sitting on 28s or better. B Gizzle also had a Dually Monster Truck that he would tow his other luxury cars around with whenever he decided to set the city on fire.

Unlike Diezel, who was a local celebrity d-boy, B Gizzle became known all across the country for shutting cities down. Whether it was NBA All-Star Weekend, The Super Bowl, a championship boxing fight in Vegas, or a major rap concert – B Gizzle was in the building and the after party killing it. Women were coming by the boatload to be the eye candy to his entourage. His VIP tabs easily ran over $30K.

Every birthday, B Gizzle threw a huge party and would fly in a major rap artist to perform, as well as one of the hottest female celebrities in the industry to be his main companion in VIP for the night. B Gizzle had the stunt game on lock. Everybody was talking about B Gizzle and how he would go "Megahard" in the paint. All the notoriety drove his celebrity trap star story and national drug ring sales to epic proportions.

Keeping his eyes on the money, B Gizzle definitely kept the "Megahard" dope business cycle growing by continuously stacking to build his empire to higher levels through Dope Boy Rule #5 – "Re Up & Flip." However, he began getting many of his shipments seized by the Navy at the border. This cost him a lot of money. After several seizures that left B Gizzle in numerous droughts, B Gizzle hit the ultimate lick when he found a way to make a serious connect with a top-ranked official in the Navy, who was responsible for drug smuggling seizures made with the Coast Guard.

B Gizzle cut a deal with the Navy official to buy the cocaine seized at $12K a key. When that happened, it was "Game Over!" B Gizzle used that superior profit advantage to dominate the competition and flood the streets across the nation with his "Megahard." At that price, which couldn't be beat, B Gizzle had created a monopoly where 80 percent of the crack in most of the cities he occupied was bought from him and his downline, saturating the market with his product.

Diezel got out of prison a couple of years early on good behavior, but when he came out B Gizzle had done a full-blown takeover. He had taken over Diezel's spot, and the next five levels above that. At only 24 years old,, B Gizzle was making around $10.5MM a month. He had moved Diezel all the way out and was moving that "Street Diesel" from coast to coast. Diezel tried to get back in the game but he had lost too much swag and respect. B Gizzle had the dope game in a chokehold. Diezel just had to fall back and witness the new king of a new era.

B Gizzle became a living legend. Everybody in the streets and beyond was talking about him. Every dude wanted to be him, and every woman wanted to be with him. He continued doing it real big...actually too big. The Feds built a major case on him, and everybody in the market began to plot on taking him down to break up his monopoly empire in the dope game. The government eventually got enough corroborators and informants to build a solid case to shut him down. Now there is no way B Gizzle will ever walk the streets again.

Crack De-Coding

The reason B Gizzle will never walk the streets again...is because he never did. B Gizzle never existed. He is a fictional character made up. However, B Gizzle's hustle and ambition is reflective of many real life trap star come-ups. What would happen if we took the fabric of this same "hustle" storyline minus the broken home upbringing, street criminality, and urban Slang—and then change the occupation from one of the biggest crack cocaine distributors to the biggest computer software distributor ever? We would have the same working model for arguably the greatest business story ever. The dope boy story of B Gizzle becomes the tech giant story of Bill Gates.

The making of "Megahard" cracked and de-coded under a different perspective and set of circumstances, highly resembles the making of "Microsoft." First, let's do the following swap-out of Bill Gates' childhood life and upbringing for B Gizzle's:

- Change Bill Gates' two-parent/upper-middle class suburban family of multi-generational college graduates and professionals
  TO...
  B Gizzle's broken home in the projects with no dad (murdered) and a poverty-stricken single mom trying to hold down two jobs with the majority of family members never finishing HS.

- Change Bill Gates' growing up in a beautiful and respectfully policed neighborhood, with elite private school education opportunities, inclusive of the most cutting-edge technology programs
  TO...
  B Gizzle's drug-infested neighborhood, inflicted with crime and broken down public schools with no resources to train young people for high demand careers – where police incarcerate, brutalize, and kill young males that look like him every day

- Change Bill Gates' young white male experience of a privileged upbringing in which hundreds of years of history, culture (lifestyle/language/religion), land, wealth, and pride is historically preserved and uplifted by the U.S. along with the global community
  TO...
  B Gizzle's young black male experience of ancestral persecution where hundreds of years of conspired destruction and mutilation of his history, culture (lifestyle/language/religion), land, wealth, and pride happened through the worst terrorist act of slavery in world history. Coupled with this is a systemic racist oppression historically preserved by the U.S. and global community at large.

Under these circumstances, it's quite possible that a perceived nerd tech boy genius like Bill Gates could've become a street dope boy genius like B Gizzle. Below are the parallel business tactics by B Gizzle in the dope game and Bill Gates in the tech game.

	B GIZZLE	BILL GATES
INDUSTRY	CRACK COCAINE	COMPUTER SOFTWARE
GENIUS TALENT	CHEMISTRY	CODING
LEARNING TACTIC	HACKING THRU BANDO & MASTERING POTENT SOLUTIONS FOR DEVELOPING CRACK	HACKING THRU COMPUTER PROGRAMS & MASTERING POTENT SOLUTIONS FOR DEVELOPING SOFTWARE
ACQUISITION TACTIC	TOOK DIEZEL'S SWAG & OPERATING STYLE TO CREATE A GREATER BLUEPRINT FOR SUPERIOR POSITIONING IN THE DOPE GAME	TOOK SEATTLE COMPUTER PRODUCTS' "Q-DOS" OPERATING SYSTEM TO CREATE A GREATER BLUEPRINT FOR SUPERIOR POSITIONING IN THE TECH GAME
STRATEGIC ALLIANCE TACTIC	MAJOR CONNECT WITH NAVY TO GET SUPERIOR PRICING FOR MASS DISTRIBUTION OF MEGAHARD CRACK	MAJOR CONNECT WITH IBM TO GET SUPERIOR MASS DISTRIBUTION OF MICROSOFT SOFTWARE ON PCs
PROMO TACTIC	SPENDING $ FOR "STUNT ADVERTISING" TO INFLUENCE THE HOOD MARKET BY BRANDING IN THE STREETS & CLUBS	SPENDING $ FOR "PRINT ADVERTISING" TO INFLUENCE THE TECH MARKET BY BRANDING IN COMPUTER MAGAZINES
MONOPOLY	80% MARKET SHARE LEADER – CRACK COCAINE (Multi-Market/National)	80% MARKET SHARE LEADER – COMPUTER SOFTWARE (Global)
ILLEGALITY	ILLEGAL DRUG BIZ NETWORK	ILLEGAL BIZ MONOPOLY NETWORK

Two separate upbringings and industries, but very similar business tactics implemented by B Gizzle and Bill Gates. Instead of being introduced to crack cocaine and developing a genius talent for drug chemistry compounds, Bill Gates was introduced to the computer software industry and became a genius at coding. Bill Gates didn't hack his way through a bando to steal exclusive crack cooking formulas, but he did spend countless hours working with companies and hacking their programs to steal exclusive coding formulas and practices as a teen.

In the same fashion that B Gizzle seized an opportunity to acquire Diezel's entire dope boy swag and style of operating his drug distribution to create a superior positioning in the market, Bill Gates acquired another company's entire operating system (Q-DOS) and tailored it to his own MS-DOS software, which he manipulatively used to corner the market. Bill Gates licensed it to computer industry leader IBM (who Bill Gates' mom happened to be on the corporate board of), as the exclusive software for their first desktop computer launch. Bill Gates promoted in computer trade magazines, which was his way of "stunting and flexing" to the tech world. He then went on to create a superior monopoly positioning of 80 percent market share for operating systems in PCs worldwide.

Like B Gizzle, Bill Gates too became a multi-millionaire in his early twenties, and by 31 became a billionaire. However, Bill Gates and Microsoft were also eventually conspired against and busted by the U.S. government for breaking anti-trust competition laws for illegally creating a monopoly that engaged in abusive business practices. In other words, from a street perspective—Bill Gates got way too gangsta with his hustler ambitions and was clocking way too much gwop in becoming a hood trillionaire (the equivalent of a corporate billionaire). In 2001, Microsoft was forced to follow a more strict compliance for business that reduced its market share and superior competitive advantage.

Although there is a drastic difference between the illegal business of crack cocaine distribution and its detrimental effects to society, versus the business of computer software technology and its remarkable benefits to society – they're both a business. Success in any business requires a certain business acumen that both B Gizzle and Bill Gates displayed. Bill Gates is currently a billionaire and the richest man in the world. Under different circumstances, without being on a misguided and dead end dope boy track, an ambitious, talented, and genius young black male like B Gizzle could possibly achieve such incredible success too.

Dope Boy Entrepreneur Traits

Motivated

Ex-NFL football player Herschel Walker said that in order to become the great bruising running back that he was, he had to be a warrior. He stated, "A warrior is somebody that can Go Get It!" An entrepreneur is a warrior, and the misguided yet ambitious dope boy with a "Go Getter" mind-set is cut from the same cloth. Most dope boys in the hood are driven by a sense of desperation, oftentimes due to living below the poverty line in a depressing environment where they have every reason to believe society has counted them out.

Life is about taking action. One thing the dope boy is all about is action. In contrast to most who procrastinate or are indecisive, dope boys make bold power move decisions and then move on it at lightning speed. They're always aware of the fact that tomorrow is not promised, so dope boys execute with a relentless drive. They're motivated and hungry—literally and figuratively. They want to eat! They want to put themselves in the best position to feed themselves, their families, and their desires to make their lives worth something. So they take the initiative to do completely radical and foolish things, like breaking the law daily by selling illegal drugs for a career. The d-boy is absurdly misguided, but very motivated. They have a drive like no other to "Go Get It"—believing the dope game is their one shot at breaking out of a hell hole, achieving real success, and becoming as rich as possible.

Risk Taker

A business principle applied to investments is "High Risk, High Return." The street saying to complement this principle is "Scared Money Don't Make Money." An entrepreneur determines in their mind that it's more worth it to chase their dreams and risk the stability of a 9-5. The Dope Boy embraces this mind-set even more because he is normally rejected by the 9-5 world. This, on top of his impoverished circumstances, puts him in a space where he feels he has nothing to lose and everything to gain. Even with the risk of death or incarceration, he feels he at least has a shot at doing it big and achieving a worthy level of success. The open application policy to the dope game where no resume or degree is needed makes this pursuit even more practical in their mind. So the d-boy goes for broke in embracing a high-risk pursuit to "ball out" where winner takes all.

Money-Driven

The No. 1 priority in business is to maximize profits. Every Fortune 500 company and global market leader embraces this to the fullest, basing every business decision made on this priority. In our capitalistic economy, the dope boy has gotten the same memo similar to the one Wu-Tang received and delivered thru the lyrics:

> "Cash Rules Everything Around Me
> CREAM Get The Money – Dollar Dollar Bill Y'all."

The d-boy has an insanely laser focus on the bottom-line profit. In the most extreme misguided, yet capitalistically compliant manner, the street hustler protects his money at all costs.

When a dope boy sees a clear way to make a lot of money, he locks in viciously like a pit bull's jaw when they taste blood in a fight. Every goal and action becomes centered on getting that money. Nothing else matters. On Wall Street, this tunnel vision drive and pit bull clamp on maximizing profits to achieve tangible fiscal results is a celebrated trait for generating billions and driving our economy.

This capitalistic ambition on Wall Street, which has also led to extreme success and prosperity in creating the most powerful nation in the world, has also created absurd levels of greed and white-collar criminality in creating the worst recessions and human disparities as well. Capitalistic ambition is the ultimate gift and curse to humanity. Just like every ambitious corporate exec and entrepreneur, the dope boy is constantly skewing this morality balance in exploring better ways to cut costs and make more money. That's the hardcore bottom line that the real world has yet to differ with.

Competitive Hustle

Rap is by far the most competitive music genre because it mirrors the competitive nature of the streets, which in turn mirrors the competitive nature of the world dominated by business. The hook to a popular street anthem by rapper Ace Hood goes:

"HUSTLE – HUSTLE – HUSTLE – HUSTLE – HARD
Closed Mouths Don't Get Fed On The Boulevard"

In this anthem a closed mouth represents an unheard, unsuccessful, unpaid, and ultimately unfed mouth because that closed mouth can't compete. That closed mouth is getting out-hustled and ultimately out-worked. This was a lyrical battle cry to the life gem that "Hard work beats talent when talent doesn't work." As competitive as the sports and business worlds are, this lesson is most brutally taught in the entrepreneur realm of the streets.

One of the most frequently used terms in urban culture is "Grind." At the heart of our culture's infatuation with the "Grind" is the entrepreneurial spirit and hustle of the dope boy. Like any person with this entrepreneurial spirit, competing like there's no tomorrow, the dope boy has to literally grind and get it off the muscle to make it happen. The drug game is a wide-open free market with life-ending risks and shifting dynamics, recklessly presented every second of the day. The dope boy is running a high-speed competitive race against countless other dealers, jack boys, killers, police-men, Feds, and ultimately time itself.

In the dope game, only the strong survive—and that's only for a limited time because most hustlers are delusional too. So when rolling the dice of life it has to be a Jigga-esque competitive spirit, embraced by these hustlers' core belief that "I Will Not Lose." This same win-by-any-means hustler's spirit to outwork the competition is, in fact, a major component to how Shawn Carter the Brooklyn Dope Black Boy suc-cessfully and legitimately transitioned into Jay-Z, the $500MM net worth, rich black business man.

People Skills

Teamwork makes the dream work. Successful entrepreneurs are able to hire and in-spire groups of people to implement a worthy vision. Leaders of businesses are able to effectively create a special culture of unique structure, motivation, and accountability that drives productivity among their team. Powerful dope boys are arguably tasked with creating an even more dynamic connection with their organization, because the workers have a stronger need for a real family to fill in the gaping holes and voids from a broken home. Ex-Kingpin Freeway Ricky Ross stated he was able to manage over 1,000 dope boys and made $2MM a day with his enterprise by taking care of his team and finding ways to make them happy so they would all produce.[1]

The other essential component to good people skills with any business is good customer service. In a straight 100 percent commission sales industry, such as the crack game, the difference in converting a serve is in the ability to connect to custom-ers and provide good service in closing the deal. This also includes being a serious closer as a salesman with an impeccable talk game, which many d-boys possess. In true hustler fashion, Jay-Z said in the song "U Don't Know":

"I sell ice in the winter, I sell fire in hell
I am a hustler baby, I'll sell water to a well"

That's a hustler! And when the hustler is winning, many around them want a piece of that energy. At the end of the day people gravitate towards people they like and admire, and the d-boy knows how to psychologically maneuver to create magnetic likeability among all types of people. That personal touch creates a competitive ad-vantage that positively affects bottom-line profits.

"IT" Factor

If you've ever been at the club when a major dope boy makes his appearance with an epic "walk-thru" around 1 a.m., you can feel the attention shift. They literally change the climate. The spot becomes hot! You can smell the difference. Recognizing a much more expensive cologne fragrance when they walk by, you can smell the money...literally. The room gets brighter from all the iced-out jewelry they're rocking, and the DJ gets more amped. Dudes start falling back—tucking in their much smaller items; and women start coming forward – sticking out their more glamorous assets. The entire crowd becomes very aware that something "real big" is in the building.

The dope boy commands attention. He is a walking movie. Men and women, especially in the hood, are fascinated by their presence. They're able to get people talking and spreading their rep in the most viral way, like a contagious virus on PR steroids. Dope boys often understand the inner and outer energy it takes to exude that intangible "IT" Factor.

Their <u>Hustle + $ + Swag = "IT."</u> That "IT" Factor is glamorized with the most luxurious material possessions they flex with 24/7.

The d-boy understands the significant influence of confidence, power, charisma, respect, and flossing, orchestrated in a manner that mesmerizes the masses who aren't able to pull it off. They set the bar so high that even celebrities aspire to duplicate and align themselves with their illuminating presence. In essence, the d-boy does what everybody can't do and makes it look easy. He is living out everyone else's wildest dreams...every day.

Business Strategist

At the end of the day, the dope boy, as misguided and doomed as he is, is the ultimate entrepreneur at heart. They come out of the real school of hard knocks with a 100 percent experience-based business education from the streets. The dope boy engages in every business function imaginable. They engage in illegal yet strategic and tactical plans of action for logistics, distribution networks, organizational management, profit maximization, pricing elasticity, product development, quality assurance, creative marketing, branding, benchmarking, feasibility studies, and so much more. They're the most innately developed entrepreneurs and business strategists within a thriving industry. Unfortunately, this industry is a product of a flawed system designed to put them behind bars or inside a morgue.

Core Business Strategy: *Find-Grind-Flip*

The illegal drug industry is a $400B dollar industry.[2] To be such a thriving business, it must operate behind the same business principles and strategies that apply to any other industry. This can be easily proven with the legalization of marijuana occurring all across the country. Professor Dr. Boyce Watkins stated, "So many black drug dealers from the inner city were locked up for selling marijuana. Now so many white business owners are becoming millionaires as the government allows them to legally operate medicinal marijuana businesses." What's the difference? Same hustle, but the government just decided it's legal versus being illegal before. Thus, most of the same business principles and strategies still apply.

Below once again is Diezel's 5 Step Dope Boy Plan:

#1 - Hit That Lick	(Plug)
#2 - Flick That Wrist	(Cook & Whip It Real Good)
#3 - Grind Till Every Pheen Get Dat Hit	(Work Hard & Catch Every Serve)
#4 - Stunt Till Every Hater Get Sick	(BALL OUT & STUNT!!!)
#5 - Re-Up & Flip	(Stack & Keep Growing)

Every successful corporation and entrepreneur uses these exact steps, just in different terms:

5-STEP DOPE BOY PLAN	5-STEP CORPORATE ENTREPRENEUR PLAN
#1 – Hit That Lick	#1 – Find The Demand & Market Opportunity
#2 – Flick That Wrist	#2 – Develop A Quality Product
#3 – Grind Till Every Pheen Get Dat Hit	#3 – Maximize Sales & Distribution
#4 – Stunt Till Every Hater Get Sick	#4 – Advertise & Out-Promote Competitors
#5 – Re-Up & Flip	#5 – Reinvest Profits & Grow Higher Returns

These five steps can be summarized by three simple words:

Find-Grind-Flip

Every business, whether on a Hood Street selling crack or Wall Street selling stocks, abides by this core strategy for successfully making money. The core strategy of business is to FIND, GRIND, AND FLIP. Find the opportunity and demand for business, grind to move the business, and flip the returns to maximize the money for growing the business.

Find

Every business starts with being able to identify and FIND where the demand is. What's needed, what's desired, and what's hot? In essence, what's the "Lick?" After identifying the product in demand and the people who want it, you have to FIND the right supplier or "plug" to supply this product to enter the market to "get in the game."

One of the primary strategies for business is finding the best opportunities to "Buy Low and Sell High." That's the fundamental model in business for maximizing profits. The more successful dope boy is the one who is able to find a plug that he can buy weight from at the lowest cost, and turn around to sell at the highest price. This is how every business maximizes its profits.

Real estate, stocks, retail, and the selling of any other product is totally dependent on this primary model of getting the lowest cost and selling at the highest price possible. The d-boy understands the Law of Supply and Demand, and he manipulates it to his advantage on a daily basis in the trap. The top d-boys are specialists at buying when no one else is able to buy, holding, and then selling when no one else is able to sell from the same position of supply power. With this position of leverage, the d-boy finds the best discounts to buy from a supplier, and has the strongest ability to make more money by selling at a markup.

As mentioned before, the drug industry is a $400B industry, which reflects a huge market demand flooded by people addicted to drugs like crack. The dope boy capitalizes on this opportunity through a viable market that is easy to penetrate in the hood. Despite the entrepreneurial landscape of the dope game, it's an illegal prison and death trap for young black males that kills our culture. So why settle for selling drugs? It's just one category of many things a true hustler can sell. It's not the only billion-dollar industry that we can tap into to make a lot of money. Homes, banks, food, clothes, phones, computers, cars, video games, websites, entertainment, music, events, and beauty services are just some of the many other categories with a high demand. The entrepreneurial skill the d-boy shows in being able to FIND ways to make money can easily be transitioned to FINDING legitimate opportunities and sources in other highly demanded industries to find even better ways of becoming rich.

Grind

The true grind in every business is finding effective ways to convince your target market to buy your product. That means the product, price, distribution, and promo points have to be tight. In a nutshell, this is the full scale of marketing. The dope boy has to make sure their dope is quality, to keep pheens hooked and coming back. Every official entrepreneur has to engage in the right product development, to ensure the quality of their product keeps a loyal and growing customer base. Both the dope boy and entrepreneur also have to set the right price that is appealing to the consumer and maintains a strong enough profit margin.

Sales and distribution is how you get the product out and bought. The product has to be available where the consumers are most likely to buy it. That's why the dope boy stays in the trap, and entrepreneurs of other businesses keep their products in other outlets like retail stores or online. That's where their greatest opportunities to sell are. When the dope boys want to increase their sales, they increase the amount of weight they buy, the number of dope boys serving under them, and the number of spots they sell at. The business entrepreneur does the same thing to increase business. They increase their product inventory, their sales team, and the amount of distribution outlets for their product.

The promo is how you influence the consumers, tapping into their emotions to leave the most favorable impression. For the d-boy, he can't advertise his crack on radio, TV, or billboards. With a 100 percent illegal operation, that would be the dumbest form of dry snitching on himself. So his way of promoting is flossing his expensive cars, iced-out jewelry, dime-piece females, and everything else he considers a luxury possession. Stunting in the club, popping bottles, buying the bar out, and staying "Turnt Up" is his main campaign to promote himself. The d-boy is a branding expert. Unfortunately, the better they are at promoting and stunting, the higher the risk their business and life is going to get shut down.

In the business world, the entrepreneur has to make his brand hot to his target audience, too. However, the advantage of an entrepreneur's promo is that they have much more creative flexibility to promote however they want, to as many viable customers as they want. They don't have to flirt with a delicate line of flossing, while staying under the radar, like the d-boy. They spend money just like the d-boy, but in a much more effective and open manner to advertise in numerous public ways. TV, radio, billboards, magazine ads, online ads, social media posts, events, celebrity endorsements, and many other promo tactics can be used. Both engage in a heavy marketing mix to beat out their competitors in the mind of the consumer, but the legal entrepreneur has a way better shot at enjoying the fruits of his promotional labor for a much longer time.

Flip

Sell product, stack money, re up, and flip! That's the cycle for the dope boy as well as the entrepreneur. Everyone wants to get bigger and make more money. The dope boy has to reinvest to continue to flip $100 into $200, $1,000 into $2,000, or $10,000 into $20,000 as many times as he can. Every entrepreneur and business in Corporate America does the exact same thing. The dope boy keeps a mental note and sometimes even a notebook of what he makes, reinvests, and flips. In the corporate world, a spreadsheet, profit and loss statement, balance statement, and cash flow statement are used to account for the financials. At the end of the day, both the d-boy and the corporate entrepreneur implement the same strategy to accomplish the same ultimate goal...drive as much business to make as much money as possible!

Success Profiles – Dope Black Boys to Rich Black Men

Dope boys are highly talented and ambitious business men. With the right life change and reprogramming of the mind, the d-boy can transition from making racks selling drugs to generating millions selling nearly anything else that's legit. They're the ultimate hustlers. Young black dope boys in hoods all across America have consistently excelled in the streets at applying the right business hustle to the wrong business. History has shown in numerous cases that when these dope boys properly channel their hustler's ambition to the right business opportunities, they become successful entrepreneurs and rich black men.

In fact, there is a company called Defy Ventures, based in New York, which only selects and trains ex-convicts to become successful entrepreneurs.[3] They recognize that many people who happen to be ex-cons have natural entrepreneurship skills and experience from running their own businesses before, which just happened to be illegal. Defy Ventures does an "Apprentice" type business competition for ex-cons selected from the application process. The winners are matched with mentors, who are successful business professionals, such as corporate CEOs, entrepreneurs, life coaches, and consultants.

A company statement about their program on their website homepage www.devyventures.org states, "We transform the hustle out of formerly incarcerated

Entrepreneurs-in-Training (EITs) by offering intensive leadership development, Shark-Tank style business plan competitions, executive mentoring, financial investment, and start-up incubation.[4] The program has produced numerous successful alumni who now run their own businesses.

There is an almost identical thread between what it takes to be an illegal street hustler and a legitimate entrepreneur. Here are several profiles of black males who successfully transitioned their business hustle from being criminal dope boys to legitimate million-dollar business owners.

NAME	JEFF HENDERSON AKA "CHEF JEFF"
CRIMINAL CHARGE	Intent to Distribute Drugs (9 years in prison)
TRANSITION SKILLS	Charisma, Product Quality, Multi-Faceted Marketing, Branding
MILLION $ BIZ TRANSITION	Catering Company, Publishing, Consulting
IMPACT	Award-Winning Chef, National TV network shows, Motivational Speaking to At-Risk Youth, Best Seller Book: "Cooked"

An article written by the *Huffington Post* described Jeff Henderson as one of the top crack dealers during his time in Southern California, making up to $35,000 a week.[5] In 1988, he was arrested and served 9 years in prison for intent to distribute. While in prison, Jeff became the prison cook and discovered a passion for it. After being released, he went on to become the first African-American chef at the Bellagio casino in Las Vegas. He began branding himself as "Chef Jeff" and launched The Henderson Group Inc., a catering, publishing, multimedia, and consulting firm. Chef Jeff has been featured on national TV, won numerous chef awards, and is author of the best seller book, *Cooked*.

Chef Jeff does motivational speaking to at-risk youth and has said the following:

"At-risk people have the gift, traits, and ability to create their own business. I tell kids I'm still a homeboy, I'm still a hustler. I just changed the products and the terminology. I tell young guys: "If you're a gang leader, you have the ability to convince people to listen to you, buy into your program, and follow you. You have great leadership potential, understand logistics, and know how to manage a diverse workforce. You just have to change your path and the type of people you deal with, and you could be successful, too."[6]

NAME	UCHENDI NWANI
CRIMINAL CHARGE	Conspiracy to Distribute Drugs (6 months/Fed boot camp)
TRANSITION SKILLS	Versatile Personality, Street Savvy Book Smarts, Strategic Management, Logistics
MILLION $ BIZ TRANSITION	Barber & Style College
IMPACT	Education, Shelter for Convicts & Addicts, Motivational Speaking, Book: "The Millionaire Barber"

Uchendi Nwani aka "Chin" was an honor roll student at Tennessee State University living a double life as a student/kingpin.[7] Uchendi had built a drug empire, anchored by a fleet of cars, with the purpose of smuggling cocaine from Miami to Nashville. In 1993, during the middle of an exam his senior year, police caught a million-dollar ship-ment of cocaine that he was tied to. Uchendi fled for 2 weeks and then turned himself in. He was arrested for conspiracy to distribute and served 6 months in Federal Boot Camp having to do 17-hour days of hard labor.

When Uchendi was released, he re-enrolled into college and focused on his bar-bering craft, cutting hair at the university salon while living in the halfway house. After graduating, he opened up his own barber shop and eventually the International Barber & Style College. Several years later, he became the largest barber school owner in the country with over 130,000 barbers and stylists.   He is also author of the book, *The Millionaire Barber Stylist*. In addition, Uchendi also bought three properties to open Opportunity House, which shelters former convicts and recovering drug addicts.[8]

NAME	TRACEY D. SYPHAX
CRIME CHARGE	Drug Distribution & Gun Charge (2 convictions/7 years in prison)
TRANSITION SKILLS	Risk Taker, Target Marketing, Situation Analyses, Investments
MILLION $ BIZ TRANSITION	Construction Company & Real Estate Company
IMPACT	Youth & Men Training Programs, Honored by the White House, Book: "From The Block To The Boardroom"

Tracey D. Syphax was a heavy dope dealer in the streets of Trenton, NJ. Tracey got hooked on his own product and became an addict as well. He did two prison bids for drug distribution and a gun charge that had him locked up for a total of 7 years.[9]

Tracey was able to transition his street hustler ambition and entrepreneurial skill sets to becoming an award-winning multi-millionaire entrepreneur. Tracey is President and CEO of his construction company, Capitol City Contracting Inc., and his real estate development company The Phax Group, LLC." He's a heavily involved community activist, founder of several youth and male entrepreneurship training programs, a White House honoree, and author of the book, *From The Block To The Boardroom*.

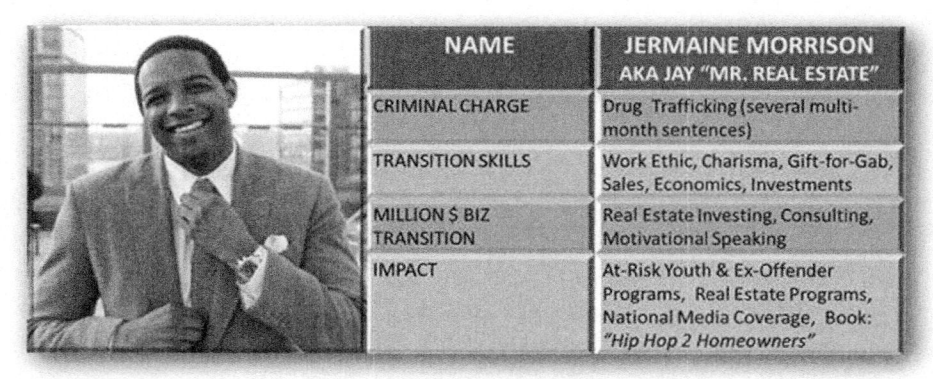

NAME	JERMAINE MORRISON AKA JAY "MR. REAL ESTATE"
CRIMINAL CHARGE	Drug Trafficking (several multi-month sentences)
TRANSITION SKILLS	Work Ethic, Charisma, Gift-for-Gab, Sales, Economics, Investments
MILLION $ BIZ TRANSITION	Real Estate Investing, Consulting, Motivational Speaking
IMPACT	At-Risk Youth & Ex-Offender Programs, Real Estate Programs, National Media Coverage, Book: "Hip Hop 2 Homeowners"

Jermaine Morrison, aka Jay "Mr. Real Estate," dropped out of high school and started selling cocaine, making $100,000 a year in New Jersey.[10] Jay racked up numerous trafficking charges and felonies in multiple states. He decided to make a change for the better and started learning finances and real estate while on parole.

Jay made a major life transformation to successfully channel his street hustle ambition into becoming a successful real estate investor, realtor, TV personality, motivational speaker, entrepreneur, and social activist. In branding himself as "Mr. Real Estate," Jay is also the CEO and Founder of The Jay Morrison Academy, an online real estate school and mentorship program.[11] Jay has been featured on numerous national TV and radio shows and has played a lead activist role for many black protests, including in Baltimore during the riots after the police murdering of Freddie Gray. Jay is also author of the book, *Hip Hop 2 Homeowners*.

Jay speaks on the superior lifestyle of selling real estate over drugs, but still credits the dope game with teaching him business skills no other school could ever have. He's fine-tuned those skills and confidently applies them towards multi-million-dollar opportunities in the business world. One of Jay's most popular quotes used during his motivational speeches is, "Think like a millionaire, dress like a millionaire, speak like a millionaire."

NAME	CHRISTOPHER FREEMAN AKA "MR. BEAUTIFUL HAIR"
CRIMINAL CHARGE	Drug Conspiracy & Drug Distribution (2 convictions/7 years in prison)
TRANSITION SKILLS	Warrior Mindset & Work Ethic, Branding, Product Quality, Unique Value Propositions
MILLION $ BIZ TRANSITION	Virgin Hair Business, Start-Up Business Investments
IMPACT	Federal Re-Entry Program/At-Risk Youth Motivational Speaker, Hair Industry/Entrepreneur Mentor, Books: "Crumbs to Bricks" and "Dope Black Boy 2 Rich Black Man"

By now you already know my story: high school dropout who started selling crack at the age of 14, became a major dope boy making upwards of $50,000 a month, and served a total of 7 years in prison for charges of drug conspiracy and distribution. I reprogrammed my mind and used absolutely every dope boy hustling skill set to fully transition into a successful owner of the multi-million dollar virgin hair enterprise, Beautiful Hair 4 U. In addition to doing motivational speaking for ex-felons and at-risk youth, I wrote "Crumbs to Bricks" and co-authored this very book written just for YOU!

Million $ Business Transitions

Everybody is not built to be an entrepreneur. Everybody can't hustle and make a way to get money for themselves by marketing a product all the way from the idea to the consumer. But the dope boy can, as well as many other street hustlers. If you have what it takes to make money as a street hustler, you definitely have what it takes to transition into a legal business realm, making even more money as a successful entrepreneur.

Below is a list of several street hustles that can transition into successful entrepreneurial careers in the business world.

Street Hustle	Transition Skill	Career Transition
Drug Dealer	Leadership/People Skills/ Hustle/Marketing/Sales	Retail Business Owner/ Real Estate Developer
Gang Member/Goon	Fearless/Protective/Instinctive/ Muscle	Security Detail Owner
Gambler	Risk Taker/Opportunity Chaser	Stock Investor
Con Artist	Salesmanship (Gift-of-Gab)/ Multi System Developer	Motivational Speaker/ Network Marketing
Stripper	Attractive/Seduction/People Skills	Business Owner (Fashion/Fitness/Dance)

A major drug dealer knows how to identify a market for drugs, create a plan for how to build a team to move the weight, lead other dealers through wholesaling, promote a street-credible image, and drive sales for his product. Those are masterful skills for any retail business in selling anything there's a demand for. You can literally set up shop and sell anything with that kind of hustle and know-how. A dope boy knows how to get in the game on consignment and then hustle to take over blocks to drive cash flow through expanded territory for cocaine sells. These same skills are used by a real estate developer/investor to buy homes on credit with no money down and buy up prime real estate on blocks to create streams of income through developing, buying, selling, or renting homes and residential properties.

That goon who's the muscle behind his gang with all types of guns and a fearless natural ability to shut it down when there's a threat, can be successful as the business owner for the most elite security detail for protecting celebrities and VIPs. That compulsive gambler who's always making a come-up on the poker table at the casinos playing for hours might be missing his true calling. The real game of gambling that produces millionaires and billionaires is the stock market. That gambler can put the same amount of time into studying the stock market as a stock investor. They can produce formulas for timing the market to make a killing off the lucrative economic engine of Corporate America.

That con-artist with the gift-for-gab of selling people dreams and hustle schemes to get money (we all know at least one) can shift that same hustle and flow towards generating multiple streams of income through one of the many legitimate network marketing organizations for ambitious entrepreneurs. Motivational speaking is also a great career for selling people dreams in a more meaningful and lucrative way. Although strip clubs are legal in most places, I'm sure we'd agree that we wouldn't want our daughters or mothers dancing at one. The seductive talent and work ethic a female stripper has can be channeled towards a business that capitalizes off her ability to look gorgeous and dance incredibly. She could become a successful business owner for a fashion boutique or clothing line because she has an eye for what is sexy. She could be the owner of a fitness club because she definitely knows how to mold a body into perfect shape, or even a Modern Jazz/Zumba/Pole Dancing instructor...for obvious reasons!

It's easy for the world to tell that dope boy to stop selling drugs. The same way it's easy for them to tell the goons to stop gang banging, the stripper to stop degrading herself for singles, and every other street hustler to stop doing what they have to do to make ends meet. I would prefer a world where no one had to sell drugs or do wrong to get by. But the reality is, the world isn't fair and most people hustling in the streets know this better than anyone.

The street hustler typically hasn't received a fair shot at life. They often come from a broken home and are ruined by a broken education system perpetuating a vicious school-to-prison pipeline, where they can easily have multiple felonies before the age of 25. In a world where all they know is doing whatever it takes to survive, illegal or not, telling a street hustler to stop hustling, with no other desirable alternatives to make money makes no sense.

Here's how this conversation between the world and the dope boy looks:

World:	HEY DOPE BOY, STOP SELLING DRUGS BECAUSE IT'S WRONG!
Dope Boy:	WTH else am I going to do to get paper?
World:	GO BACK TO SCHOOL OR GET A MINIMUM-WAGE-TYPE JOB AT BURGER KING.
Dope Boy:	*Looks at his True Religion outfit, goes in his pocket to hold his fat knot of money, flips the world the middle finger, & proceeds to keeps hustling*

The world is telling the dope boy and street hustler to stop making money hustling, but never teaches them how to make good money any other way. In fact, the world rarely ever recognizes the skills and courage it takes to successfully make money trappin' or hustlin'. They never give props for their entrepreneurial "make-it-happen" skill sets, which are identical to the business owners who create million- and billion-dollar business.

The dope game is arguably the hardest business to work within. Forget just going out of business, drug dealers and street hustlers are literally "killed" on the daily in what one could call "going out of life." But like Chef Jeff has said, "The same traits that a successful drug dealer has are the same traits any legitimate entrepreneur has. You have a product, you have a marketing plan, you have a vision, you build relationships. You outsmart and out-strategize the competition."

Young black male caught in the streets, illegal trades, or the prison system, due to your hustler's ambition and street-savvy entrepreneur skill sets, I believe in you and your ability to be a successful entrepreneur in transforming your entire life around 1,000 percent. You're a great business man, just in the wrong business. Switch up the game. Focus on putting that same ability to FIND, GRIND, & FLIP into a business that can officially fulfill your wildest dreams. There is an alternative way to make a significant impact and feed your seeds for generations to come through your genius hustle. Let this chapter be motivation for taking those exact skill sets that you have to grind in the streets, and make them shine within another official business realm so that you can take over the world.

CHAPTER 8

Thug Life vs. Real Life

Every male desires to be respected and successful. Men of all races throughout all of history have gone to great extremes to achieve this, especially in the face of oppression. Even religion has historically been used by men in the bible to create a culture of empowerment for fighting and winning wars. The American Revolution was based on a culture of fighting, by any means, to achieve freedom and liberty from British rule.

Every ethnicity has a rich historical culture in which boys are taught to embrace, at an early age, the process to manhood that most contributes to collective value and power for their ethnic group. Unfortunately, worldwide acts of oppression have been forcefully applied against blacks for centuries to destroy black culture more than any other. Black culture has always had to re-emerge from the depths of overbearingly difficult circumstances.

In so many ways, we were robbed of our culture during slavery when our ancestors were stolen from Africa and brutally separated from their families, languages, customs, religions, lifestyles, and legacy. Because of this, every era of black civilization in America from slavery to today has been a twisted combination of culture "co-creation," between blacks striving to regain a sense of self and the system that has been in place to unjustly define and undermine blacks. One of the products of this complex dynamic has been "Thug Culture."

Thug Culture

Aggression is a masculine characteristic that has always been admired in pursuit of power. The aggressive domination of another has been the primary tactic for most cultures in gaining power. Thug is defined in the dictionary as a brutal assassin. Where in history have we seen our most brutal assassins? Most often we can look behind our most powerful regimes and nations.

Contrary to popular belief, "thug culture" did not start with blacks hustling and saggin' our pants while committing acts of crime in the hood. Domination through brutality has been a tactic for acquiring power amongst the earliest empires. Egypt, Mesopotamia, and many other early ruling civilizations developed superior armies to destroy others, while taking over land and resources to amass even more power.

Christopher Columbus led a movement of annihilating Native Americans to take their homeland, which we now know as America. Even today, when push comes to shove amongst global forces, the ultimate threat is war. The brutal killing and total domination of another is the way empires have always been built in world culture. Read a history book or bible, and you'll find war to be one of the most prevalent activities. Historically, world culture has always inspired "thug culture."

In the book, *Brainwashed*, by marketing guru and founder of Burrell Communications, Tom Burrell, he states "one of the greatest propaganda campaigns of all time is the masterful marketing of the myth of black inferiority."[1] Mainstream media has created the impression that outside of terrorists, young black males are the epitome of thug life in the most negative context imaginable. Despite the respect and power pursued by every other ethnicity that has ever existed for engaging in "thug" tactics, black males have been most characterized as bad criminals and hoodlums for doing the same. History shows that the most powerful threats and enforcers of domination are most successful, yet black males are most ridiculed whenever operating from a similar barbaric mind-set.

Thug Life in Rap Culture

The demeaning modern image of the criminalized "young black thug" has been heavily influenced by the rap music industry. The profanity, vulgarity, violence, misogyny, drug hustle, drug use, street image, and reckless celebratory lifestyle characterized by so many black rappers with ties to the streets has been promoted to the world as the main prototype of the "dangerous black male." This perspective is unfortunately what mainstream America most likes to project and invest in regarding the young black male. Despite some of the root purposes of positive black empowerment for which hip-hop was created, mainstream America benefits most from exploiting the negative image it amplifies of young blacks.

All rap fans are not thugs. By some music industry estimates, 80 percent of rap music is bought by white consumers. As black males, we love rap music so much because it's our very own style and culture that uniquely expresses our thirst for self-actualization. It also expresses our aggressive masculine desires for money, respect, power, success, swag, and ultimately happiness. Hip-hop reflects the challenge we face as a people in striving to make it from the bottom to the top, rags to riches, and struggle to triumph.

The power in being a rap fan is in maximizing this empowering energy to be successful and feel good, despite whatever your life challenges are. Although rooted in reality, rap is most useful for its symbolic and metaphorical value. The true value in bumping Young Jeezy is to embrace the energy of his "thug motivation" trap stories of hustling, as inspiration for grinding and reaching the top of your own positive endeavor. The value in bumping Lil Wayne or Young Thug is to embrace the energy of their "thug rock star lifestyle" as entertainment and motivation for creating your own means to achievement and celebration within your own positive life endeavor.

The mistake is in idolizing a rapper's street depictions as a literal, criminalized model for how you should get yours. The harsh realities of the hood depicted in rap are very real; that's why we connect so deeply to them. The blessing to recognize regarding renowned rappers is that despite some of their tough upbringings in the streets, they are now free, alive, and successful as music artists — not current dope boys.

They make a lot of money and file their taxes as entertainers and business owners. That's why they're at liberty to create music about the streets or "thug culture" versus having to live it on a daily basis. They have put themselves in a position where their real life is all about being a recording artist who can talk about the streets, not literally engaging in "thug life" for a means of daily survival. The areas that they intend to dominate are primarily musical, entrepreneurial, and most of all financial. Despite some of their current encounters with the law, I'm sure they would tell you that they would much prefer to be rapping versus trapping, experiencing freedom versus prison, and being alive versus dead.

Rap captures the urban attitude and spirit of greatness in being young, gifted, and black. I'm all about being able to succeed against all odds, and my personal testimony is one big rap trap story in of itself. Rap, just like life, is tough and vulgar; so I don't mind the vivid depictions. Rap is realism art, which is a great source of entertainment and inspiration.

In light of these great attributes to rap music, I know it can also be disturbing and unproductive in content. There's more to life than the killing, drug dealing, and sexual overdoses that many rap songs perpetuate. When I was hustling, rap seemed to be more about the empowering mind-set of "the dealer" to come up and get money. As wrong as drug dealing is to glorify, at least rap had a hustler's ambition reflected in it, which could translate into success in many other ways. Now rap music seems to be more about a user/abuser lifestyle — "the stoner." That mind-set could never be productive. It's the opposite of a come-up and has me all the way confused as I hear it in the tone of rap music today.

Consequently, as we mature at various points in life, our perspective on rap has to be adjusted to use it for our best interests. We have to wire our minds and emotions to get the most out of the power of rap, while minimizing the negative ways it can influence us. I am very mindful of when I need to turn rap music off, when it no longer serves my purpose for handling my business. Rap music, just like any other art form or activity, must be absorbed with the proper perspective and discipline to know when and when not to use it to be productive versus self-destructive. I'm the sole controller of how I allow myself to be influenced by rap music, not the other way around.

I would be absolutely stupid to look at a Michelangelo painting of nude David and then go stand on a park bench posing butt naked because I was influenced by the art. It would be even dumber to watch *The Terminator* or *The Purge* and then start going on a wild killing spree because I was influenced by the movie. Young black male, be wise enough to know these rappers' intentions are to inspire, entertain, and most of all make money.

Many rappers will exaggerate or lie to make money and be successful as a famous artist. That's their prerogative, because that's their job as a creative artist. It's not their job to tell you the real truth about what they aren't really doing in their raps. Just like it's not John Cena's job as a WWE wrestler to tell you how all their matches are scripted and planned out. However, as a young, intelligent black male, it is your job to be wise enough to distinguish between musical "thug life" and official "real life," in order to find the true value of rap in its entertainment and inspirational purposes.

2Pac

The term Thug Life became popular in part by the renowned rapper 2Pac. Despite the derogatory meaning mainstream seemed to pick up from this term and 2Pac's image, 2Pac was a brilliant revolutionary. Despite his conflicts, he always stood for knowledge of self, justice, activism, social consciousness, and black empowerment. As the son of a black panther, 2Pac was aware and furious about the oppressive system used against blacks in American society.

The book, *Tupac Shakur Legacy*, shows in his own words how 2Pac was even more deeply concerned with "the escalation of black-on-black crime, including senseless drive-by shootings, drug dealing from and to kids, and the disrespect of women."[2] 2Pac began endorsing "T.H.U.G.L.I.F.E.," a code of street etiquette through rap culture, to build stronger respect and unity amongst everyone from righteous leaders to gang members for taking back our communities. T.H.U.G.L.I.F.E was also an acronym 2Pac created that stood for "The Hate U Give Little Infants F's Everyone." It was a "chickens coming home to roost" statement to society, reflecting the boomerang effect of society hurting young people in poverty, specifically blacks. 2Pac explained this perspective on T.H.U.G.L.I.F.E by stating "what you feed us as seeds grows and blows up in your face."

2Pac is to many the greatest and most purposeful rap artist ever. Despite his aggressive lyrics and run-ins with the law, 2Pac did not stand for killing and drug dealing amongst his own black brothers and sisters. His purpose in rap was not to promote an ignorant, uneducated, and reckless lifestyle amongst young black men. In 2Pac's last interview ever recorded, he mentioned he would love to lead rap culture to a monumental point where we launched our own political party.

All of his music and projections of aggression, violence, sexuality, partying, and being hardcore were all symbolic of the energy he felt was most influential in leading Black America to a place of economic, political, educational, and socio-cultural power. For any current rap artist or fan of rap to mimic 2Pac's hard-surface exterior image and style just for their own street thug glorification purposes would be totally flawed and the complete opposite of "keeping it real." 2Pac's T.H.U.G.L.I.F.E stood for being the strongest urban hip-hop blend of Jesus and Malcom X, making a positive impact on the black community as a strong enlightened black man.

The encoded definition of T.H.U.G.G.I.N amongst enlightened minds in rap culture is "Taking Hardship Using God's Gift In-spite of Negativity." 2Pac's version of T.H.U.G.L.I.F.E represented this mentality as a message for converting hopelessness into hope. 2Pac described T.H.U.G.L.I.F.E as the abstract urban portrayal for how a rose grows from the concrete. The rose is the ambitious young black male, and the concrete is the hard, cold ground of American society. Our history and struggle is our unifying connection, and our collective triumph as a people is our destiny.

Dope Boy Hustle Vs. Grown Man Purpose

Let's be honest, as a young male coming up, what is there not to like about the image of a dope boy? Ninety percent of what we see in the lifestyle of a glorified dope boy does not show them actually selling drugs or hurting someone. That info normally comes to us through word of mouth and their reputation. However, what we do see are the fresh new Jordan kicks, True Religion outfits, luxury cars sitting on chrome, countless beautiful ladies on thirst mode, iced-out jewelry, and VIP "Turnt Up" privileges in the club whenever they want.

These privileged abilities give us the powerful perception that they have a lot of MONEY!!! With money comes power and respect, something every man wants. The hood is mesmerized by this lifestyle. Most of us see struggle and lack amongst the majority of people we know. Even if we know others who are doing well for themselves, most are not able to really "stunt" in our eyes like the dope boy.

In general, it's natural to want to show our successes in life by showcasing our material possessions. That's what the world often judges us by. Why do companies even make mansions, yachts, private jets, and Rolls-Royce Phantoms? They make them because that's what people want to attain to show off a certain perceived level of status. Why have options of coach versus first class? The options are available because they separate people and create a culture in which one group of people is more privileged than the other.

Self-esteem is one of the highest levels of need, only second to self-actualization according to "Maslow's Hierarchy of Needs." Status is one of the primary ways our capitalistic society categorizes people. Systems of separating people by class and wealth have been the way of the world throughout history.

Young black male, you're not crazy for wanting the finer things in life. To desire your own fetish material possessions to make you feel more privileged, fulfilled, and worthy of status is very natural in this world. The global economy, driven by capitalism, primarily seeks to "capitalize" on this human need. But we can't be stupid by living and spending way beyond our means. This is one of the biggest misconceptions of the dope boy hustle image in the hood. Many think dope boys have all this money to splurge without breaking themselves. This is absolutely false! Most times it's all a big front.

Dope Boy $ Myth

The infatuation with being a dope boy is due to the fast money and plush lifestyle they're perceived to have. Growing up in the hood, we see the materialistic success of these young flashy hustlers and believe that most of them are in route to becoming a kingpin who is mega- rich beyond our wildest dreams — much like the ones glorified in street lore and movies.

On the contrary, this couldn't be further from the truth. Based on my hustling experiences, I found that 80 percent of dope boys never elevate to buying drug weight at a level above 1 oz. In many scenarios, it's less than this, oftentimes just 10 rocks.

Here's a chart that shows the money most dope boys, at what I call Level 1 and Level 2, were able to make on a monthly and yearly basis when I was hustling:

DOPE BOY – LEVELS 1 & 2

Level	Oz/Rocks	COST	FLIP	PROFIT	TIME TO FLIP	MONTHLY INCOME	PROJECTED YEARLY INCOME
1	10 Rocks	$100	$200	$100	3 days	$1,000	$12,000
2	1 Oz	$800	$1,600	$800	1 week	$3,200	$41,600

The reality is 8 out of every 10 dope boys are nowhere near a kingpin level and never will be. Most are stuck on this Level 1, because the drug game, just like most other business industries, is not set up for everybody to be a boss. To be a boss, in fact, is to be a real exception to the mass population. For you to be able to excel in the streets at a major level, it's almost impossible. There are thousands of drug dealers, or at least they consider themselves drug dealers, most of whom are poor hustlers competing for little bitty crumbs of the pie. Plus, many underestimate what it takes to sell drugs. It takes some sense of work ethic, skill, and resourcefulness that the typical low-educated person cutting corners in life doesn't have.

A petty hustler selling in increments of 10 rocks, which we called "jugglers," account for many small Level 1 dope boys claiming they're hustling. These jugglers are able to make double from their initial investment of $100 in flipping it on average about every 3 days to $200. A lot of young hustlers at this level would go around and brag to their boys about how they made $400 over the past couple of days. But that is not all the way accurate, because they had to put up half of the cost. They really just made a profit of $200. Over the course of a month, that turns into $1,000 a month.

Here's how this Level 1 Dope Boy's monthly budget probably looks (monthly income of $1,000):

MONTHLY EXPENSES	
New Kicks	$150
New Clothes	$300
New Jewelry	$300
Phone Bill	$50
Total	**$800**
$ Left over to Turn Up (Profit from $1,000/month sales)	**$200**

An income of $1,000 a month is cool for just splurging, and that's normally the only thing this dope boy can do with this money. So $1,000 spent on the new KDs, a couple of polo outfits, and a new chain, while flexing with a Metro PCS Mobile plan looks real impressive to the average young person. Plus, you may have a little change left over to get in the club and take your girl to Zaxby's a couple of nights throughout the month. But that's all you can do with this amount of money, as a little dope boy trying your best to stunt.

In the adult world, $1,000 alone is not even chump change. As a small-time hustler, walking around with a stack in your pocket comes across as impressive in the hood like you're holding real money. But if that's all the money you have, it's really small-timing it and fake flossin'. Most responsible adults put that kind of money in the bank or towards real bills they have every month. Having a huge knot of one to two Franklins covering a bunch of twenties and ones is something that only impresses a jit with no income. Any adult could hold that if they wanted to irresponsibly floss.

Real adult bills normally start around at least $2,000 a month. The poverty line in America is a little over $23,000, and many dope boys are below this line living in serious poverty. In some households, welfare benefits can total $1,600 a month, which is more than a lot of dope boys are making.

A study of one particular gang's finances showed that their foot soldiers made, on average, $3.50/hour selling drugs. This is way lower than the minimum wage of about $8/hour. That $3.50/hour is not even half of minimum wage. Keep in mind it's not just lil dope boy jits at this level. Many grown men in their twenties and thirties are hustling at this level of low payout. Due to all the risk one takes with their life and freedom for such a petty-paying hustle, it would make way more sense taking a minimum wage job at McDonald's and working your way up.

At this level of petty hustling — which, I reiterate, is the level at which many claiming to be dope boys are at – you have no funds to pay any serious bills. Although you're trying to flex in public as a dope boy, it's a totally different situation, more like a little boy, when you go home. You're trying to flex, but in reality you're really living off your momma. You're living in Momma's house because you can't afford your own. You're using Momma's car because you can't make enough to save and cop one. You're only able to put food in your stomach by the grace of Momma's home-cooked meals. Plus, you're borrowing money left and right from Momma whenever things get tight. In essence, you're more of a Momma's Boy than a Dope Boy — especially since you have to call on her every time for bail money to get you out of jail.

Yes, bail money is going to be required very often, because as a small-level dope boy foot soldier, you're always getting caught trying to sell hand-to-hand. To make that $1,000 profit, you have to sell at least around 100 rocks, meaning you have to sell hand-to-hand to numerous people and really get it out the mud. That's numerous different situations a month in which you're at risk of being jammed up by the cops.

One thing about the dope game is the smaller dope boys at the lowest level are caught and go to jail the most, because they have to always be out in the streets hustling. You're in the grimiest environments and have to deal with the greatest risks of getting caught by the cops. You're also at the highest risk of getting killed over any of the petty beefs that can easily pop off in the streets.

In the midst of depending on Mom for everything, you're going to dirty your little record up, while putting yourself in low-return/high-risk situations where she could easily be crying over your grave sooner rather than later. To go through all this for $12,000 a year and a closet full of overpriced kicks, it's just not worth it. Frequently, you're getting jammed up by the cops so often that this projection of making $12,000 in a year is never realized. You're hit with so many jail setbacks that you're not even free to be in the streets hustling a lot of times.

Now the dope boy at Level 2 moving weight at increments of 1oz (28 grams) is making more and profiting on average $3,200 a month. I remember when I was hustling at this level. That dope boy's expenses look something like this:

Dope Boy Level 2 Monthly Expenses (Monthly Income: $3,200)

MONTHLY EXPENSES A: NO MOMMA'S HOUSE	
New Kicks	$300
New Clothes	$600
New Jewelry	$600
Phone Bill	$70
Rent	$500
Utilities	$150
Baby Expenses	$150
Gas	$200
Chicks/trickin'	$500
Total	**$3,070**
$ Left over to Turn Up (Profit from $3,200/month sales)	$130

MONTHLY EXPENSES B: MOMMA'S HOUSE	
New Kicks	$300
New Clothes	$600
New Jewelry	$600
Phone Bill	$70
Car/Rims (Savings)	$500
Gas	$200
Chicks/trickin'	$500
Total	**$2,770**
$ Left over to Turn Up (Profit from $3,200/month sales)	$430

Now although more money is being made to splurge on the hot boy material possessions to floss with (kicks/clothes/jewelry), other responsibilities kick in, too, like rent and utilities if you want your own place as shown in Monthly Expenses A. But with only $130 to turn up in the club, plus no car to flex hard in, a dope boy is more likely to change to Monthly Expenses B. This means living with Momma and putting extra money towards a hood-flashy whip and rims to promote status with. Plus, this allows for more leftover funds to "Turn Up" in the club.

Therefore, even as a Level 2 Dope Boy, you're still living at home with your Momma and relying heavily on her. This doesn't feel good for a grown man who's putting on a persona as the No. 1 Stunna Boss in the streets. Plus, now you're at an even greater risk of getting jammed up in the streets, more than the Level 1 Dope Boy. This is because you're making more money by doing way more transactions, which makes you an even bigger target in the streets.

Your hand-to-hand sells may be with over 300 people a month, tripling the amount of risk. So you'll more than likely get caught by the cops and do various sentences of 9 months to a year at a time. Levels 1 and 2 dope boys are getting caught all the time by undercover cops roaming the streets incognito and getting caught more often for trafficking. In addition, you're on the radar for jack boys to rob you. Heated beefs are coming your way on the regular, because your slightly elevated position makes you a target in dangerous street territory.

You're absorbing all this risk of being arrested, robbed, hurt, or killed — for what? $3,200 a month and a projected $42,000 a year if you don't get caught, which is highly unlikely? In the real world, that's not really ballin'. You're only able to put on a front for ballin', because you're not paying taxes and still relying heavily on Momma for covering your adult bills and responsibilities.

There are many jobs that don't even require a college degree that pay much more than what 80 percent of dope boys make. Below is a *Forbes* magazine 2012 list of America's highest-paying blue-collar jobs:[3]

Top-Paying Blue-Collar Jobs

Rank #	Job Position	Avg. Annual Salary	Avg. Hourly Wage
1	Elevator Installer	$73,560	$35.37
2	Powerhouse Electrician	$65,950	$31.71
3	Transportation Inspector	$65,770	$31.62
4	Petroleum Pump System Operator	$60,290	$28.99
5	Electrical Power-Line Installers	$59,450	$28.58
6	Subway & Streetcar Operator	$59,400	$28.56
7	Commercial Divers	$58,640	$28.19
8	Rotary Drill Operator (Oil & Gas)	$58,540	$28.15
9	Boilermaker	$56,650	$27.13
10	Aircraft Mechanic	$54,500	$26.20
11	Railroad Repairer	$54,210	$26.06
12	Locomotive Engineer	$52,940	$25.45
13	Electrician	$52,910	$25.44
14	Telecommunications Repairer	$52,870	$25.42
15	Electronics Repairer	$52,420	$25.20
16	Pile-Driver Operator	$52,140	$25.07
17	Precision Instrument Repairer	$51,970	$24.99
18	Plumber	$51,830	$24.92
19	Brick mason	$50,760	$24.40
20	Millwright	$50,650	$24.35

Being a dope boy is supposed to be all about the paper, right? The main reason to hustle is because it's the only way to put food on the table for you and your fam, right? That's BS! Here are 20 jobs that pay way better than what most dope boys make with absolutely none of the foolish risk that goes along with the street hustle. All that's required is getting some trade schooling and experience under your belt.

The same type of initiative and work required to get any fake temporary success in the streets by selling dope can be used towards a professional trade. With this smarter option, you can make enough money to provide for yourself, move out of Momma's crib, cop a nice car in your OWN NAME, and still put money aside for future savings. Plus, you can engage in some hot boy splurging to flex whenever you want to Turn Up! Young black male, there is no excuse for getting caught up in the allure of the drug game. You have so many options to live the good life without losing it.

DOPE BOY LEVEL 3+

Below is a chart that shows income potential for the next Levels 3-6 based on my hustling experiences:

Level	KILO	Oz/Rocks	COST	FLIP	PROFIT	TIME TO FLIP	MONTHLY INCOME	UNREALIZED YEARLY INCOME
80% of dope boys								
1		10 Rocks	$100	$200	$100	3 days	$1,000	$12,000
2		1 Oz	$800	$1,600	$800	1 week	$3,200	$41,600
15% of dope boys								
3	0.11	4 Oz	$3,000	$4,500	$1,500	1 week	$6,000	$78,000
4.9% of dope boys								
4	0.25	8.82 Oz	$6,000	$18,000	$12,000	30 days	$12,000	$144,000
.1% of dope boys								
5	0.5	17.64 Oz	$11,500	$14,000	$2,500	2 days	$37,500	$450,000
6	1	35.27 Oz	$22,000	$27,000	$5,000	2 days	$75,000	$900,000

As mentioned before, I found that 80 percent of dope boys never escalate beyond Levels 1 or 2 in the game where they sell more than 1oz. The big myth is that they're ballin' when the reality is they are making less than most of the working class and are living at home with Momma. Only 15 percent are at a Level 3, buying dope in increments of 4 ounces.

When I was at Level 3, I was able to flip my product for a profit of close to $1,500 on a weekly basis. This put me at a monthly income of $6,000, projected out to $72,000 a year. In the hood, you're able to stunt and go ghetto fab. You can trick out your whips and officially move out of Momma's house into your own place. But the reality is that, you're making the same type of money as many everyday working professionals.

Most who enter the dope game ideally see themselves getting to a Level 4 where they're able to buy a ¼ key. That was my goal. I was one of the few hustling in my area to get there. I've found that a little less than 5 percent of dope boys are able to reach that level.

At that point, I began wholesaling to other smaller dope boys. On a good month I was able to move that ¼ key in 30 days for a profit of $12,000. The higher you go up the dope boy food chain, the more wholesaling a hustler does. So by the time I was buying ½ Key at Level 5 and a whole brick at Level 6, I had a small organization under me made up of other dope boys who were doing most of the street hand-to-hand transactions.

At that level, I was primarily concerned with flipping wholesale dope every other day as much as possible. Level 6 is the highest I got to as a dope boy, and based on my experience only 0.1% or 1 out of every 1,000 dope boys get here or higher. There are extremely few dope boys beyond a Level 6. The famous kingpin Freeway Ricky Ross was able to make as much as $2 million a day while managing over 1,000 drug dealers. But the far-fetched reality is he may be 1 out of every million dope boys. And even in the best-case scenarios, making the most amount of money, it's all fast money that never lasts. He had to do a serious bid in the pen just like any black man at that level. The harsh reality is you're always bound to get caught.

Blowing Money Fast

When living in the moment at these higher levels of pushing weight, you can make a gang load of money. But these are fleeting moments that come and go, because the money is coming and going so quickly. On paper and in the charts, the annual incomes are projected but rarely ever realized, because it is very rare that you're able to keep all that money being generated. At Level 5, you may think that based on being able to make $37,500 a month you'll be able to come across a total of $450,000 for the year ($37,500 X 12 months). But the real is, it's being blown so fast, with your world spinning out of control, and so much trouble coming down on you that you never really see that. It's a false hope that's never realized.

Below is a tab of two consecutive monthly expenses typical for a Level 5, making on average $37,500 a month:

MONTHLY EXPENSES – A		MONTHLY EXPENSES – B	
New Kicks	$600	Bail/Lawyer Fees	$20,000
New Clothes	$1,500	House Expenses	$1,000
New Jewelry	$2,500	Phone	$100
New Car/Rims/Audio	**$25,000**	Gas	$1,000
House Expenses	$1,000	Girlfriends' Bills	$1,500
Phone	$100	Chicks/trickin'	$1,500
Gas	$1,000	Robbery	$10,000
Girlfriends' Bills	$1,500	Family	$1,500
Club/Turn-Up	$3,000	Traffic Girls	$1,000
Chicks/trickin'	$500	Guns	$750
Family	$1,500		
Total	**$38,200**	**Total**	**$38,350**
$ Left over (less $37,500)	($700)	$ Left over (less $37,500)	($850)

An income of $37,500 should be more than enough to work with, especially when you don't have to pay taxes on it, right? Well check out the expenses during Month A, while you're spending crazy money to flex. Flossing has to be a part of your monthly expenses at this level of hustling, because it's the way you promote. You have to flex so hard and show that you're the man all the time, to maintain respect and power as the top dope boy.

During Month A, you even cop a new ride with rims and sounds for $25,000. In addition, you have all your other bills, including "Club/Turnt Up" and other random bills. You're covering the tab for chicks and family members leaning on you for all types of favors. When all your expenses for that month are added up and subtracted from that $37,500 you're bringing in, you're actually in the hole $700. Sure you have a stash somewhere with cash saved up from previous months of hustling, but you really have to hustle hard and "go get it" the next month to stay on top of all these expenses.

Now when you're on to the next Month B you're about to grind out and make a serious come- up right? Wrong? Although on average you're making about the same money in flipping the ¼ key, you get arrested and catch a charge for intent to sell. Now you have to pay $20,000 in bail money and pay off some good lawyers to get you off. So for that whole month, you can't buy any fly kicks, clothes, jewelry, or anything to floss because handling this case is your top priority.

Because you can't go out to the club and turn up, you're doing more trickin' with females at home. But in the midst of it all, you slip up and get robbed when someone breaks into your crib and takes your stash of cash and product. This could've been a setup by one of the random stripper chicks you were messing with. You cop some more guns for extra protection and, long story short, find yourself again taking an "L" at the end of the month, going in the hole an extra $850.

That's why the fast money is such a false fantasy. Nothing in life illegally done fast happens without harsh consequences. The faster the money comes for a dope boy, the faster the money goes. It's recklessly spent trying to prove you're the man, and to provide for others relying on you because you're the man. You feel the pressure of having to protect yourself, while watching your back from every direction because you're a target to "get got."

Meanwhile, the Feds are tracking your every move and building up a huge case against you. Yeah, I was the man, but not for long. I was able to beat the smaller cases by paying off lawyers who were experts at finding loopholes in my cases to get me off. But while getting even cockier about my hustle power, I had no idea the Feds were on me like a cheap suit plotting the big moment to take me down.

No Love for a Hustler

Part of the American Dream is being able to work your way up through society and make enough power moves and money to acquire the things you want in life. This includes a wonderful family, beautiful home, nice car, or significant career title. You want to max out on all these things, while making the right financial investments to create a comfortable safety net for you and your family that will last as long as possible. Everything you do ideally contributes to having more finances, acquisitions, and opportunities to set yourself up with greater value and comfort in life for you and your family.

However, as a drug dealer, there is no comfort or value that can carry over to pursue this American Dream without consequences. Regardless of how much money you make as a dope boy, it can never work for you in the long term. You just have to be a fast-money illegitimate hustler with no long-term security.

Young black male, society has no love for you once you turn to the streets as a dealer. For one, society doesn't even recognize that you work, so your money is not accounted for. Although you're keeping more money in the short term by not paying taxes, you're setting yourself up to become an enemy to the biggest thug in world history. That would be the American government. Uncle Sam and the IRS require every working person making a certain level of income to pay a certain percentage in taxes to the government. By operating outside of this law, the American government will hawk you down and have no mercy in finding a way to punish you.

Also because of the manner in which you make money you're unable to legally account for, society will show no love in viewing you as an illegitimate who is less than an adult. Most major purchases you make as a drug dealer will have to be in cash, because you will not be able to establish any line of credit with the occupation of a dope boy. One of the more demoralizing feelings I had as a dope boy was making all this money and having to ask family members who made way less to come with me to a car dealership to put it in their name. I had to ask older relatives to co-sign my leases, because on paper it looked as if I was unemployed and broke. As a man and adult, we always want to be respected; but a dope boy only gets that respect from the hood.

When you learn about savings and financial investments, channels through which money is able to increase by itself, placing thousands of dollars under a mattress becomes real wack. There are so many financial investment opportunities to maximize on the American Dream where your money works for you, but dope boys are rarely given the opportunities to take advantage of these instruments the way respected working-class citizens are.

Putting away $500 every month in a retirement account (IRA) as a legitimate working-class person, at 8 percent interest can turn into over $148,000 in 20 years. That is a stable, secure way of looking at finances and life in the long term. You can't retire at 50 and live off a crack cocaine distributor pension. As a dope boy you have no long term. Plus, your short term is always in jeopardy; and you can't even really consider what you make in a month a reliable amount to project out a yearly income, because you can and will face a serious setback at any moment.

Young black male, if the long-term effects are a loss, it's NEVER worth it. The dope game is the biggest example of this. For one, an overwhelming majority of dope boys never make a lot of serious money selling drugs; that's the honest reality. And for the few who do, you have no rights to that money or anything acquired with it. In Jay-Z's first album, *Reasonable Doubt*, he lyrically portrays his life as a hustler in a song called "Can I Live" and states in the intro:

"Well, we hustle out of a sense of hopelessness, sort of desperation.
Through that desperation, we become addicted
Sort of like the fiends we accustomed to serving

But we feel we have nothing to lose, so we offer you, well...
We offer our lives, right. What do you bring to the table?

Society would respond to a young Jay-Z hustler (one that would never have made it if he hadn't quit selling drugs completely to pursue a legitimate career as a rap artist and business mogul), along with any other street hustler and say "ABSOLUTELY NOTHING. WE'RE GOING TO TAKE ABSOLUTELY EVERYTHING FROM YOU AND REDUCE YOU TO ABSOLUTELY NOTHING!" The governmental powers of our society will literally take your table and everything else you think you own.

As a dope boy, when you get in the game you forgo your civil liberties. When you get robbed by some jack boys, you can't file a report with the police and pursue legitimate justice for someone jeopardizing your life. You can't get insurance on any stashes of cocaine as your main business asset. If a server shorts you on money off product, you give them on consignment, you can't sue them in court. No civil liberties, no rights. You're the only one who can protect yourself.

When I made over $10,000, I couldn't even put it in the bank because it would have to be legitimately tracked. That would've put me on the radar for a lifestyle and earnings level that I couldn't prove without going to prison and having everything taken away from me. Hustling becomes one big bad dirty joke played on you. You think you're stacking money and making the most of your life, but the more you do to come up the more you're increasing the chances of being brutally set back.

Young black male, there is absolutely no love for a hustler. The homeys, women, and entourage around you are mostly there because they need your money and influence – not necessarily because they have genuine love for you. Your customers are addicted to a substance far beyond anything that has to do with being loyal to you because you're a good businessman. They'll flake out on you whenever the opportunity presents itself.

Worst of all, cops and federal agents are paid salaries they depend on to take a chunk of your life away, by catching you and sending you to prison to do hard time. Plus, there are an increasing number of envious competitive hustlers and jack boys in the streets putting a price on your head. They're looking to get seriously paid by taking your life. The whole world begins to plot against YOU to take YOU OUT!

The only reason why such a dangerous high-risk/low-return, short-term hustle is pursued so often by so many naive ambitious dreamers is because every hustler thinks they can beat the system and not get caught. Every hustler thinks they can plot to make major dough and beat the addicts, hustlers, criminals, cops, court systems, Feds, and ultimately the U.S. government. Dope boys always think they can beat the odds and live the good life without doing time in prison or getting killed.

This is the biggest illusion of all for the ambitious street hustler. The most significant stat I discovered from all my experiences as a hustler is the following success rate of a dope boy:

0%

Of all the dope boys that I knew who were hustling during the same time that I was, and who never quit on their own, NONE were able to escape prison or early death – including myself.

Young black male, a life of crime as an over-glorified dope boy has a zero success rate. You will be broken down to zero. You will be broken down to absolutely nothing, because you will be sent to prison, or killed!

CHAPTER 9

The Trap Pt. 1: Prison & Death

TRAP HOUSE

I n the hood, the spot where you cook, stash, or distribute drugs is known as the "Trap House." That's either the actual crack house or the area in which a dealer is serving his product. Often the surroundings of these places are highly enclosed with a one-way entrance and exit. In a trap house, you're in essence "trapped" if you ever get jammed up by jack boys or the cops. "Trappin'" insinuates going into this hood spot to put in work knowing that in the mix of grinding for a come-up, all around you are the dangerous elements of getting hurt, jacked, caught, or killed. In the streets, anyone trappin' must be aware of this danger 24/7. This is why it's called the Trap House.

Unfortunately, young blacks engaging in this criminalized way of thug culture is nothing but a literal "trap house." We live in a world that has conspired so much against us on such enormous globalized proportions that we can never win that game of "thug life" the way we normally engage in it. The energy of respect, swag, money, and power, by any means, is indeed an empowering one for any male. However, attaining these desired attributes through the streets comes with fatal consequences.

We all desire to have control, status, material possessions, beautiful women, riches, titles, followers, fans, honor, and ultimately our way with this world. That is a natural aggressive desire of all men of every creed and color. However, when we fall too deep into a thug life persona, which leads to trying to dominate through criminal activity in the streets, the system is historically against us and always wins in punishing us with "real life" consequences that are never worth it. That's the ultimate trap, being tricked into a bad situation that you can't get out of. Thinking you can achieve long-term success and happiness by trappin' is a "trap house" of the mind and unavoidable circumstance.

The Fall

I was a "trap star" who thought I could beat the system and never get caught moving weight. Go to prison and do time? Me? "The Champ?" Yeah, right! You couldn't tell me I wasn't a young Cassius Clay, dancing my way around the dope boy ring without being touched. I felt I had enough money and enough muscle to buy or push my way out of any trouble. I just knew I was too illusive, strategic, and resourceful to ever fall off. Like every other ambitious hustler in the streets, I was delusional to think I could continue this full-time hustle of committing multiple crimes on a daily basis and not feel the repercussions of the law. I was literally in a mental "trap," where I saw nothing but these bright "stars" for my life without realizing the inevitable surrounding darkness I would soon become victim to.

One evening I was with my first wife eating at Sneakers Sports Bar. We were enjoying our food during a date night out. After we finished our food I noticed a lady and man begin walking towards our direction from the bar. They came to my table and said, "Christopher Freeman!" I was thinking in my head, "How do these people know my name?" I quickly scanned them up and down and knew they were some form of law enforcement. Then the man flashed his U.S. Marshall gold badge. Deeply concerned at this point, I said to myself, "WTF Did I Do! WTF Have I Gotten Myself Into Now!"

Immediately, they grabbed me and the man said, "Do Not Make a Scene." They sat down at our table and said, "If you have anything on you, pass it under the table." I knew they were referring to drugs or a gun, and I told them I didn't have anything on me. They told me to get up from the table and walk with them. I glanced at my wife, who was looking terrified and left her the keys. They escorted me into a van and took me to the DEA building. I had been arrested by the U.S. Marshalls.

At the DEA building, I found out they had been tracking me for 6 months to get an indictment. I was arrested and investigated for two different conspiracy charges with different groups. They knew everything about me. They knew my movements over those months and all about where I would go. They knew exactly where I lived and all about what was inside of my house. They knew about the rifles I had and my pit bull. When I saw how long and how strong their investigation was on me with the multiple hands they had against me, I knew several people close to me had folded and snitched.

My lawyers were quick to tell me what I already knew, the Feds don't lose cases. With my conspiracy charge, all they had to do was prove I "conspired" to sell cocaine. This was something very easy to do, and something they prove all the time, especially with informants working for them. My lawyers stated it would best serve me to cop a plea and settle for a shorter sentence.

The Feds have a 95 percent conviction rate for cases that go to trial. It's so high because they're brutal manipulators at jamming someone up in your circle and squeezing them to sing. The Feds make agreements to reduce their sentence or let them off in exchange for personal intel about you. The 95 percent conviction rate means that in 95 out of 100 cases there is somebody supposedly "real," snitching on somebody, oftentimes someone close in their camp. Ninety-five percent of gangstas and dope boys will fold and become the softest most selfish corroborators for the DEA when facing serious time. I knew the game but fell victim to this 95 percent snitch rate that inevitably catches up with most hustlers.

Ninety-seven percent of federal cases are plea bargains, because it's nearly impossible to beat a case. Knowing this, I took the plea bargain. Before I was sentenced, I tried to stack as much money as possible to leave with my pregnant wife, so that she would be able to hold it down in raising our first son without me. I also wanted to put some aside to be able to make moves when I got out. I left her with close to $100K and gave my brother 12 stacks to put away for me. I tried to put everything in place so that when I got out everything could be the same. But it never was, and it never is. I was sentenced to do 78 months in the Jesup, GA, Federal Prison. Life would never be the same.

Prison

To sell drugs and think prison time isn't about to be your new reality is beyond ridiculous. I got caught, most of my partners got caught, the small petty hustlers got caught, the major-level dope boys got caught. The kingpin street legends, like Frank Lucas, Big Meech, and Freeway Ricky Ross, all got caught. EVERYBODY gets caught. Selling drugs has a 0 percent success rate and 100 percent rate of failure. If you stay alive and don't quit, you will get caught; that's a fact. If YOU sell drugs YOU will get caught. And prison will be the worst and possibly last experience of your life. It's not worth it at all.

Trust me, as a man who was forced to give years of my life to the prison system, you NEVER want to be behind those bars in that 6 X 8 cell surrounded by steel walls. It's no place for a free-thinking man. Before going to prison, I would often hear about the deadly shanking or raping that could take place. Those activities do go down because you have dangerous men from all different walks of life who are encaged for a great part of their life. They must find out how to survive within their own imprisoned means to exist mentally, physically, spiritually, emotionally, psychologically, and sexually.

My first bid was in the Jesup, GA, Federal Prison, which was a medium-low security prison. Although there is always a threat of violent breakouts occurring in the pen, it was nothing I had to worry about consistently at this prison. The guards seemed to have everything under control, and most of the inmates were just serving their time without creating much ruckus. It was more civilized than I had expected.

Although constant fights and murders weren't happening in this particular prison, it was still a miserable experience. Violence is not what breaks down every man who enters the pen. The absolute worst part that breaks down every man is the loss of his freedom. You never realize how incredible it is to have your freedom until it is taken away from you. The time on your hands, as a man who's no longer able to live freely, when totally isolated from the world you were meant to live in, is what kills you.

Freedom is better than anything. It's what allows you to do everything you do in life. Without freedom your whole life is nothing. You have the opportunity as a free person to pursue happiness and do whatever you want to do. You don't even understand that until you lose it, and it's all taken away in prison.

In prison, you can't just up and watch your favorite TV show, surf the web, listen to the new hot mixtape your favorite rapper dropped, spend quality time with your loved ones, make out with your lady, play pickup ball whenever you want, turn up with the homeys at the club, start a business, go to Walmart at midnight for some munchies, go out of town, hit a BBQ for Memorial Day, watch your children open their Christmas gifts, or just take a stroll in the park. Jeremiah, my closest homeboy who I sold blow pops with and put on to sell weight, died while I was in prison. Not being able to go to the funeral to pay my last respect burned me inside. As a prisoner, you forgo all the big and little things you cherish in life. Even your name is reduced to a series of numbers. I was inmate # 29269-018.

I run across young guys that'll say, "Man if I can get 3 good years of ballin', pushing this weight, I could do 25 in the pen." My response is "NO YOU CAN'T!" Lil buddy, every hustler says that and feels like getting that fast money while living that fast life is worth whatever prison time comes along with it. And that's "if" they get caught. But there's no "if"; you will get caught.

Dead Man Walking

I know it's easy for most young jits out hustling to say, "So what, I don't see the pen." But young black brother, if you try to make a life out of selling drugs, you're gonna see that pen. You're gonna see it, and it's gonna see you all the way out. You will feel that hurt. You think you're people are gonna hold you down? It's gonna hurt to find out nobody is gonna ride for you like that. Your Mom might, but NOBODY else will; they'll all forget about you. You know why? You're DEAD to them.

Ever wonder what your own funeral will be like when you die? Well, in prison you no longer have to wonder — YOU GET TO LIVE THROUGH YOUR OWN FUNERAL. Yes, being incarcerated is like seeing your own funeral but even worse. In fact, it's more like seeing your own grave site, because for the most part NOBODY is going to be checking on you. Every day you're on your own, rotting in a living cemetery. You get to see who will really be there for you and who won't. The reality is, you've been removed from the living world just like at a grave site, so you no longer exist for anyone in that world. That pain right there is worse than any physical harm that could violently pop off in the pen.

Deep within every man, we all want to provide for our family. I had created a "ballin'" lifestyle for my wife and son on the way, but that money flow was cut all the way off in prison. You aren't there for your family physically or financially. When I was first locked up I was trying to hold on and make moves for my family behind bars. I still had money that I left with my wife, and I would try to tell her how to pay the bills; but the money was running out so fast because none was coming in.

Keep in mind, I was locked up during my first bid for almost 5 years. On a small scale, the minimum bills to pay were $3,000 a month, which comes to a total of $180,000 over 5 years. As much ballin' as I was doing, I still didn't have 180 racks stashed away. The money I left quickly ran out for my family, and there was nothing I could do about it. I was unable to be there for them. In the streets I was the man, but in prison I was reduced to nothing. For all intents and purposes, I was dead to them and of no value to the world or my loved ones.

My first year in prison, my wife visited me regularly. I saw my son Chris Jr. 2 weeks after he was born, and what carried me through was knowing they would regularly be coming through to see me. I would mark off on the calendar when they were going to come through each month. My wife would pick up all my calls and keep me motivated, assuring me that she loved me and was going to hold it down.

But by Year 3 things had really fallen off. She stopped visiting as often, stopped writing, and it became harder and harder to reach her by phone. She then began telling me to stop calling after 5 p.m. At that point I knew why. She was definitely seeing another man. Not only had the money run out, but her patience in holding it down while becoming terribly lonely and depressed wore thin as well. I knew this and there was nothing I could do.

I saw my marriage falling apart. The streets also began to talk, so I was getting word from outside that she was seeing another man. Women can be very vulnerable, and this is fully exploited once their man gets sent away to prison. After years or in many cases months a woman begins to think "why should my life be put on pause just because my man is locked up."

My wife was 22 when I got sentenced, so she was young with so much life to live. She still wanted to live her life, plus she had major bills and a lifestyle to maintain. Before I got locked up, I paid all of the bills and provided for an extravagant lifestyle as a major dope boy bringing in all the bread. She was dependent upon me for all of her needs, especially financial. So when I was sent away to prison, the pressures of being able to provide for everything by herself were overbearing. I wasn't there as a devoted husband to give her nor our son what was needed.

My wife married me to be with me for life, not without me. So in my absence she desperately desired attention and affection from a man. What attractive woman in her early twenties doesn't want to spend time with a man, be courted to dinner, catch the latest movie at the theater, go on vacations, get help with the bills, receive flowers for Valentine's Day, while having her needs fulfilled in the bedroom? Unfortunately, it was only natural that she eventually chose another man who could fulfill these needs and desires.

As hard as this decision was for me, I told her she could see other men. Just don't let anything happen that would all the way ruin our marriage, as if being locked away for years didn't already have that effect. While I was in prison, my wife ended up falling for another man and got pregnant. That was it! I had lost my marriage and my family.

Being the alpha male that I am, that broke me inside. When I was released from prison, I knew I couldn't accept what had happened and I divorced her. But we were doomed as soon as I got incarcerated and removed from her life. The reality I had to come to grips with of failing my family as a man and provider is what I had to violently wrestle with in my mind every night in prison. It even haunts me at times to this day.

Young black male, if you want to keep your chick, don't go to prison! If you want to keep your wife and family, don't go to prison. If you mess around and have to do some time, your main lady will start loving another man who's taking care of her and your kids. She'll also probably have a child and family with him. She's not going to be able to ride for you the way you wish she could. Being sent to prison, for the most part, makes your wifey a widow. Sure she loves you, but you're dead to her and she must move on with her life.

Same goes for the bulk of your family, homeys, jump-offs, and everyone else you thought cared about you. One of the worst parts about prison is you lose your loved ones. Without them life becomes a deadly cold place, and that's exactly what prison is. You feel like a dead man walking in prison, because while incarcerated a part of you literally dies. When you get locked up, the prison system becomes your father, mother, brother, sister, wife, husband, boss, president, minister, best friend, and most of all worst enemy.

In prison you lose all control and someone now controls you. Somebody, in some cases even younger than you, is telling you what to do all the time. In taking orders, you'll have to endure much disrespect, something that goes against every instinct to being a man. Prison is the most dehumanizing experience there is.

It's infuriating when a guard with power over you requires you to do a strip search. It's not normal for you to stay cool, while your cell is randomly searched by guards throwing your belongings around, running through all your stuff however they want. Plus, your time will not just be spent playing spades, weightlifting, hooping on the yard, drinking coffee. Much of your energy will be exhausted within your own mind, trying to figure out how you're going to stay sane. "Doing Hard Time" is no punk.

Doing Time

Chris on the yard with some of the homeys "Doing Time"

"Doing time" is a verb and a skill. When sentenced to prison, you have to learn how to do it. You have to try to figure out a routine and purpose, or you'll go crazy. Luckily, I was able to find a purpose and source of sanity by reading books, getting an education, and staying focused on having a legitimate plan to succeed in life without resorting to crime when I was able to get out. However, most people can't handle doing time.

Many inmates contemplate suicide because the time they have to serve eats them alive. At the end of the week, you can't just go ride out to the club downtown or go on an out-of-town trip for the weekend. You never go anywhere. You're disconnected from your comforts and norms to a breaking point that can be unbearable.

Try going without your smart phone for a week. Just in that short period of time, you'll feel a huge level of discomfort. Now multiply that times the pain of someone taking away your clothes, music, friends, family, computer, job, sex life, sports, cable, TV, parties, birthdays, holidays, favorite food, favorite drinks, favorite vices, and anything else valuable you can think of. Then lock yourself in an encaged place where you can't leave. This may give you a small dose of the psychological torture an inmate faces when doing time for several months, years, or in some cases the rest of their life.

When I was locked up, inmates were given 300 minutes a month to make collect phone calls in 15-minute increments on the prison phones. These phones are referred to in the joint as the "stress box." Also every hour there is a 10-minute time frame called "Move." This is a controlled movement where you can go anywhere on the yard.

Daily showers, three square crappy meals, recreation on the yard, and jobs where you get paid peanuts are the main daily activities you're allowed to do. Otherwise you stay in your cell keeping yourself occupied. Education, group meetings, and church can be thrown in the mix, but this is the gist of what you do every day by yourself or amongst your segregated group. And under certain prison circumstances, it can only get worse. You can find yourself in a prison that is a straight-up jungle! Every day you could be fighting for your life.

Hell in a Cell

Back in the day, HBO had a popular show called Oz. It was a wild and crazy prison show about a max security prison where men were constantly shanked, raped, and murdered. It was super entertaining, but I just knew it was over the top and probably not realistic. When I did my first bid that prison was nothing like Oz. Outside of some minor fights that would break out, it was quite civil. The guards had everything under control for the most part. It felt like a college campus in some ways, which is partially the reason why I got my G.E.D and A.A. degree in prison.

But when I got locked up for the second time, my prison experience was much different, the complete opposite in fact. I was sent to Coleman II U.S. Penitentiary in Florida and got thrown into a real zoo. It was the jungle. All the messed up stuff that happened in the show Oz happened here. It was "Hell in a Cell!"

When I set foot on the compound of this high security prison I was looking around like "WTH is this?" It looked like the worst projects. A mix between what used to be the Cabrini Green projects in Chicago mixed with the Magnolia Projects in New Orleans. Inmates were drying their clothes on the rails, smoking cigarettes inside, and drinking wine. Whereas the guards ran the prison inmates during my first bid, the prison inmates ran the guards at Coleman.

The guards were scared to death. They stayed in their place and basically let the inmates handle themselves within their own jungle. Inmates would curse at the guards, rank on them, and talk about their mothers. They would threaten to smack them, shank them, piss on them, and everything. There was no respect for authority in there, except for the inmate shot callers really running the prison. Some of the more serious dope boys, white-collar criminals, robbers, rapists, and murderers doing decades to life were here in this prison. Many were doing life with no parole, which in the joint is called "A Day & a Night." So these dudes would get it in because they had absolutely nothing to lose.

I've never seen so much blood in my life. The ground was stained with blood. There could be three or more stabbings in one day. People were getting killed. Rapes and murders would happen to grown men in the kitchen. Fights and riots would go down out of nowhere. Guards would get handled and hurt. I've even seen inmates throw objects at the Warden, who is like the President of the United States in a prison. You had to stay on guard at all times. The smell of danger and potential death lingered in the air.

The worst riot I've ever seen jumped off at Coleman Prison in 2009. It started due to a direction given that was sent by letter in what is called a "kite." Leaders of a Mexican gang from another prison gave the order to go to war against a rival Mexican gang. For a couple of days it got real quiet. It was like the quiet before the storm. Everybody was on guard and taking short breaths. No gangs or races were co-mingling; everybody knew to stay with their own group, strapped up with whatever body armor you could put together to brace for when things popped off.

Then all of a sudden one day out on the yard a riot broke out. The two rival Mexican gangs started going at it, using their shanks like swords. It looked like a war scene straight out of the movie, 300. We all ran to our separate groups and huddled up to defend ourselves. Bodies covered in blood were flying everywhere, and all you could hear was yells and screams. The riot went on for hours. Officers started shooting with AK-47s and helicopters began flying over the compound. It was the most dangerous thing I've ever seen. Every inmate and guard was in serious jeopardy for their life. The riot got so big and out of control that it was covered on CNN.

Before I was supposed to leave Coleman for the R.G.A.P. mind reprogramming program that reduced my sentence and would have me out of prison in 18 months, I found myself caught up in a beef. Many inmates I was cool with supported the fact that I would be out soon, but there were a few that were hating. This one dude started trying me to provoke something that would mess up my situation. He was disrespecting me by calling me all types of stuff that nobody was supposed to tolerate in the pen. Whatever disrespectful words would get under any man's skin, that's what he was calling me in front of everyone every day.

I tried to keep it moving without getting at him, but the OG shot callers told me I had to "do something," which was code for "get him." So my homeboy Wax gave me a knife and when dude wasn't expecting it, I ran up in his cell. He suffered some serious stab wounds from me stabbing him in the side of the body and the neck.

The officers caught me on video leaving his room. I was put on investigation and sent to the hole in solitary confinement for 90 days. Dude never told on me, primarily because he wanted me to go back to the general population where I could be exposed for him to get some get-back.

Being in the hole was the absolute lowest point in my life. I knew I was in jeopardy of ruining getting out of prison, and all my prison privileges were taken away. Being by yourself amongst your own thoughts with no interaction can eat you alive. I got depressed and thought about how much of a failure my life had turned out to be.

I literally had nobody. For one, my second wife that I married in-between bids when I was out couldn't hold on. She went through a similar cycle of visiting me less and less, similar to what I experienced with my first wife. She ended up divorcing me while I was in prison. So it became real hard putting my mind around something to live for. I didn't have any distractions or even prison friends now to help me "do time" while I was in the hole. I was confined to this miserable hole where I was only allowed to come out for a shower two times a week. I hated it. Over the course of those 3 months, I felt myself losing my mind.

Being in the hole was like being in the worst form of jail within a jail. I felt like I had died and gone to hell. It was a real "Hell In A Cell." It was during this time that I found the only source that could help me through anything and never leave me. It was the one source that no one could ever take away from me that could have my back whenever I needed. GOD! I prayed heavily to God to help me get my life right. I asked God to bless me by getting me out and keeping me from doing the same things in the streets that got me in this Hell Hole.

It took being in the hole at my lowest low to find God and come to the realization that I never want to do anything that could possibly put me at the mercy of a prison again. Through those prayers, I made a commitment never to drink or do drugs again. I found the motivation to be productive in the hole by finishing my book, *Crumbs to Bricks*. When I got out of the hole, I survived the next 2 weeks before being sent to the R.G.A.P. program.

Young black male, prison is not the life. In fact it can be your death. It's hell on earth. Prison life can break you into pieces and ruin your head. Even your subconscious begins to change. You won't even dream the same dreams, because your world is reduced to the prison your mind has become enslaved to. Your dreams aren't out in the world any more, they're in prison. You'll no longer have dreams about living the life with beautiful chicks. You'll begin dreaming about getting in a fight on the rec yard because a guy stole your cigarettes. Prison breaks down your mind, body, and soul. In prison you're the opposite of free. There is no freedom of the mind or body. In prison you're in fact a slave.

Modern Day Slavery – The New Jim Crow

The 13th Amendment to the Constitution, which was put in place to abolish slavery, carefully states:

> "Neither slavery nor involuntary servitude, **except as a punishment for crime whereof the party shall have been duly convicted**, shall exist within the United States, or any place subject to their jurisdiction."

The "except as a punishment for crime" part is often overlooked. What this means is that the U.S. government legally recognizes the prison system as an institution to enforce a form of slavery. A slave by definition is someone who is legally owned by another person and is forced to work for that person without pay. Slavery was initially instituted within this country as a capitalistic means for driving the economy to extremely profitable measures. Today the prison system significantly contributes to the U.S. economy under a very similar business model.

According to the U.S. Bureau of Justice Statistics, approximately 1.57 million adults were incarcerated in prison and jail in 2013.[1] Despite the U.S. population only accounting for 5 percent of the world's population, the U.S. holds the largest number of prisoners with 25 percent of the world's prison population. In 2013, blacks made up the largest portion of male inmates in U.S. prisons at 37 percent, almost three times the percentage of the entire black population in the U.S. reported at 13 percent.[2]

Michelle Alexander states in her book, *The New Jim Crow*, that the U.S. imprisons a larger percentage of the black population than South Africa did during apartheid.[3] A disturbing statistic from the U.S. Bureau of Justice Statistics also reports that one in three black men can expect to go to prison in their lifetime.[4] Alexander states the mass incarceration of blacks is not just a criminal justice issue, but a serious civil rights issue as well.[5]

According to the Human Rights Watch and an article written by Sophia Kerby highlighting criminal justice facts about blacks in the U.S., "people of color are no more likely to use or sell illegal drugs than whites, but have a higher rate of arrests.[6]

African Americans comprise 14 percent of regular drug users but are 37 percent of those arrested for drug offenses.[7] From 1980 to 2007, about one in three of the 25.4 million adults arrested for drugs were African American."[8]

It's also reported that, "Once convicted, black offenders receive longer sentences compared to white offenders.[9] The U.S. Sentencing Commission stated that in the federal system black offenders receive sentences that are 10 percent longer than white offenders for the same crimes.[10] African Americans are 21 percent more likely to receive mandatory-minimum than white defendants and are 20 percent more likely to be sentenced to prison."[11] This goes along with research done by the American Psychological Association that found black boys are more likely to be mistaken as older, be perceived as guilty, and encounter violence from the police if accused of a crime.[12]

Crack-cocaine conviction discrepancies stand out as some of the more obvious cases of racial discrimination within the legal and prison system. Crack has historically been considered a drug more prevalent amongst poor blacks versus cocaine powder, which has been perceived as a more socially acceptable drug amongst more financially stable whites.

Before President Obama signed the Fairness in Cocaine Sentencing Act in 2010, federal law stipulated 5 years in prison without parole for possession of 5 grams of crack in comparison to a possession of 500 grams of powder cocaine for the same sentence, a quantity 100 times more than rock cocaine. The Fairness in Cocaine Sentencing Act reduced this disparity from 100:1 to 18:1, but it's still a major disparity reflecting racial discrimination and a "trap" in place for young black males.[13]

Felony disenfranchisement is amplified by racial disparities in the criminal-justice system. In *The New Jim Crow*, Michelle Alexander states once you're labeled a felon you're legally barred from many civil liberties and subject to legalized discrimination regarding denial of the right to vote, employment discrimination, housing discrimination, denial of educational opportunity, denial of food stamps and other public benefits, and exclusion from jury service.[14] "Today it is perfectly legal to discriminate against criminals in nearly all the ways that it was once legal to discriminate against African-Americans.[15] As a criminal, you have scarcely more rights, and arguably less respect, than a black man living in Alabama at the height of Jim Crow."[16]

A year after release from prison, up to 60 percent of formerly incarcerated people don't have jobs, and over two-thirds of the 650,000 people who are annually released from prison will be rearrested within 3 years.[17] These stats are even worse for black males. After serving a second prison sentence, I knew there was no way I could go back. I could not fail again. But I also saw firsthand how incredibly hard life is as an ex-felon. Everybody stigmatizes an ex-offender and nobody wants to hire you.

I had to become successful starting my own business because nobody was going to think twice about giving me a job with my prison record. You're really making it hard for yourself when you get caught up in the system. Young black male, that's the trap you want to avoid at all costs because it's extremely hard getting back on your feet as a black ex-convict. With a skewed percentage of black men incarcerated, racial discrimination has clearly not been eradicated but more so redesigned in a very "industrial and complex" manner.

Prison Industrial Complex

The Prison Industrial Complex is the network of privately owned prisons that are operated for profit by a business that is contracted with the government. Privately operated prisons grew from 5 prisons with 2,000 inmates to 100 prisons with 62,000 prisoners in 2014.[18] The prison industrial complex is big business and is one of the fastest-growing industries in the U.S. Prison industrial complex companies, such as The GEO Group and the Corrections Corporation of America, are publicly traded on The New York Stock Exchange on Wall Street.

Capitalism built off slavery was based on the high profitability of building a workforce that drove production without having to pay the workers adequately or provide fair working arrangements. Inmates working within prison are often paid below minimum wage and earn a measly $150-300 a month.[19] In an article written by Vicky Pelaez of Global Research, inmates within privately-run prisons can receive as little as 17 cents per hour for a maximum of 6 hours a day, the equivalent of $20 per month.[20] These low paying and enslaving conditions in which prisoners by law have to abide by are worse conditions than sweat shops in third-world countries. However, it provides a profit-maximizing opportunity for major businesses in the U.S. and the economy as a whole to operate at extremely high cost advantages.

According to the *Left Business Observer*, the federal prison industry produces 100 percent of all military helmets, ammunition belts, bullet-proof vests, and many other military supplies. Ninety percent of the entire market for equipment assembly services, 36 percent of home appliances, 30 percent of headphones/microphones/speakers, and 21 percent of office furniture are produced in prison as well.[21] Powerful multi-billion-dollar businesses that use prisons for manufacturing products include

IBM, Microsoft, AT&T, Motorola, Intel, Dell, Compaq, Nordstrom, Macy's, Target, and many more.[22]

The key to business and capitalism is profitability and growth. A threat to the U.S. economy has increasingly been the need for its largest corporations to remain globally competitive by outsourcing its labor and materials overseas to low-cost suppliers in countries such as China, India, and numerous third-world countries. Thus, the prison industrial complex is an obvious national strategy for the U.S. economy to create an even lower-cost supply option — the creation of its own "Third-World Country" business operation by building an underworld nation of prisons filled with enslaved black men forced to work for the most minimized pay and no benefits.

Between 1980-1994, profits went up within private prisons from $392 million to $1.3 billion.[23] Ironically, this same time frame of explosive growth simultaneously occurred during the time when crack spread viciously throughout the black community when the "War on Drugs" was introduced by the government to put tougher laws in place to punish related offenders. As professor Dr. Boyce Watkins has stated, "The real War on Drugs is the War on Black People."

During the 80s with Nicaragua being a battleground for the Cold War between the United States and Russia, each country was trying to gain control by funding the revolutionary forces fighting to take rule over the country. The U.S. funded the Contras, and Russia funded the opposing Sandinistas. In 1986 the Ronald Reagan administration admitted that money from cocaine smuggling into the U.S. helped fund the Contra rebels' military activity.[24]

The black market they were allowed to make billions from to fund this geopolitical revolutionary war in Nicaragua was indeed the "black market." They were allowed by the U.S. government to create a massive drug flow in urban black communities across America. The mission became to turn as many blacks into crackheads and drug dealers for mass killing and imprisonment purposes. As Malcolm X stated, "They will sell you the liquor and then arrest you for being drunk."

The Secret Rap Meeting

What was also ironic during this same time frame was the explosive growth of "gangster rap" in hip-hop. During the late 80s-early 90s, rap began to shift towards a much more aggressive criminalized style where gang banging, violence, and drug dealing was glorified and promoted. Rap music began to project these images in mainstream culture while glorifying such lifestyles in the black community. Was this shift driven by more than just the entertainment business?

In an anonymous letter that became viral on the internet, entitled "The Secret Meeting that Changed Rap Music and Destroyed a Generation," an alleged former influential record company employee discussed a strange secret meeting he was invited to amongst other tastemakers in the music industry in 1991.[25] No one in attendance was told about the topic of the meeting until it started. The room was also guarded by men with guns and all in attendance were required to sign a confidentiality agreement. The speaker at this meeting informed the few elite music influencers in attendance about how the major record labels they represented were investing millions into the building of privately owned prisons. They were told their positions of influence in the music industry would impact the profitability tremendously.[26]

They were informed that the business model of these prisons was "the more inmates incarcerated, the more money the government would pay these prisons." They could even own shares of stock once publicly traded. They were then told that their role would be to begin marketing rap music that promotes reckless criminalized behavior to drive up arrests and the expansion of these privately owned prisons. The writer of this letter goes on to say how rap indeed took a huge shift towards what he considered the worst. He was compelled to quit the music business within 2 years of that meeting.[27] Even though this letter is anonymous and not fully authenticated, it's compelling food for thought that makes sense.

Prison Trap

Young black male, it doesn't take being a rocket scientist to know that getting caught up in a "trap-star" lifestyle is a vicious trap that will land you in prison. Unfortunately, history shows that there are many forces in place that benefit enormously when you don't succeed and are disenfranchised from society. As a young black male, the legal, political, socio-cultural, and prison systems all possess detrimental "trap" dynamics that can hurt you and take you out of a winning position in life.

Within the stock market there are forms of investments called derivatives. With derivatives you, in essence, have several ways of betting on whether a stock is going to go up or down. Thus, there are ways of making money on stocks that grow or stocks that fall. It's an amazing way of covering your bets and finding a way to win even when a company is losing. Young black male, society has numerous "trap" derivatives in place to make a profitable come-up at your expense. If you drop out of school, become a dope boy, get caught, and lose your whole life and family because you're enslaved in prison – there is a large part of this nation that gains tremendously from your loss in life.

Young black male, do not fall for the enticing fast lifestyle of a dope boy trap star like I did. It's literally a trap to give up all your freedom and power to someone else, who will control you for their own purposes. The hardest thing for a male to be without is his freedom. It's the worst feeling in the world, and you will feel this pain within every inch of your mind, body, and spirit. You're not a slave, you were only meant to live happily as a powerful free black man.

Our ancestors fought centuries of oppression, enslavement, and institutionalized discrimination to put us in a position where we could experience something they were robbed of...freedom. Young black male, prison is not for you. It's definitely not for me and I have no intentions of ever going back. It's the second to last place in the world you want to be. The last place you want to be is in the grave.

Death

As the popular saying goes, everyone wants to go to heaven, but nobody wants to die. Thug life mentality is a false delusion that you can accept consequences of death to live a hood-rich lifestyle. It's typical for guys in the streets to say they don't care about dying, but that is far from the truth. Dudes think they want a thug's life, but never want a thug's death when it hawks them down. In that moment it always becomes clear that YOU DON'T WANT TO DIE!

The first law of nature is self-preservation. The human spirit only wants to live. While in human form in a human body it's only natural to do whatever it takes to live. When you're born as a baby nobody tells you to breathe; it's all a part of your natural instincts. Babies cry when they want food because they're instincts tell them they need that to live.

Hold your breath for as long as you can right now. How long are you able to hold it? Maybe 30 seconds, 60 seconds, or even longer. But to get to that point where you're turning red and can't hold your breath any longer and tell yourself, "Oh, let me go for five more minutes" is nearly impossible. Something will kick in so fast and you will say "forget that" and open your mouth to breathe in as much air as possible. We're wired consciously and subconsciously to breathe, eat, and drink because they're all natural instinctive activities for living.

Unfortunately, mortality is engrained in the minds of young black males. Our upbringing is entirely unique from any other race partly because we're saturated with so many circumstances that produce the death of young blacks that look just like us. By the age of 13 the average young black male has been inundated with the death of many young blacks through headlines or first-hand accounts of knowing a peer who was killed. Whether it's a highly publicized wrongful death in the media or an unfortunate, senseless black-on-black crime, it becomes a part of our psyche to accept the possibility of an early death. Reaching 25 as a young black male is something we process much differently than most others. For many of us reaching 25 is either viewed as a huge goal, or not even a reality we can see.

When the future appears so bleak and the only way we see ourselves as successful and happy is by hustling in the streets living a fast life of crime, we naively tell ourselves we can accept the consequences of death, similar to a heroic soldier courageously fighting a war on the front lines. But even in the military, 80 percent of the jobs are non-combat operations. Most who enlist in the military never intend to expose themselves to combat where the outcome could be getting killed. Similarly in the streets, most hustlers don't intend to get killed. But when you enlist in the streets, you are enlisting in a very combat-heavy operation where, at various points, people will want to kill you and you will have to deal with it one way or another.

The myth is, you can deal with dying if it comes to that; but the truth is, you can't and that's the last thing you ever want to accept. Natural survival instincts will force you to fight death to your last breath. So often in our community, as young black males, we're influenced to sacrifice looking at the long-term consequences — all because we're infatuated with the now. We want to be young, flashy, and rich with all the cars, jewelry, women, swag, and popularity that kind of lifestyle can afford.

At 20 years old, a misguided dope boy's mind-set is "I don't care about reaching 30, 40, or 50. I'll do whatever it takes to get it in now; and if I die, at least I balled out." But when you turn around one day and you're 30, you have a whole new concept of life and how to exist. You will not hit 30 and say, "Yeah, that was a good run. Go ahead and shoot me jack boy, because I was ready to die right around this age anyway." That is your NOW and you will not want to let it go. Same at 40, 50, and even 60+, because it will always feel good to be ALIVE versus the alternative.

If you were staring down the barrel of a gun with nowhere to run because someone wanted to take you out and take over your spot, you would do anything to see another day. Regardless of your religious beliefs, all you know for certain is this life.

You will not want to have taken away 100% of everything you know about this life to experience a whole other realm you know absolutely nothing about. You will not want to be gone from here forever. Nobody wants to accept never, and once someone leaves this earth we NEVER see them here again.

A heartbreaking story I read about, was a man who was driving and got run off a bridge. His car flipped over the railing and sunk into the St. Johns River in Jacksonville, FL.[28] The man escaped out of the car but couldn't swim. Most people driving pulled over and tried to help in some way, but nobody jumped in. The man kept being taken under by the strong waves and would come up to scream, "HELP ME, I CAN'T SWIM!" He continued being taken under and would come back up screaming for his life. He was fighting with all his might to survive in the midst of not knowing how to swim, but his fight was becoming more and more dreadful and hopeless.[29] He then screamed, "TELL MY DAUGHTER I LOVE HER!" He was taken down again by the waves and his final scream before he went down for the last time was, "JESUS!"[30]

He had no clue when he woke up that morning to go to work that it was his last day on earth. Most times people never know. Death is something we do not expect to happen today. We all must meet our fate, but we will postpone that date as far out as we can. In addition, it's a horrifying experience to die violently. Unfortunately, in the streets a violent death is normally the only way to go out.

Don't Let Me Die

I had a homeboy that I hustled with; his name was Fatboy. He was a big, cool, yet aggressive d-boy, who had a lot of street cred from roughing up people around the way. He would always joke around with me and say, "Boy, always keep on a fresh pair of tennis shoes, because you never know when you'll have to run from the police or go to prison. They will be the same shoes you go in with." He had always accepted prison as a consequence that could go down at any time. He was always prepared for it.

It still saddens me to this day that the big homey Fatboy had to encounter a different fate that he wasn't prepared for. One night we were in the club with several other homeys from the block getting it in. Someone Fatboy had pissed off wanted to get revenge on him that night. While we were partying and having a good time in the club, a dude ran up in the spot and shot Fatboy.

Fatboy got shot six times in his chest. When he got shot, everyone started screaming and running. Fatboy was slumped on the ground with his eyes wide open and scared. He began wheezing in a terrible panic, because he was choking on the blood that kept coming out of his mouth. He couldn't breathe! Someone ran to call the ambulance, and we were all terrified trying to help however we could. But no one was more terrified than Fatboy. He continued to choke, making a horrible sound as he was gasping for air. Fatboy then struggled to yell out to us as best as he could in his husky voice, "Don't Let Me Die! Y'all Better Not Let Me Die!"

Fatboy's gasps got slower and slower. He then slumped all the way back and stopped breathing completely. Fatboy died. He was laid out on the ground with blood leaking as his eyes remained open with a blank stare of death. It was a look I had never seen before and never want to see again. It was the most horrific thing I've ever seen in my life.

The big homey Fatboy did not die quickly, and it looked like the worst pain he had ever experienced. Sadly, that was his last experience as well. There is this delusion that when you die it will be quick and somewhat painless, as we see so often in the movies. In real life, many times a person does not die instantly. They often go thru turmoil, especially when shot. In the world of a dope boy, murders happen every day. Regardless of what Biggie said in his first album, you will not be "Ready to Die."

No Swag in Getting Shot

When a person is a victim of a gunshot, it can be extremely painful and fatal, depending on the size of the gun and the bullets. The body begins to hurt badly because the bullet rips through the flesh, leaves a hole, and is burning inside the body. The bullet can crush serious body tissue, blood vessels, bones, and vital organs. The bullets may also shatter on impact sending fragments through the body, and bones can get chipped while driven through the body's tissues.

This is worse in situations where there are multiple gun shots. That person can then suffer from drowning in their own blood like what I saw happening with Fatboy. They can't breathe and begin wheezing because their lungs are filled with blood. Oxygen can't get to the brain forcing them to pass out and the body shuts down. That's often how one dies from gunfire, and serious gunfire is how most die in the streets.

Young black male, YOU DO NOT WANT TO DIE! Especially not violently and early in life. Seeing your kids, grandkids, and great grandkids grow up is a beautiful thing that we mature into desiring with age. Even in a dream, we're often sweating bullets and wake up in a cold sweat if someone tries to shoot us. When that time comes, you don't want to go.

I grew up around a lot of hard dudes in a lot of tough places; but whenever someone starts shooting, NOBODY is sticking around to get hit. Nobody is standing around trying to be Superman, seeing if bullets will bounce off their chests. EVERYBODY is ducking and running low, trying to escape. The hardest thugs give Usain Bolt a run for his money in trying to escape those shots of death. In the heat of the moment when death is right around the corner, your survival instincts always kick in.

I've also seen many become paralyzed as victims to the streets. This can ruin a person, because life drastically changes once a person is severely immobile — no convenient clubbing, sex life is ruined, unable to have kids, even urinating in the car because you can't make it to the bathroom fast enough. Being paralyzed affects your subconscious as well. You may dream of driving a nice car or running in a football game, then wake up with no legs to a reality that is your real living nightmare.

Every drug dealer I knew either got sent to prison or is dead. Once you're gone, you're out of here! There is no coming back from death. You're gone man. You will not get to turn your life around like I did, it's OVER! Everything you know and have ever been for all human purposes is OVER! If you choose a life in the streets hustling, there is no way around it.

You will be facing death daily, and one day it may not be on your terms. You may want to stunt and ball to look good, but nobody looks good in a casket. Nothing is cool about being stiff and cold with all your blood drained out in exchange for embalming fluid. Nothing is cool with your eyes shut in a coffin around loved ones crying their hearts out because you were too young to die. They will never see you again. IT'S NOT WORTH IT!

Young black male, LIFE is truly a gift from God. That's why the now is called "the present." The future becomes your present much sooner than later so it's important to make the right decisions that direct you towards life blessings versus curses and regrets. Although we all must transition from this life at some point, it makes no sense to live a delusional trap-star life of crime, jeopardizing your life every second while recklessly playing with a situation not to be played with — DEATH.

Young black male, you are special and placed on this earth for an incredible purpose that far outweighs any illegal hustle and early grave. Never fall prey to the trap of a fake short-term balla' lifestyle as a drug dealer. That is really a "deathstyle." In every experience you have, always choose LIFE.

CHAPTER 10

The Trap Pt. 2: Alcohol, Drugs, & Dope Boy Hollywood

Alcohol & Drugs

Alcohol and drugs are the worst substances to be addicted to. They alter the mind and body in a way that can make you highly unproductive and even destructive. I've found that alcohol and drugs contribute to some of the main shortcomings with people in our world.

An addiction is composed of the following:

1. Engaging in an activity consistently
2. Producing negative results from it
3. Not being able to stop engaging in that activity.

We're all supposed to have a natural self-correction mechanism within us that tells us to stop doing something if it hurts us. To experiment is human nature as well. But if you touch a stove and burn yourself, there is a "survival instinct" protective mechanism that should kick in and tell you "I shouldn't touch that stove while hot anymore." However, if you continue to touch that hot stove, say "Ouch" because you hurt yourself, but continue to touch it over and over again, you have a serious problem. One may even call you a pain freak.

All addictions follow this same illogical pattern where a person is doing something they often see is damaging themselves and their life in one way or another, but there is some addictive craving for the immediate effects from that activity, which severely impairs them and keeps them from making the self-corrective decision to stop.

Then the addiction becomes even more of a problem, because they're impaired and too delusional to realize they even have a problem.

Addiction is a disease that affects both the brain and behavior. People with addictions lose control over what they're doing. Bad habits that are initially self-controlled can lead to bad addictions beyond any self-control. Nobody aspires to be an abusive, sloppy drunk alcoholic hitting on women. Nor does anyone plan to be a 90-lb. crackhead who steals TVs from their mother just to sell them for a $5 crack rock hit. But they're brutal examples behind how substance addictions can spiral out of control.

Peer pressure is the desire to assimilate with others in a particular setting. The reason why people begin experimenting with alcohol and drugs is usually because of peer pressure. We all are vulnerable to some extent and desire to belong as a means of feeling accepted, which boosts our self-esteem. People addicted to alcohol and drugs use these substances because it makes them feel good or stops them from feeling bad.

There is usually either a boredom or depression mind-set for their current reality, and they're looking for an escape from this reality. Or they desire to fill an extreme void to artificially enhance their reality. It reflects a serious weakness, because you're going so far outside of yourself and reality to alter your mind so that you're comfortable with a fake reality and fake version of yourself. Whenever you back down from your delusional high and altered reality, there's the real world with those same real problems waiting on you that you'll still have to face. You go through withdrawal and serious depression, because your ability to cope with reality or enjoy it gets worse and worse. When you can't deal with real life, it will brutally deal with you.

I made a street-glorified living off addicts when selling drugs. I know the behaviors, mannerisms, habits, and movements of a substance abuse addict. Plus I personally was a substance abuser of alcohol and weed. As a past alcoholic and smoker, I know the unproductive and harmful effects they can have. Now 100 percent sober, free of any substance addictions, I have no problem dispelling the myths of alcohol and drugs. I will keep it all the way "100" on why these are weakening agents that produce sickness and failure that young black males should totally avoid.

Alcohol

Often I hear the saying "all things in moderation." This is most often used when discussing alcohol. Society says it's fine to drink alcohol, just in moderation. I, however, think differently and ask myself, "what am I gaining by doing this" and "what am I risking in doing this." I was a heavy drinker for years. But as a sober man now for 6 years straight — the empowering feelings I have of genuine peace, control, and true fulfillment are night and day verses back when I was an alcoholic. Alcohol never measures up to a worthwhile winning advantage, so I go against the grain and ask, "Why even do it at all."

I was a functioning alcoholic back when I was hustling. A functioning alcoholic is defined as someone who can hold down a job, pursue a career (or hustle in my case), and care for children while continuously drinking alcohol. I would drink a bottle of fifth every day. I was never sloppy drunk, but would drink beer, Cognac, Hennessey, and a gang load of other drinks. Although I didn't consider myself addicted, because I wasn't falling out in the clubs or being abusive, I would often start my days off early in the morning drinking. In the afternoon I would drink. Definitely in the evening wherever I was, I couldn't feel comfortable unless I had some liquor.

I started drinking just because everybody else on the block was doing it. I was following the crowd and succumbing to peer pressure. But as I drank more, it became a weak remedy that I needed to dull my senses in filling certain voids in my life. It never made me a better person in any way; but for the time I was liquored up, it made me feel good about myself.

Alcohol is legal, but it's still a drug. The addiction becomes mental just as much as physical. The mind as well as the body begins to crave alcohol to destructive extents. The body becomes so addicted to it that it can't function without it.

I have someone in my family whose body has reversed in such a dysfunctional way that they can't even eat, because the only thing their body desires now is liquor. It attacks critical functions of the mind and body invoking thinking impairment, memory loss, and a lack of motor coordination. Laws are in place to arrest you if you drive while drinking, because under the influence of alcohol you're a high-speed mobile weapon behind the wheel. Another car or walking child could cross your path and your cognitive abilities could be so weak and slow that you wouldn't see them until it's too late. Every day in the U.S. 28 people die as a result of drunk driving.

In addition to destroying your mind, alcohol is one of the most destructive drugs to the body and many of your organ systems. It tears up the stomach, creating ulcers; plus, it damages the pancreas and liver. The liver is responsible for clearing toxic things from the body, so when that shuts down due to liver disease, it's a very serious physical problem that breaks down many other vital functions.

So why do people get drunk? It starts off from peer pressure. Then it becomes a way to escape reality and all your problems. It's also a fake confidence booster. In the hood, we call it that "liquid courage." Throwing back shots will give a guy the courage to holler at girls he normally would never approach. It will also have him talking trash and ready to fight a dude he would normally be too scared to confront.

In many situations, I've seen dudes get laid out because their mind was altered to act like somebody they were not. Mentally, they were Mike Tyson in his prime — but physically they were weaker, less coordinated, and less prepared than a person who hadn't balled his fists up ever in life. Drinking excessively can get you in a lot of trouble. Someone suffering from alcohol addiction can lead to ugly scenes of domestic abuse, child abuse, and so many other forms of aggressive behavior that can tear your family apart and land you behind bars.

Drinking and getting "F'd Up" is exactly that, screwing your life up for the moment. The addiction leads to a downward-spiraling, depressive lifestyle with no good ending unless you quit. As an alcoholic, you're also screwing up the lives of those around you. It's the worst to be the child of an alcoholic. It's unbearable to be married to an alcoholic. Alcoholics lose their families and friends all the time, because they're reduced to just being sad, depressed, slurred-speaking drunks, who are unproductive and emotionally unfit for holding down a family.

Sure there are ways to drink in moderation, but there's a slippery slope between moderate and excessive. It's all good to have a good time poppin' bottles. However, when it becomes the only way to have a good time or stop feeling bad, that's a problem. Alcohol addiction is a path to destruction and a loser lifestyle.

Weed

The popularity and frequent casual smoking of weed as a recreational drug, in addition to the legalization of weed throughout the country, are all reasons why many think there's nothing wrong with it. THC is the main psychoactive ingredient in marijuana, which acts on certain parts of the brain responsible for pleasure, memory, concentration, and sensory areas leading to a "high" experience. Weed is the most widely used drug in the U.S.

When I was young and hustling in the streets, I would get high all the time on weed. I would smoke a ¼-pound of weed every week. It was my drug of choice for being high in chill mode, club mode, ladies mode, trickin' mode, deep-in-hustle-mode, and philosophical professor mode. In the hood it was almost mandatory to smoke weed and get high. The thought was, "Who would ever be such a peon that they wouldn't want to get high?"

I was a follower and smoked weed because it was considered cool and everybody was doing it. Whether you were a dope boy, rapper, junkie, teenager, OG, 9-5 worker, stripper, college student, athlete, or just a regular person, anybody with any cool bone in their body was down for smoking weed. The first time I got high I was with a homeboy joking around, and I started laughing out of control. My stomach was about to explode from laughing so hard. Afterwards, when I came down from my high, I was like "Man that was weird." But I kept on doing it to be cool.

My homeboy Bubba was the only person I knew and respected as a cool hustler who never smoked weed. Bubba sold drugs, too; but he was the only exception to never getting arrested, because he QUIT. I believe his key to never going to prison or getting killed was that he never did drugs. My other homey Jeremiah and I were always the ones high, but Bubba never was. While Jeremiah and I were always in and out of jail, Bubba never got caught. He was able to do his hustle and exit the game as he smoothly transitioned into real estate.

In the early 2000s, way before the market crashed, Bubba told me he was getting out of the game to buy properties, as a real estate investor and I should think about doing the same. I said, "yeah whatever," and even lent him money for one of his first investments. He started flipping profits on property and paid me back the money. I didn't even think to enter the real estate business with him, because I was still conditioned to the "trap" game. Plus, I probably wasn't thinking straight because I was always high.

Till this day, he is a successful real estate investor with a clean record who has never spent a day in prison. Everyone else who continued selling dope, including myself, either went to prison or was laid to rest six feet deep. He was able to see the inevitable tragedy that came along with being a dope boy more clearly than others and stuck to a plan to get out of the game. I believe strongly that this was because he did not paralyze his mind or distort his clarity with weed or any other drugs.

He was always clear-headed, never got caught up in any BS, and was able to jump into the housing market at the absolute best time, because his senses weren't blurred by any mind-altering substances. During that time, houses were selling in 30-90 days; so he was able to flip houses really quickly and make great profits. Bubba legitimately found a way to live an even better lifestyle with a legitimate hustling occupation. He saw how his talents for hustling in the streets were much more effective in the real estate market. He had the ability to channel his ambition towards a much more productive career with long-term benefits. His discipline to refrain from weed gave him a life advantage compared to everyone else around him getting high.

There's this false myth that weed makes you think on a higher level. Weed smokers often feel like they're enlightened. Weed does make you "think" in your own head, but it's a completely isolated perspective from what the world thinks. It's not incorporating how the real world works. Much of life is based on being able to process your surroundings and perspectives outside of yourself. When you make a decision, you shouldn't just base it on your own thoughts without considering other perspectives and thoughts. With marijuana, you don't see things outside of your own brain and thoughts. You are under a delusional spell that your thoughts are the only great thoughts that matter.

I remember I was getting high chilling with the homeys back in my hustling days, and I began discussing random stuff. We were smoking for about three hours, and then I started trying to be a philosopher in breaking down things in nature like I was the black Leonardo Da Vinci. I started telling them, "The ocean is blue because the way the sun is hitting it, it's a yellow light mixed with the green coral in the ocean." Looking back on that now, I just scratch my head! It took me three hours to come up with that. I could've gotten that same thought, plus way more factual insight in way less time by reading a book or website. Reading will educate you way more than getting high.

At Beautiful Hair 4 U, I had a hair stylist who was a customer and bought hundreds of dollars in hair. She was a very talented hair stylist as well. But she smoked so much weed that she was always off her square. One time she came in the store red-eyed and high out of her mind. She came all the way from the other side of town to pay for the hair that she needed for a client waiting in her chair. She paid for the hair and then left the store without it. She realized 20 minutes later that she didn't have the hair and had to come back to get it. She was laughing and saying how crazy she was, but she failed to realize that it's not cool to leave a client sitting idle in a salon for an hour. Needless to say, she did not stay in business long at that salon. She was so high that she was continuously messing up left and right. That's no way to keep a job, clientele, or money coming in.

There's also this perception that weed makes you so relaxed. The reality is, weed gets you a relaxed high because weed really makes you lazy. You'll put off stuff you could do right now. You need urgency for effectiveness and greatness. Weed smokers are often underachievers due to laziness. Marijuana makes you think in a carefree "lawless" way, because it makes you feel like everything is alright. You could be in a piss-infected alleyway, broke after your wife left you; but when you're high, it's alright and even funny. How delusional is that?

Many think weed is okay because it's not a biological addiction. But smoking weed becomes a very potent physiological addiction that greatly alters the mind from its natural state. It becomes your great mental escape from reality. Medical marijuana is primarily for people suffering from an illness with no other way to cope. Many have chosen to clock out of life due to an extreme medical challenge, and marijuana helps them escape from what they believe is a bleak reality. For those who can medically benefit, that's fine. But in general, I believe legalizing marijuana will just make the rich get richer. The wealth divide will get even greater. It will create more weed heads who will be underachievers.

So become an underachieving weed head if you want. Meanwhile, we clear-headed thinkers of the world will be overachieving. We'll be getting up earlier, getting more done, and getting much further ahead in life than you.

I never see anyone at their best when they're high. No pro athlete ever does a "puff puff pass" in a huddle before the last winning play in a championship game. No President ever looks like they hit a joint before a national debate. So how can you ever become the best by beating the best when you're high. You can't! All you can do is fail and feel okay about it. Young black male, that's a loser's mentality and no way to achieve greatness.

Cocaine

Cocaine is a powerfully addictive stimulant drug. It's made from coca plant leaves mostly from South America. Cocaine increases levels of dopamine in the brain that amplify pleasure, senses, and movement to create a high. Powder cocaine is normally snorted, while crack cocaine is a freebase form of cocaine. Crack is coke mixed with baking soda that can be smoked. It's called crack because of the sound it makes when being cooked.

Crack cocaine is so potent because when smoked it hits the brain and creates a high in as fast as 7-10 seconds, whereas powder cocaine is snorted and takes closer to 10 minutes.[1] The crack high lasts about 10 minutes, and then it's a serious drop to no high at all. This extreme roller-coaster high, followed by an extreme drop-off, is what messes people up and makes them addicted. It's like immediately busting in your room and celebrating because you won a million dollars, buying all the things you could ever want, and then having it all taken away from you in a matter of minutes.

A crackhead is one of the most messed up people on the face of the earth. Their addiction to crack ruins their life and reduces them to being a zombie who has no purpose in life other than trying to reach that first high they got that they can never fully get again. They throw away their entire life chasing that unconquerable high.

Crack addicts become delusional, paranoid, irritable, and pretty much inhumane. Men and women addicts throw away all their morals if it can lead them to another hit. They will have sex with whomever, wear whatever, live wherever, go without brushing their teeth or taking a shower for however long – all because nothing else in the world matters but finding a way to get that next hit. They're not just addicts, they're slaves to the drug and whomever can provide it. They'll steal from their momma, child, employer, neighbor, or anyone else to get whatever it takes to buy some dope. When you see a crackhead scratching and biting themselves all the time, it's because the effects of the drugs make them feel like they have parasites crawling under their skin.

The strongly addicted consumer base of crackheads makes selling dope appear to be very lucrative. There's a customer base that's a slave to the product, so they'll keep coming back over and over again, finding a way to pay for their fix. But they're in such an irrational state of dysfunction that they ultimately become a person you don't want anything to do with. You don't want to touch them, you don't want to be around them, you don't want to inhale their awful smell, and you don't want to be a victim to the dumb and dangerous energy they carry, which comes with being a lost soul. This is an unhealthy way of viewing your customer base.

Pheens are a slave to crack in general, but not necessarily your crack when you're a drug dealer. They're addicted to any crack at any time, however they can get it. Young black male, there is no high in the world ever worth destroying your life like a crack addict. Crack, cocaine, and anything else related that has such a destructive effect on one's life is something you want to stay as far away from as possible! Never experiment with it, never try it, and never sell it. If you're doing either, STOP IT NOW! Get help, rehabilitate yourself, and never look back.

Although the high with powder cocaine is not as extreme, powder cocaine users suffer from similar effects of chasing what they feel is a needed high to cope with reality. Powder cocaine is perceived as a drug for more affluent people who can function normally while taking it. But they too can fall off their square and spiral out of control.

I've seen businessmen take a bump before a meeting, lawyers come into a court room after a hit, as well as other people in the streets and other different walks of life. Never were they on point. They were always in an altered mental state and weren't on top of their game. Many use it as a recreational drug to chill, socialize, or party. In each of those settings, I don't consider it productive at all. I need all of my wits, instincts, and intelligence, because I need to know what exactly is going on in my surroundings. I need to always be able to size up every opportunity and threat on sight.

Heroine, ecstasy, molly, codeine (lean), flakka, and any other drug illegally used can alter your mind and body to an extent where you're a different person. You become totally off track from who you're intended to be. They're all destructive shortcuts to stimulating pleasure in the mind and escaping reality. Reality is something you're supposed to deal with. Reality is where real problems are solved and where real results and success are achieved.

The mental and physical damage these drugs can have on you are always life-threatening in one way or another. Placing yourself in a delusional mind-set is seeking a way to leave this earth. Decomposing in a destructive, unnatural way is exactly what you're doing when you mess with these drugs. You're becoming addicted to losing yourself, losing in life, and ultimately killing yourself.

Dope Boy Hollywood: Why Don't Dope Boys Leave the Game?

The plan in the back of every dope boy's head is, "I'm a hit this lick just a little longer before I go legit." Despite seeing countless stories daily of dope boys getting caught up or killed, every dope boy thinks they have a little more time to hustle without getting caught. They think their clock has a little more time to operate in a kill or be killed environment, without someone catching them slippin' to clean their clock. They think that fast money will roll in a little bit longer without everything just bottoming out.

That's more of a false delusion than the addict thinking they'll stop doing crack. At least the crackhead has accepted the fate that they're a wasted junkie. The dope boy rarely ever leaves the game, even though he's doomed to be imprisoned or killed. This is because...

THE DOPE BOY IS THE BIGGEST ADDICT OF THEM ALL!

The dope boy is the most delusional. He's the biggest addict, who is helplessly addicted to the lifestyle. I know this because, as a fully recovered street hustler, the dope boy hustle game had a hold on me worse than any addiction I could ever imagine. The worst kind of addiction is the one you have absolutely no clue you're addicted to.

It's similar to the guy who gets dunked on in a basketball game. He's the last person in the gym who sees that sledgehammer coming down on his head. It's a fast break that the whole opposing team sees coming; the fans get excited and stand up because they see it coming, plus the guy dunking on you sees the whole play unfolding 10 seconds before it goes down. Even your own teammates scoot out the way to avoid getting "posterized." However, when you get dunked on you're in the worst position possible to see it or defend it. You're the last one to see it coming; and once you realize what's happening, it's too late. You're already done.

I had no idea I was going to get caught when I did. The Feds knew everything about me and all my movements. To think someone within your hustle circle won't snitch on you when their jammed up facing serious time is the epitome of being naive. To think you can sell drugs to so many unreliable crackheads, commit a felony every time you walk out the door, floss your big money lifestyle to so many other hungry up-and-coming hustlers plus all the cops on to you, and think you can come out clean is as delusional as it gets. To see every other hustler get locked up or killed and think you can do the same hustle, while avoiding those consequences, is straight up stupid. But when you're addicted like the dope boy is, nothing is processed with a clear mind.

Beyond just an addict, I was a slave to the dope boy lifestyle. I needed the entourage and flunkies I thought would hold me down, but who were just freeloading. I needed the fly cars, clothes, jewelry, and all the other material possessions I could throw money at to make me feel like the man. I needed the false illusion of popularity and power. I needed all the chicks to sweat me and make my name ring bells in the streets.

These were no longer desires; I desperately needed all of it. The more money I made, the more I had to get, and the more I had to flex. Paying all the expenses for wifey, baby momma, strippers, and other miscellaneous female bills was an addiction. But I couldn't stop, because I was addicted to every high I got from being a dope boy living the fast life.

My biggest fear was becoming regular. I didn't want to become one of those hustlers who used to be respected but fell off. They got moved off their blocks and dwindled down to a petty hustler or a regular guy who had no more respect. Their funds were low, and their swag was all gone. I would've rather died or gone to prison than fall off like that at the time.

In Jay-Z's song, "Hollywood," he raps about how celebrities can easily become addicted to "the lights" of Hollywood and end up blowing their whole lives away. Jay-Z refers to it as a killer and the most addictive drug in the world. In this same way, I became addicted to "the lights" and fame of the "Dope Boy Hollywood." Every dope boy ends up blowing his life away from this addiction.

At the peak of my hustling, I couldn't afford to fall off and lose all those things of purely perceptional value from the streets, because I was addicted to creating this flawed perception that I cherished as my only means of self-worth. I was addicted to the "Dope Boy Hollywood" drug. I was addicted to getting power and attention, because it was my validation to the streets for how successful I was. I needed to feel good about myself and continue an unrealistic high for being the ultimate dope boy. I couldn't afford to get out the game, because I would lose the Dope Boy Hollywood fast life and everything that came along with it.

The more money I made, the more I spent. Because I was selling illegal drugs that also meant the more trouble I was getting into. It was a vicious cycle of trying to keep up with the delusional Dope Boy Hollywood lifestyle that could never last. I did more wrong and tried to sell more weight, digging an even deeper hole that was inevitable. My mind was so messed up on a Dope Boy Hollywood "lifestyle crack" that I couldn't see the danger in the fatal consequences that would hit at any moment. A hit that would take me from the opposite of high and Dope Boy Hollywood fly, to the lowest low, destroying me and my family. The dope boy story may be one of the saddest, because he has no idea that in the midst of servicing a bunch of pheens, he's the biggest addict of them all.

Get High Off Success

Sobriety changed my life. It cleared my mind so that I could see good things for being good, and bad things for bad. I had moments of bottoming out and being extremely depressed, especially in prison. But the removal of alcohol and drugs allowed me to deal with my own demons in doing some heavy soul searching. It opened my mind to seeing all I had done wrong in life so that I could get on the right track to success by removing the delusional irresponsible filter I was processing everything with.

I was no longer desensitized about my destructive lifestyle and decisions that reduced me to zero. In addition, I was able to become more disciplined, ambitious, and strategic in pursuing success the right way. Drugs and alcohol are a temporary means to a fake feeling of being unstoppable. But removing these addictive substances, which create false highs, is the only real way to get a "natural high" and feel a true existence of being unstoppable.

There's a reason why the richest, most powerful people keep liquor stores and trap houses out of their community, and why there are so many allowed in the hood. Drugs and alcohol are "trap" substances, designed to keep certain people dumb, delusional, and underachieving. While these alcoholics and addicts are distracted, the winners in society gain even greater competitive advantages. When these drunks and pheens are acting wild, distracted, or succumbing to pressure — a sober person is clear-headed to the highest degree in order to consistently pursue success.

You see everything when you're drug- and alcohol-free. You see all the strengths, weaknesses, opportunities, and threats. A mind that's not altered is really keen and able to maximize the use of all the senses. You see and hear everything. All smart people know no person can function to their full capacity under the influence of any mind-altering substance. You could be a chess master; but if you're high, I'll beat you all day. To consistently succeed in life, you need real energy that doesn't burn out. You need the ability to use all your natural intelligences and senses on demand. Handling your life business, in general, is too complicated to try to get everything done while intoxicated or high. You will lose.

Young black male, you can find a wild escape to feeling free and liberated within the excitement of exploring the unlimited realms of your wildest, most ambitious imagination. Your high can come from every intriguing moment involved in running a successful and fun business, marrying the love of your life, looking out after your younger siblings and eventually raising your own beautiful kids, working hard and buying your dream car, graduating from college, or working on a way to finding the cure to cancer. Discover your own puzzle of life to put together, and have a blast finding your great escape with that.

I no longer drink or smoke; I just get high off success. I get high off getting into either one of my BMWs and riding out. I get a high off copping a new crib when I bring Beautiful Hair 4 U into a new market. Above all, I get high off being able to take care of my children and family. To be able to take care of their needs all the time and address any matter with a sound resolution is a long-term high for me. To be able to take care of my people, that is a high that is extra rewarding to me. That makes me get up and go get it. Love for my people is an ultimate high, which drives me to being the best man and provider I can be.

Competing against these other beauty supply stores masterfully, while making them squirm and capturing more market share, is how I get my rocks off. Securing a luxurious future when I retire, by making great long-term investments in companies like Apple, while seeing my net worth expand beautifully is a high like no other. Striving to be a multi-millionaire who might one day grace the covers of *Fortune Magazine* one day is a high that lifts me up above the atmosphere and beyond what any pile of cocaine could. That's true success to me. My mind-set is that I own success and I make success addicted to me.

Marcellus & Chris at the Beautiful Hair 4 U 3 Year Anniversary Celebration

Making a difference in the lives of other young black brothers and our community means the world to me. That gives me an incredible high. It places me at the highest mountaintop of satisfaction to give back in ways that count.

Young black male, always look at the long-term perspective. What will it cost you in the long run? Is it worth it? Ben Johnson broke a world record in the 100-meter dash in the Olympics, but was disqualified and stripped of his gold medal and place in history, because he used steroids. Lance Armstrong overcame cancer and was recognized as the greatest cyclist ever, but took a huge legacy hit for being accused of using performance-enhancing drugs. I believe those athletes were great enough to accomplish those feats without the drugs. Instead of finding their own high within their own mind, they relied on illicit drugs to trigger things within them that I feel they could've done naturally and gotten full credit for.

Life comes down to determining if you will bet on yourself, or bet on something outside of yourself. We all have doubts — even great talents like the ones just mentioned. But they didn't bet on themselves and went through illegal means where there were consequences. Too often you get caught. Even when you don't get caught you're cheating yourself and ultimately fooling nobody but yourself. A short-term gain and long-term loss is never worth it! Any bad alteration to your brain or body will not allow it to work right to its full capacity. You become addicted to something outside of yourself, when the only source of power you ever need is always within you.

Dopeness!

Every drug ever created is an external agent intended to trigger something that naturally occurs internally within you. Cocaine, weed, alcohol, pornography, and any other addictive substance or activity you feel pleasure from has some effect on the brain. Dopamine is the natural "dope" chemical activity in the brain that stimulates reward-motivated behavior. Dopamine is released in our brain to motivate us to accomplish the smallest things in life as well as our greatest aspirations.

Dopamine stimulates us to accomplish something on our to-do list like pick up an item from the grocery store, study for an exam to get a good grade, score a basket during a game, get dressed in the flyest outfit to turn up at the club, pursue a woman we're attracted to, wake up early to go to work and make money, in addition to pursuing whatever our biggest life dreams are that we are motivated to accomplish.

Whatever degree of motivation you have towards accomplishing anything on any level is a direct reflection of your dopamine levels. Dopamine drives our productivity and ambition on the smallest and greatest levels. It stimulates us to perform the same activity in the future if it makes us feel pleasure. The more dopamine produced in association with an activity, the more we're motivated to do that activity and achieve that sensational reward in the form of a "high."

There are good highs and bad highs. Addictive drugs prey on this dopamine system within your brain and aggressively reinforce bad behaviors to an addictive extent. You no longer just desire a certain type of destructive high, you feel you need it. Good highs allow you to feel good and still face reality in a productive way without producing bad consequences. Bad highs associated with these addictive drugs make you escape reality, becoming that much more vulnerable to negative consequences. So when this artificial high leaves, it makes it hard for you to be turned on by reality or to cope with it.

The science behind an addict is that their "dopeness" is associated with an artificial euphoric high that removes them further and further from reality. True "dopeness" within the mind creates a euphoric, sustainable high. It's an authentic high. It empowers you to break through challenges in reality, while still being productive and rational within the real world.

The brain is an awesome phenomenon. We have been given the most powerful gift of being able to control it in creating our own life experiences. Shown below are the two parts of the brain: the Pre-Frontal Cortex and the Limbic System:

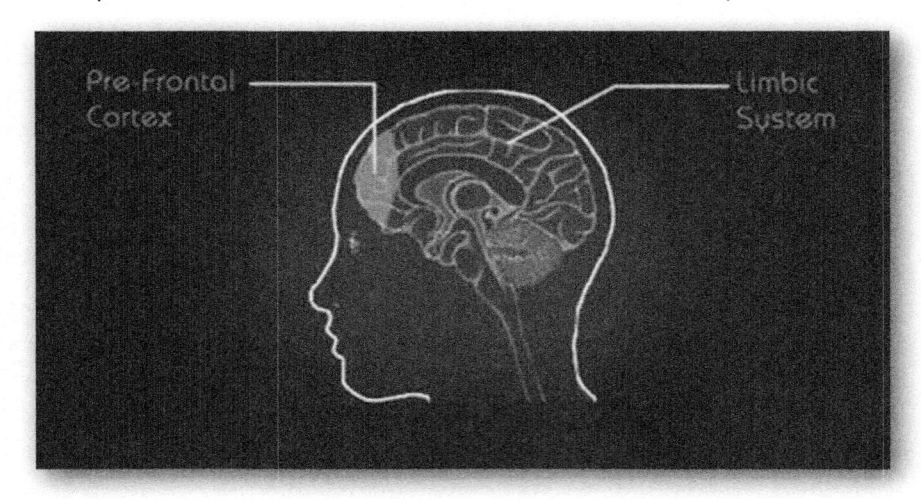

Ninety percent of subconscious human behavior — like breathing, heartbeats, and pleasurable urges — is driven by the Limbic System, which is the reward-stimulated side where your "dope" chemicals of pleasure operate. This "reward-dope" part of the brain does not care about what's right or wrong, good or bad, and moral or immoral. It just alerts us if what we feel is desired and needed to survive.

The Pre-Frontal Cortex is the rational side of the brain that uses logic. It allows us to reason and understand consequences. So a bulk of the brain is wired for instinctive necessities and emotional pleasures for experiencing a "high." This "reward-dope" side of the brain is not controlled by the conscious mind. What separates us from animals is the "rational" side, where we can consciously process our decisions and think to our fullest capacity. The rational side is the master of our brains. Anything the "reward-dope" side wants to do must get clearance from the rational.

These two sides of the brain are the source of our greatest internal conflicts and mind battles in determining what's right from wrong. One of our most powerful abilities as humans is being able to keep a healthy balance, allowing rationale to dictate and control what pleasures are best for us to experience or not. When addicted to drugs, the brain is thrown off balance by producing a recklessly high amount of dopamine from the impulsive and emotional "reward-dope" side.

Crack has one of the worst effects because it stimulates an insanely high and instantly rapid release of dopamine greater than anything else in life – including your career, ambition, family, favorite deserts, and favorite hobbies. The rush from crack can be significantly greater than that during sex, which is where most people experience their highest rushes of dopamine stimulation from an activity. With this dangerous rush of dopamine stimulated by crack and drugs, the "rational" side of the brain is uncontrollably dominated and overthrown. You no longer have a thinking mechanism operating correctly for determining what's a good high to experience or a bad high to prohibit. Without this thinking ability in place, your life is in serious jeopardy.

Drug abuse also ruins the ability to enjoy natural high experiences in reality. Addictive behaviors create a pleasurable experience by unnaturally overstimulating the dopamine "dopeness" within you. It makes you a slave to your own "dopeness" and your own ability to achieve a healthy, productive euphoric high.

Young black male, you're not a slave. You're more than a dope black boy as well. You're built to be a successful, rich black man, who is strong and intelligent enough to rely on your own natural "dopeness" to create the right results in life. It's quite natural to want to feel happy and experience a high like no other. Your power lies within the higher-functioning part of your "rational" brain, which can create the best experiences for achieving genuine highs in life that feel good but are still controlled on your own terms.

The same parts of the brain that cause bad, unproductive habits can cause good, productive ones. The same "dopeness" that can make you an addict and failure, uncontrollably committed to doing things the wrong way is the same "dopeness" that can turn your life around. You can experience a high on success, with a relentless ambition for producing great results the right way, without ever resorting to drugs or alcohol again.

The greatest high you could ever experience is a high you can generate independently within your own mind. This power can never be taken away from you when you choose to control your own mind the right way. You're the sole controller of this inner phenomenon. Any other artificial, excessive, and delusional way of experiencing your own dopeness is just a destructive trap. Young black male, you're DOPE! Get high off your own success, and rely on your own mind to be the absolute best man you can be.

CHAPTER 11

Intimacy: Bridging The Gap Between Love & Sex

Sex is man's greatest desire and downfall. It's also society's greatest marketing tool that triggers an automatic emotional response. That trigger can lead to our greatest joys in life, or our most painful mistakes. Images of sexuality are constantly presented to us on our timelines on Instagram and Facebook, websites, TV shows, movies, commercials, music, radio, shopping malls, workplaces, events, and throughout our entire culture. Sexuality is the most puzzling and provocative desire for man, especially when packaged in the beautiful expression of a woman.

In the book, *The Way of the Superior Man*, author David Deida states as men we are ultimately driven by our purpose and mission.[1] By nature, we're hunters driven to conquer. The words "I came, I saw, I conquered" embody our deepest desires to be kings amongst our own empire. This is most evident in a man's lustful pursuits.

The energy we use to pursue various life missions is transformed to even higher levels of intense pursuit in our desire for women. Sexual energy within a man reflects our intense attraction to beauty, passion, opportunity, accomplishment, and freedom. It's an erotic adventure, full of lust and seduction which fulfills that inner lion within every man who desires to be king of his own jungle.

But beyond those animal instincts and cravings is something deeper. Sex is such a powerful outlet because we literally can create life from it. I believe it's a symbolic force representing how we pursue our life mission. Deeper than just the physical thrills with sex is the euphoric intimacy of a universal energy that drives the human soul experience and beyond. That energy is the true intimacy of LOVE!

Cycle of Life & Love

Every person you've ever seen or known was created by sex between a man and woman. There is an evolving sexual drive within every person of every race, religion, and culture. Every time you see anyone anywhere, it's a reminder of how natural sex is to our world. There's only one way we all got here.

Our parents did it, our grandparents did it, our great-grandparents did it, and so on back to the beginning of time. If they're not Jesus from Nazareth, they exist or existed because somebody got it poppin'. As the most intelligent and sophisticated species on earth, sex is still the fundamental act required for our existence. It's how we build our beloved families, communities, and evolve as a human race.

In Maslow's *Hierarchy of Needs*, the renowned psychologist placed sex in the most critical category of needs for human survival, along with air, water, food, and sleep. Maslow then placed it in the category for the need to love and belong. So young black male, when you feel a certain way about a female you're attracted to, that is perfectly natural and normal. This desire alone does not make you a pervert, thirsty, nasty, or a bad person. It makes you straight up human like everyone else. It's a part of what makes you a man. It's all a part of the remarkable cycle of life and love.

I'm a keep it real. Sex is the most amazing, righteous, and natural human expression all in one. This incredible experience is also the most necessary for continuing the human race. I hear so many supposedly "righteous" people who speak of sex as if it's the worst thing in the world, unless you're married. There's absolutely nobody I've ever known who didn't have sex before marriage, to my knowledge. NOBODY! And the past history of most of the so-called "righteous" ones shows that they were getting it poppin' as a "playa" during their teen years, wild frat house college days, or even in some cases "big pimpin'" outside of their first or second marriage, which led to a divorce.

Don't get me wrong, marriage is the most ideal relationship for love and intimacy. The intentions of the "righteous" are good for promoting a message to not have sex under non-marital conditions. However, I just find that the discussion is too often unrealistic and untrue.

Nothing is more special than intimacy and love. All sexual activity is definitely not always this, but under the right conditions it's exactly this. There's a natural desire and "need" regarding sexual expression, which becomes important to us in the same way food and water is necessary. I know I had my fun when I was younger and hustling in the streets going from female to female. Sometimes, I was with multiple females within the same 24-hour period. I'm not justifying these actions, but I also know some of the greatest men in world history have fallen prey to sexual infidelity and lack of control.

Sex is a very mystifying sensation that man, in general, has shown a very inconsistent ability to control. Despite these dynamics, I never want to become that old head who's telling the young bloods to stop chasing women just because, as an old head, my big pimpin' days have passed me by. In contrast, I also don't want to be that irresponsible old head still practicing and promoting reckless promiscuity, even though he has ruined every relationship he's been in because he can't let go of his destructive played out pimpin' ways. I personally prefer to just be a voice of reason in reflecting upon some insights to sexuality as it relates to a higher understanding of its purpose within the cycle of life and love.

A Mother's Love

I once heard a man say, "If you don't love yourself, your neighbor is in trouble." I will go as far as to say that not only is your neighbor in trouble, but so are all the people closest to you. This includes your family and those you're supposed to love the most. Loving people love people, hurt people hurt people, and confused people confuse people. My experiences with women have proven all of the above.

They say a male's first love is his mother. Looking back on everything now, my relationship with my mother Tina affected how I pursued girls. As a young mother, Tina spent a lot of time going out. So although she loved me and looked out, our quality time did not equate to a lot of quantity time.

It was like having a celebrity singer for a big sister who was always on the road living the life without you. It was fun when we could hang and spend time together, but most times I had to stay with my grandparents so she could roll and do most of her hanging elsewhere. As I grew older, I found that I would become most attracted to the "hot girl" that was always going out and was perceived as "the baddest." In fact, I became that dude who could attract that specific prototype of the "baddest chick," looking for an escape through the fast lifestyle that I could provide.

During those times, I treated every female I got down with very similarly to how my mother Tina treated me. Love for the moment, but gone before you know it. In a twisted way, I now realize I was seeking short-term jump-offs I could keep and reject on my own terms, because deep down I felt some sense of rejection all my life from my mother. I equated real intimacy and quality time with short fleeting moments with no need or desire for real quantity time.

Females would desire my presence more and more, and I would just become more detached, seeing them less and less. I wanted 100 percent commitment from them but gave them very little in return. I mainly just gave them some trickin' money and bedroom action. Eventually they would be upset with the treatment and I would cut them off, quickly moving on to the next one.

I built up my roster of women like luxury material possessions. Their main purpose was to fulfill my need for sex, ego boosting, and stunt power. Sex became a weapon. It was one of my "Art of War" tools for increasing the power I felt I needed to be that official boss in the streets. The facade I would put on included running through as many beautiful chicks as I could — not Christopher Wallace aka "Biggie," but another Chris getting his "Big Poppa" on.

Back then I was a rolling stone. Wherever I laid my fitted cap was my home. But the more I laid up with women, the more I felt alone. Luther Vandross sang "A House Is Not a Home." In all the spots I was running through – nothing felt like a home. Running through random chicks' spots, night in and night out, got played out because it was all temporary and superficial. They were purely sexual relationships with no substance.

The more women I was with, the lonelier and more depressed I would get dealing with all the inevitable drama. It became just another dirty street game, where everyone was looking for a fast come-up. I came to realize that sex was becoming a revengeful self-destructive weapon. It became a numbing drug, stimulating an adventurous high, followed by a depressive low. Sex became another version of crack; but instead of just being a seller, I was a junkie. I was addicted to a fleeting high that would always fade away.

As hard as we are as men, there's a Mary J. Blige singing deep down in our hearts for a "Real Love," too. For us to feel good and secure about our mission in life as men, whether in the streets or in the corporate world, we want true stability with a love mate. We want a real home — not a whore house, strip club, or never-ending twerk fest.

Sure, we might fantasize about women throwing themselves at us in the hot tropical remote islands, or getting "turnt up" making it rain around a bunch of sexy women taking their clothes off. But the reality is, we want the intimacy of a woman who will love us and ride or die for us until the wheels fall off. We can kid ourselves and run around the block all we want with every jump-off we can slide through with a cute face and bangin' body. But something is going to tug at us deep within to lock down something more meaningful and lasting.

My greatest experience of real love and intimacy is with my current wife Sherrina. She's allowed me to fill a void in my heart for genuine love and stability. For the first time I feel I have a hold on a powerful type of love that can last forever. She's the first woman I can honestly say I love, trust, and respect. Overall, she is a phenomenal woman and mother. I am truly blessed to have her as my wife.

Beauty of Women

Women are without a doubt the most beautiful beings ever created. Just on the surface alone their attractiveness, softness, vibrant glow, grace, and curvaceous symmetry are mind-blowing. I get goose bumps when I see gorgeous women all across the country posting pics on Instagram, rocking my Beautiful Hair 4 U. I am honored to the highest degree, because they connect their amazing world of beauty to my brand to showcase.

Women are masterpieces and the most vibrant form of living art. But what lies within a woman is so much deeper and even more amazing. Their ability to nurture, care, and love is what fuels us all since the beginning of our birth and inception. A woman will spend countless hours for 2 days straight cooking a Thanksgiving meal just so the entire family can feel an unconditional nurturing and blessing through a memorable feast. There's no way I could do that. There's not enough nurturing in me or most men to even try.

Women are designed by nature to be very emotional, much more so than men. That emotion a woman provides is the spark to nature, life, and love. It's what holds our families together, and it provides the love that makes the world go round. A woman's emotional capacity for love balances us, and we balance women with our logical capacities for strength. When done right, it's a match made in heaven, happily experienced right here on earth.

Sex: The Incredibly Good, Bad, & Ugly

The Good

Just from a physical standpoint, sex is meant to feel really good. Everything that leads up to it - from the initial attraction to a woman - to the entire build-up process of penetration mentally, emotionally, and physically, are an explosive journey and a high like no other. Sex allows a man to feel confident, accomplished, happy, and ultimately free.

But sexuality alone is only one component of many facets required to feel whole and complete. To try to satisfy our sexual urges without satisfying our mental, emotional, financial, aspirational, communicational, social, cultural, relational, and spiritual aspects is nowhere near a full or ideal life experience. Sex alone, without fulfilling the other dimensions of our existence, is like eating dessert alone for dinner. Sure we love apple pie, sweet potato pie, or chocolate cake and would love to get right to it before anything else a lot of times. But even a kid given only dessert for dinner all the time will begin to ask, "Where's the real food?"

True unconditional love and intimacy involving sex is what makes the entire process incredible. Random sex by itself is like going to the Burger King drive thru all the time to get an apple pie for dinner. At best, sex by itself is going to the Cheesecake Factory for your favorite over-the-top cheesecake. Yes, it tastes good, but you can't live off cheesecakes and apple pie. A man needs some real food, and a man also needs some real love.

A man can make use of this "real love" to literally create a love child and have the most amazing family experience in life. Everything created and shared in a family is based on love. As men, we have the power to create a family that extends our greatness and happiness beyond ourselves. We can create our own empires and carry on our legacy through the love creation of our own families. We have the power to create beautiful kids with our very own blood running through their veins. This very blood of our own will run through every child and family created by them until the end of time.

I know how fun it is to knock down as many beautiful chicks as possible. Every day every man is tempted by another woman for purely sexual reasons. So young black male, I'm not saying pursuing a bunch of women sexually is not exciting or temporarily gratifying as heck. I'm saying the pursuit of true intimacy with a real love soul mate is that gratification plus so much more. Why settle for a bunch of random one-course sexual apple pies when there may be a 5-star five-course woman of a lifetime with your name all over her.

The ultimate woman for you is not only one who fulfills your physical needs, but also a woman who supports your ambition, talks with you for hours and stimulates your mind, shares life responsibilities with you so that the burden is not all on you, has your back and is there for you during your toughest battles, beautifies your house into a loving home, provides lasting memories and moments as a best friend, all while being the absolute best love of your life and mother to your children.

The *Science of Love*, by John Baines, quotes Archimedes in saying, "give me a means of support and I will raise the world."[2] Baines states Archimedes was not referring to a physical phenomenon. The lever is an analogy of man's will, and his means of support is the woman.[3] Behind every great man is a great woman. Our ability to conquer the world is often directly related to the woman we have supporting us with a fulfilling all-around love to do so.

I don't think Barack Obama becomes the first black President of the United States of America without a ride or die wife like Michelle who can hold it down as his closest confidante, best friend, and nurturing backbone to their family. I don't think Magic Johnson makes it through life to evolve beyond a great NBA basketball player, who courageously overcomes a diagnosis of HIV to become a great entrepreneur and ambassador to the world, without his wife Cookie by his side, loving him every minute despite any life-altering mistakes.

Life is rarely a blowout game where you win by a landslide. A man is faced with some real tough life moments and decisions in the clutch. During these moments, great sex alone won't get you through. That ride-or-die woman becomes your backbone and provides a love source for a long-lasting bloodline to your family and dreams that no random apple-bottom shaking by itself can support.

A healthy, intimate relationship with a soul mate helps give you that all-encompassing energy of love and happiness, to break through all life's obstacles to becoming the most successful man you can be. This intimacy and love is the fabric behind building a family of kids and a household that will be your true legacy. The impact of this legacy through your family is worth more than anything else in the world. The creation of this once-in-a lifetime love experience is what life is all about. This intimate love in its entirety, which creates pure euphoric happiness beyond the physical, is what makes sex ultimately worthwhile and incredibly good.

The Bad

Sexual energy if used in the wrong way can lead to very undesirable situations. A woman is driven by the pursuit to love in a manner much more open and direct than men. So despite a woman's initial interest in just having a casual sexual relationship or being that "side chick," most women will eventually want much more from you. If by chance she doesn't, that's a woman who may be using you and manipulating you to get what she wants.

That woman could be playing the role of a vampire and hypothetically killing you by sucking your blood and leaving you lifeless, so to speak. The blood she's taking is in the form of trickin' money, power, status, comfort, or bounce-back revenge from another man doing her wrong. Either way she's playing you.

She'll play with your heart, emotions, and money. She'll break your heart and bank account all in one sexual fiasco. As a man you never want to be in a situation where a woman misuses you and turns you into a feminine victim. That's the opposite of what you're designed to be as a strong man. Women with ulterior motives are often a trap.

This kind of woman can seriously set you back and hurt you to a point of no repair. That's not real love. Most times it's a dangerous game. Just like selling crack, you will eventually get caught. Most men have at least one woman in their past or current life who is too fast for them. That woman sets up shop in their head and manipulates it to a point of no return.

Playing the sex game with a woman like this never preserves your best interests. It's embarrassing and heartbreaking for a man to be sprung out with a woman he thinks is only loyal to him — only to find out she's sleeping with another man or other men. You don't want to fall in love with a woman who's scandalously giving up what you thought was yours to someone else. It's very wise to avoid these situations so that you don't get hurt and played.

On the other hand, when you have a good woman that you hurt by misleading her, you'll often have a problem on your hands as well. Regardless of what the casual terms of non-commitment are supposed to be; in her mind, those terms become null and void once you all become intimate. A woman is a receiver by nature, and as men we are the giver. So somewhere within the dynamic intricacies of sex is an energy that is transferred by a man and consumed by a woman. Even the physical nature of sex proves this. Oftentimes, when a man's love activity ends in intimacy, a woman's deeper yearning for love is just beginning. As the saying goes, "Men hold to have sex, and women have sex to be held."

A woman once explained to me that intimacy for a female can be compared to gum sticking on carpet or a Kool-Aid stain. Once gum or Kool-Aid is on the carpet, it's hard to get all of it out. You can come back over and over to try to remove it, but it seems like you can never get it all out. If you continuously stain the carpet or leave new gum on it, it makes the process of removing it even harder. When a man is with a woman, he leaves something behind within her mind, body, and soul that can never totally be removed as well.

A mistake that many of us men make is to believe we can be intimate with a woman and leave it there, with no strings attached. No good woman who likes us, in a way that a quality man attracts, can leave it at that. It's not just physical sex but an intimate act of lovemaking for her. So it's natural for that woman to want more of you and a commitment, especially if the intimacy is consistent. This is true regardless of the supposed "terms to engagement" or lack thereof.

This creates extreme frustration for a woman, and that leads to a lot of DRAMA for you. Dramatic outbursts, leading to the keying of cars, busted windows, public episodes, where you're getting cursed out in front of the homeys, or getting a drink poured on you in the club. Even physical altercations start from this hurt that a woman feels. The emotions and drama these experiences bring into your life can set you back from your purpose, peace of mind, and well-being. A distracted man is often an unsuccessful man. So despite the temptation of conquering various women for various reasons, these sexual pursuits leading to overwhelming drama are not worth it at all.

The Ugly

Lost Soul Mate Forever

Oftentimes in life, if you don't determine what you truly want and what you're willing to sacrifice, you may end up losing something special that you'll never be able to get back. I was chopping it up with an OG in the barbershop, who was in his mid-40s. He was bringing up different situations he had with past and current women in his life, but I could tell he wasn't all the way happy. I asked him if he had ever been with a woman who was worth giving up all the other random women for. He sat back in his chair, slightly grinned, and said in a very reflective tone, "Yeaaaahhh, Man!"

He began to tell me about a woman he was with over a decade ago, whom he now can say was the love of his life. At the time they were together, he was entertaining some other women as well. At first the woman was cool with the casual relationship but as they grew more in love she began to pressure him to be with her only. Even though he felt that she would be "the one," the OG had too many other "bad chicks" on the roster and wanted more time to sow his wild oats before settling down.

He ended up getting another woman pregnant and the woman left him. A couple of kids and divorces later, the OG said if he knew then what he knew now, he would've locked it down with her all the way and cut off the other women. "She was my soul mate man; we were really in love, and she really held me down."

I asked, "So if you could go back in time and never be with another woman just to be totally committed to her for life, you would?"

The OG said, "Hell yeah! I wouldn't wanna be with any other woman in the world but her."

That man found out she was his ultimate soul mate after he lost her for good. After her, he had plenty of jump-offs and good times, momentarily; he even had kids he loves. But he would contemplate changing all of that to go back and have a family with the soul mate he knew was his greatest love. He thought he had time to play around, lay up with numerous women, and still keep her; but he was wrong. His greatest opportunity for "real love" was gone and lost forever.

Young black male, you do not want to get old in the game as an OG running from chick to chick, carelessly disguising the fact that you're depressed and unhappy. When you run across that woman who makes you feel good in every healthy, productive, and exciting way – you may be experiencing a once-in-a-lifetime love that you want to hold on to. But when you're sexually reckless, and running around trying to get with every chick in town, that woman and the life you could happily live with her will pass you by.

Like R. Kelly said, "When a woman's fed up, there ain't nothing you can do about it." That can be a heartbreak that haunts you all the way to the grave. Don't let the undisciplined desire for sexual variety, fantasy, and pleasure keep you from experiencing an unconditional love of a lifetime. When you lose a soul mate you're in love with forever, due to some frivolous BS, part of your heart and soul goes with her. At the end of the day, "real love" is all there is.

Unwanted Pregnancy

Having a child with a woman you've been intimate with should be one of the happiest times in your life! There's nothing that can make you more proud and satisfied as a man than the lifelong opportunity to raise your own flesh and blood with the love of your life. Creating a family in this way is awesome!

But finding out you're having a child from a woman you have no real interest in other than those weak moments of wanting sex can be the worst thing you can imagine. The lifelong turmoil, frustration, pain, and drama of having to deal with a woman for the rest of your life because you all brought an innocent child into this world that requires your involvement for a lifetime, or at least 18 years, is a new, ugly reality to a living hell. Sadly, many men are living in this hell right now.

Sex is often a very mutual decision between a man and woman, but the decision to go forward with having a child after pregnancy is totally up to the woman. The woman is given this right because she's the one giving birth to the child and responsible for carrying it for 9 months. Regardless of whatever a man's short-term intent is behind sex, a woman has full authority over deciding whether to have a child once pregnant. So young black male remember that at the point where a female is pregnant, she literally holds much of your own fate in her own hands – without requiring your say so.

These are the initial components to becoming a deadbeat dad. Young black male, just as I did, many of you know the angry feeling of not being with your biological father because he didn't want to be in your life. The sad reality is that dad chose to be dead to us the minute he realized he created a child by having sex with the wrong woman — a woman he determined was not worth being with, let alone creating a family with. This has to be the weakest moment in the world for a man, to turn his back on his own flesh and blood. No sexual experience in the world is worth being dehumanized and emasculated to this point.

Young black male, if you grew up without your real father like I did, you know that deep, ugly hurt of having to find your way through this cold world knowing that 1 man, 50% responsible for your existence, wants nothing to do with you. You have to go through getting beaten up at school for the first time by a bully without your dad. You have to struggle to learn how to ride a bike or tie a tie without your dad. You have to play football or basketball your entire childhood without your dad seeing you play once.

Growing an interest in a female, and not having dad around to give you some game. Having to go to the funeral of a homeboy who was killed senselessly in the streets, without dad around to console you — that's that hurt! As in my case, you either know this firsthand, or you've seen a situation very close to you where this is the case. You never ever want to be that dude.

However, all black men who aren't with the mother of their kids are not deadbeat dads. Many black men step up to the plate and take care of their responsibilities in providing for their children, just as I have for my first two beautiful children, despite the relationship ending with their mothers. Luckily, everything works out well with their moms, so that I can maintain a wonderful relationship with them. Unfortunately, the misery many other men have to go through in being handled by the court systems, put on child support, given weak custody privileges, and having to deal with all the drama in the world just to pursue having a relationship with their own child becomes a living hell for those men.

It's hard to take these potential concerns into consideration when feeling the sexual desire to be with a female. But it's a million times harder trying to live a life as a halfway decent father under the worst co-parenting conditions. Sure sex can be casual, fun, and for the moment. But it becomes an entirely different situation when a child is created. That's a life that should be happily loved and cared for by its father. If that's not your intention, you have to be wise enough to not only protect yourself at all times in every way possible, but gain control of your sexual urges so that you don't create a lifetime mistake.

Now it's never a mistake for a child to be born. That's always a God-sent blessing for me, you, and anyone else, regardless of if the father sticks around or not. But it's a life-altering mistake for a man who can't come to grips with creating such a blessing because he's not ready.

Young black male, you always want to be as ready as possible for creating and raising your own child when that time comes. But that time is not to be rushed. It's one of the most important decisions in your life that should be responsibly managed. Control yourself and avoid making your most precious gift an ugly nightmare. A nightmare you can never wake up from.

STDs

Imagine going to a party and meeting the baddest dime piece, who is dancing all over you. Afterwards, she invites you to her crib and long story short – you have the wildest one-night stand of your life. Everything happens so fast that you don't even bother to use protection. But you're so lost in the moment that it doesn't even matter. You're still shocked that you were able to pull such a banger on the first night. You leave her crib afterwards feeling like the man.

However, when you try to call her on the way home to get some positive reinforcement on "how hard you went in the paint" you realize she gave you the wrong number. The following day, you wake up and feel a horrible burning feeling in your throat and assume it's the flu. You go to do your normal routine in the bathroom and feel the worst burning sensation ever. It literally feels like you're urinating fire and razor blades. You're holding in a scream as you try to tinkle little by little. The entire area feels painful, and as you look down you almost faint after seeing this nasty greenish-yellow stuff floating in the toilet.

All day you're feeling pain and trying your best not to go to the bathroom. All you can think about is how trifling this chick was for burning you, and more so how stupid you are for getting down with someone you barely knew without using protection. You would do anything at this point to never have had the sexual encounter with the female. The pain and fear of what you've contracted is not worth it.

This is the experience of catching the clap, also known as gonorrhea. Fortunately, by going to the clinic, medication can be given to cure this. But in contracting other Sexually Transmitted Diseases (STDs), it can be quite worse.

STDs are transmitted by sexual contact. According to the journal "Sexually Transmitted Diseases" more than 110 million men and women in the United States experience a sexually transmitted infection.[4] That's almost 1 out of every 3 people. Another alarming statistic is that there are nearly 20 million new infections each year, and half of those occur among young people aged 15-24.[5] One in four American teens contract an STD every year.[6]

The most widespread forms of STDs that cannot be cured are herpes, HPV/genital warts, and HIV/AIDS. Genital herpes is an STD where small painful blisters can break out on the genitals. Medication can be prescribed to treat and prevent outbreaks, but once contracted it cannot be cured.

According to Justherpes.com 25 percent of women (1 out of 4 women) and 20 percent of men (1 out of 5 men) in America have genital herpes.[7] That's over 50 million Americans, and it's estimated that 85 percent of those who have it don't know. Despite genital herpes not being as contagious when there is no current outbreak, these alarming statistics are nothing to be played with.

Human papillomavirus (HPV) is the most common sexually transmitted infection in the United States. It's so common that nearly all sexually active men and women get it at some point in their lives, with 79 million Americans currently affected.[8] Most people with HPV do not know they're infected and never develop symptoms or health problems from it. But it can develop into genital warts, cervical cancer for women, and genital cancer for men. Unlike most STDs that can be prevented with use of condoms, they do not provide complete protection against HPV. The virus can spread through skin-to-skin contact with infected genital areas.[9]

The most deadly of these STDs is HIV (Human Immunodeficiency virus) and AIDS (Acquired Immune Deficiency Syndrome) which is the final stage of HIV. This disease attacks the immune system. As the immune system weakens, the body is at risk of getting life-threatening infections and cancers that can lead to death. According to the Centers for Disease Control and Prevention, more than 1.2 million people in the United States are living with HIV infection. Of those, 1 in 8 is unaware of their infection.[10]

The highest growth rate reported for new HIV infections in the United States is with African-Americans. Unless the course of HIV in the United States changes, it's predicted that at some point during our lifetime an estimated 1 in 16 black men and 1 in 32 black women will be diagnosed with HIV infection.[11] That means in a club that's jumping with 500 men and 500 women, 31 men and 16 women would be infected with HIV.

In 2014, my hometown, Jacksonville, was ranked No. 3 in highest HIV/AIDS rate in the country, only behind Miami and Baton Rouge.[12] Despite the advancement of medicine that has allowed for many infected to live longer than before, some have to take over 20 pills a day. HIV/AIDS is an extremely serious and rampant growing disease in our community, which can put your life at extreme discomfort and serious risk when contracted by being sexually irresponsible.

Young black male, this info is given to you to make sure you know sex is not a game. Every sex-related decision you make can affect your life. The viral spread of STDs may be the most ignored issue in all of society. With all the sexual hype, sensation, and influences we experience - STDs are what we naively choose to neglect thinking about when getting lost in the heat of the moment.

Every time you explore fulfilling a sexual fantasy, regardless of how "hot" that woman is, there is an ugly reality that you could be putting your health and life at risk. These numbers prove that there are many people you know right now with STDs, HIV and AIDS included. You just don't know they have it. Most people infected don't go around telling everyone they have herpes or HIV, it's their darkest, deepest secret. Young black male be responsible, wise, and disciplined enough in protecting yourself so that this type of secret doesn't have to become yours.

4P Code: Purpose/Perspective/Personal Responsibility/ Protection

Here's my recommended 4P Code to bridging the gap between intimacy and sex, so that you explore the happiest and safest way to enjoy all it entails:

#1: Purpose

Young black male always keep in mind that the ultimate purpose of sex is to create a love experience and a child. This outlet best serves as a cornerstone for establishing your own family, legacy, and empire. Sure sex can be enjoyed for so many other reasons, but in holding on to its real purpose you can best direct your energy towards mature experiences that can serve your greatest expression of love and happiness when you're ready.

#2: Perspective

Young black male, you're not a wild naked animal that lacks control over your inner urges. You are a sophisticated, intelligent, and superior being who must always use his mind to determine the best action for every situation. Sex should not be a candy, drug, weapon, or forced act of twisted bondage you feel helpless to engage in upon arousal. Sex is a powerful energy that should be wisely guided and absorbed.

There are all types of permanent life or death consequences to it — so it should never be entertained with an immature, childish, and temporary mind-set.

#3: Protection

Young black male, the first line of protection is abstinence. If you are too young to responsibly raise a child you are more than likely too young to engage in activities to create one. For any male who finds himself desiring a woman who is not his wife or a long-term mate, while at a mature place in life, protection is mandatory. Condoms are a man's best friend in every and all sexual situations in which no child or STD is desired. Condoms prevent pregnancy 98 percent of the time and significantly reduce the chances of transmitting an STD. But nothing is ever fool-proof, as slippage and breakage can occur. Communication is also vital with a partner regarding other forms of birth control, in addition to open dialogue about past experiences and current health status.

#4: Personal Responsibility

Young black male, at the end of the day, you're responsible for your own actions. What you become in life is totally up to you and the decisions you make. Sexual decisions account for some of the most important decisions a man can make. We're in pursuit of life goals that far exceed sexual pleasure alone. The level of responsibility we use for controlling and guiding our sexual desires can lead to the greatest complements to achieving our life dreams. They can also lead to our biggest regrets and failures.

Having a stable relationship with one loving woman does enhance your focus and ability to get things accomplished without the huge distractions that come from chasing a lot of women in the streets. Sex in general takes up a lot of a man's energy, especially when chasing numerous women. Champion boxers are often known for refraining from sex during training leading up to a title fight to preserve their strength. Young black male, we are champion boxers at the sport of life and must maintain the same type of discipline required to achieve our goals as well.

Symbolic Value of Sex

Trust me, I know controlling our sexual desires as men is an extremely difficult task for us all. However, I believe a man who can control and productively channel his sexual energy is as powerful as any other man on the planet. Sex represents opportunity and challenge, just like life. This power to control the deepest desires of our body with the strongest capabilities of our mind is the epitome of real power for a man who can conquer his own worldly ambitions. The way we approach sexual intimacy with a woman reflects the way we approach life. It can symbolize our breakthrough power for experiencing unconditional happiness, or it can be a depleting dumping ground for being unsuccessful and weak as a slave to bad conditions.

Being good and faithful to our woman is a challenge for any man on the planet. However, for black men I think we have a unique opportunity to strengthen ourselves in our collective empowerment as a people by strengthening our ability to control our sexual decisions. What if we started with the black woman as the highest complement to our pursuit of love and success in life? I know the black woman can be a handful, but I also know I have no interest in a world without her. I love the black woman, and I know she loves the black man!

They can play all the "Independent Women/Single Ladies" anthems all night in the club. But after the party ends, that independent black woman would much rather be coming home to her devoted black man (for all the ladies reading right now, I'm preaching way louder than you all are saying Amen! Lol.).

CHAPTER 12

Our World History in Black & White

The Human Genome Project, which studied the entire make-up of the human DNA, discovered that every human is 99.9 percent the same, with all our differences accounting for only 0.1 percent of our DNA make-up.[1] So from a biological standpoint, we are all very close to the same. We have overwhelmingly way more similarities than differences. However, over the thousands of years of existence, human society has configured separatist states of grouping, where various worldwide powers have been predominantly concerned with manipulating and exploiting every difference between people that can possibly be imagined.

Further genetic studies show that race has no true biology behind it.[2] "In the face of our advancing knowledge, race emerges less as a scientific reality and more as a cultural construct."[3] The DNA of humans today is intermixed with different biological traits, representing numerous types of ethnic descents. Therefore, there is no valid, clear-cut way to intelligently label a person biologically by any racial group— Black, White, Hispanic, Asian, Arabian, or Native American. Research has shown that in some cases a person of European descent can have more DNA similarities to an African-American than another European.[4] Racial classification, specifically black and white, is not at all a science. It's a sub-rudimentary way to label people based on a false perception regarding physical features and the complexion of one's skin.

This leads to an understanding that race is just a social concept made by man to create categories of biased separation. The terminology "Black and White" is most accurately used for describing a variation of color optics. Black is the color that results from the absence or complete absorption of light creating total darkness. White is the color that results from the combination of all the colors of the visible spectrum.

To use these terms for categorizing people is one of the most idiotic ideas ever! I have never in my life seen a black person this color:

Nor have I ever in my life seen a white person this color:

The level of ignorance it takes to classify a person by black or white is ridiculous. Furthermore, the sickness to use such classifications to discriminate against a particular group of people, creating bias associations with these colors is wrong to the worst degree (i.e., Black being associated with bad, dangerous, wicked, and dirty — versus White being associated with good, pure, innocent, and clean).

Regardless of the origin of this biased racial categorical system based on unrelated colors, I am proud to say I AM A BLACK MAN! My pride comes in knowing and constantly developing a greater level of truth about myself through my people. The world began and will end with my people. "True history" proves that Black is synonymous with beautiful, powerful, intelligent, pioneering, successful, and great beyond measure. Young, black, and gifted male, this history is yours too.

With this all-powerful feeling, we can always tap into ourselves. Young black male, I also know the pain and frustration of trying to process questions like, "Why does it feel like the world has turned its back on us?" Why has the White versus Black plight been formed to systematically discriminate and work against us just because of the color of our skin? Why were we most abused during the worst slavery of mankind, which lasted for centuries and set us so far back? Why were some of our greatest leaders assassinated during their prime while trying to further our movement?

As young black males, why are we still currently abused and discriminated against today? Why do we so often have to face the unjust fates of a Trayvon Martin, Oscar Grant, Michael Brown, Eric Garner, Walter Scott, Tony Robinson, or Freddie Gray? Most painfully, "Why do we mistreat, hurt, and so hatefully kill ourselves within our very own communities? All are very hard questions to ask — even harder to answer and resolve. However, in life when we remove the "less" from what's "senseless," we're always left with something we can use to make "sense."

The purpose of studying history is to gain a better understanding of OUR world as a self- discovery mission in learning more about "who we are and where we come from." This is so we can better determine "who we want to be and where we want to go." Our knowledge of our true selves is the most powerful key to being free from any of the shackles of history, oppression, discrimination, poverty, institutionalized injustices, police brutality, drugs, broken homes, black-on-black crime, and any other deviations from our true greatness.

The purpose of this chapter is to provide critical insight into exploring the real truth behind our "real world" and our "real history." Together we're going to take a trip. Let's navigate from the beginning of mankind, all through the manufactured "black and white" challenges, to our current state today in gaining a better understanding of truth and self.

Greatness of Africa

Birthplace of Mankind

Hundreds of thousands of years ago the origin of mankind began in Africa. Through the process of human evolution, the modern man, also referred to as homo-sapiens, evolved. The earliest fossil evidence for mankind was found within the area of Ethiopia.[5] This time period is considered pre-history. Numerous genetic studies over the last few decades have shown that human genetic diversity is greatest within African populations.[6] These facts further support that modern humans first appeared in Africa and then spread out to populate the rest of the world.

Historical evidence proves that Africa is the birthplace and true "motherland" for every civilization, race, and religion. It's from the original African man and African woman that all people evolved. Geneticist and anthropologist Spencer Wells says that through DNA analysis of thousands of people around the world, he's discovered that "all humans alive today can be traced back to a small tribe of hunter-gatherers who lived in Africa 60,000 years ago."[7] This is not just black history; this is the entire world history of mankind. Europeans, Asians, Hispanics, Native Americans, and all other ethnicities come from the African.

Young black male, be proud and know that you're from the direct lineage of the creators of mankind, Africans and black people. Also take pride in knowing, despite any racial separation you see in our society, every other person of any other ethnicity shares this same special lineage with you too. The history of whites and all other non-whites begins with blacks. If every family on the face of this earth traced its ancestry back as far as possible, we would all start from the same African man and woman. There is even strong support that the Garden of Eden, the location for the biblical account of the first man and woman Adam and Eve, was in a region of Africa.[8]

The first classified civilizations recorded in history began in Ancient Mesopotamia (now modern-day Iraq, Kuwait, and Syria within the Middle East) with the Sumerians, Babylonians, and Assyrians.[9] These civilizations existed over 6,000 years ago from around 4,000 BC to 300 BC. Many historians consider the original settlers of Mesopotamia to be of Ethiopian descent.[10] These Ethiopians took on the name of the cities they developed and inhabited (i.e., Sumer, Babylon, and Assyria).[11] The following is their blueprint mastered for building these powerful civilizations that would be used by all other future empires till this day were:

1. Natural Advantage - surplus of natural resources & land
2. Economics - business, commerce, trade, & capital
3. Civilization Structure - leadership, government, roads, religion, culture, education, etc.
4. Superior Military – war-ready armies and protectors of the civilization

5. Conquest - dominant conquering of other societies, people, lands, and resources

Because of its unique geographic position perfectly located between two rivers, The Tigris and Euphrates, the soil was extremely fertile and ideal for farming. This was their natural resource advantage. Instead of being preoccupied with hunting and killing animals, like most prehistoric populations, they were able to grow crops creating a surplus of food sources and means to creating an economy through advantageous trade.

Their abundant supply of the most basic needs, food and water, allowed them to evolve in becoming more "civilized" in using their minds. This enabled them to develop other components to society such as buildings, tools, infrastructure, schools, writing, language, government, religion, marketplaces, art, culture, and army defenses. These armies were used to take over other cities and rulers. World history has proven that a powerful nation is created by conquering land and people. The conquest of people and land is achieved by military expansion, and in order to do this economic dominance is necessary. This became the blueprint for how the greatest empires gained power, and is still the blueprint for nations to this very day.

African Kings, Queens, & Empires

Young black male, you come from a lineage of royalty. The first and some of the greatest kings and queens to ever exist were from Africa. Our bloodline is not of the falsely portrayed Africans we see in misguiding infomercials showing poor malnutrition people with gas stomachs and mosquitoes living on their foreheads. We come from the most beautiful, successful, intelligent, and powerful rulers in history, who created the blueprint for all other nations to exist. Molefi Kete Asante's book, *The Egyptian Philosophies* and the African Holocaust website www.africanholocaust.net provide great content on several of the following summaries regarding some of the brilliant greats in African history:

Imhotep (2700 BC)

Imhotep is credited for being the first philosopher in human history.[12] He is considered the father of medicine, architecture, politics, and philosophy. Imhotep pioneered in the area of medical science for healing and was well-trained in all of the scientific practices of Ancient Egypt.[13] He was the great King Zoser's prime minister in Egypt and was tasked with being executive supervisor of everything in the entire land. Imhotep also invented many of the earliest instruments of measurement and architecture, which led to the genius science behind the complex structure for the creation of the "Step Pyramid."[14]

Akhenaton (1375-1358 BC)

Akhenaton was a pharaoh of Egypt. He's known as the founder of monotheism and the first ruler in recorded history to believe in the concept of one God.[15] A quote from the African Holocaust website eloquently states, "1,300 years before Christ he preached and lived a gospel of perfect love, brotherhood, and truth. Two-thousand years before Mohammed he taught the doctrine of the One God. Three-thousand years before Darwin he sensed the unity that runs through all living things."[16] His marriage with beautiful wife Queen Nefertiti is one of history's first well-known love stories as well.

Makeda, "Queen of Sheba" 960 BC

Makeda is the Ethiopian Queen who is believed to have had a royal and ceremonious love union with King Solomon of Israel in the bible, which produced what many scholars say is the longest line of royalty descendants.[17]

Hannibal (247 BC)

King Hannibal is considered by many to be the greatest military leader and strategist of all time. As ruler of the Carthaginian Civilization, he had 80,000 infantry, 12,000 cavalry, and 40 African war elephants.[18] Hannibal conquered all of Italy and major parts of Spain and France. He's most noted for brilliantly "marching his entire army and elephants through the Alps Mountains to surprise and conquer his enemies."[19]

Cleopatra VII, "Queen of Egypt" 69-30 BC

Cleopatra was the last active pharaoh of Egypt and is regarded as the most celebrated African Queen. Cleopatra is known for her incredible beauty, charm, knowledge, and overwhelming influence. She persuaded the well-renowned Julius Caesar to renounce Roman allegiance to fight on behalf of Egypt.[20]

Ancient Egypt

Egypt is regarded by many as the most extraordinary civilization in ancient world history. The awesome capabilities to create the great pyramids that stand today with such limited technology is a historical mystery that reflects a highly advanced mastery of architecture, science, mathematics, and art, superior to any other ancient civilizations. African people are too often not fully credited for developing Egyptian civilization because of its current Arabian population considered "non-African." However, during Ancient Egypt the men were described as having black skin and wooly hair. Original art pieces also consistently reflect images of people with obvious indigenous African features.

Egypt had 31 dynasties from around 3200 BC until 332 BC.[21] Its hot climate and geographic positioning by the world's largest river, the Nile, in addition to its close proximity to the Mediterranean Sea, created extreme natural advantages for anchoring its remarkable civilization from ideal farming conditions, trade, transportation, and means to build powerful armies. The annual flooding of the Nile River stimulated the learning of astronomy and mathematics to develop the 12-month calendar of 30 days, which is the exact calendar pattern we use today. The skills of engineering, geometry, and construction were advantageous for the system building of an advanced society in developing trade by ships, as well as superior resources for warfare.

The Egyptians were specialists in the medical field, which was pioneered by Imhotep. They developed extraordinary expertise in understanding the vital organs and systems of the human body. Egyptians further inspired the concept of religion by embracing mythological gods — such as Osiris, Isis, and their son god by immaculate conception, Horus, which closely resembles the life story of Jesus Christ thousands of years before him.

The most amazing symbol of Ancient Egyptian greatness are the pyramids. Their massive size and near perfect proportions make the pyramids one of the Seven Wonders of the World. The Great Pyramid of Giza in Egypt, which is 481 feet high and 756 feet long, has endured for more than 4,500 years as a marveling representation of the Egyptians' extraordinary mastery of construction, engineering, and mathematics.[22]

The building of this pyramid required the genius transporting and construction of over 2 million stone blocks, weighing on average 3 tons each, for a total mass of over 6 million tons.[23] It's estimated that the cost to build such a pyramid today, with our advanced technology, would be $5 billion.[24] The ability to develop such perfectly structured pyramids during such ancient times, with very little technology known to us, is still an awe-inspiring mystery to this day.

With the later Egyptian dynasties that emerged in "The New Kingdom" of Ancient Egypt, conquest continued with the development of more elaborate governments and sophisticated armies. This began a rise of "nationalistic government" in which there was a prideful spirit of ethnic privilege and homeland superiority, at the expense of other civilizations and ethnicities. This led to more systematic practices of slavery where the conquered were forced to work as slaves in building even more infrastructure for their nation, which included elaborate temples, pyramids, and statues. Egypt experienced unprecedented levels of extraordinary prosperity, advancements in society, and power. However, they began to suffer internal revolts and were eventually taken over by a series of conquests from other nations that ultimately ended their rule.

African Exploration

Ancient Africans were the first migrants. If Africans hadn't left the continent of origin, there is a strong chance that Europeans, Asians, and the rest of the world's population wouldn't exist. Some historians suggest that the first wave of African migrations took place hundreds of thousands of years ago. There is no place in the world one can travel and not find indigenous African people.[25] This is so everywhere from the Philippines, India, Iraq, Russia, Iceland, Mexico, South America, Siberia, China, to the Islands of Fiji.

It is well-known now that history was absolutely wrong in giving Columbus credit for discovering America, a land he thought was India that already had native people greeting him with a civilization of their own. That would be like saying I was the first to discover a basketball court at a spot full of hoopers already running a full court. Numerous resources including the book, *They Came Before Columbus*, by Ivan Van Sertima provides support that Africans had sailed across the Atlantic to America centuries before Columbus.[26]

According to an article by Harvard scholar Garikai Chengu of Global Research, Columbus even wrote in a journal that "black-skinned people had come from the southeast in boats, trading in gold-tipped spears."[27] Chengu states that "The great ancient civilizations of Egypt and West Africa traveled to the Americas, contributing immensely to early American civilization by importing the art of pyramid building, political systems, religious practices, mathematics, writing, and sophisticated calendars."[28]

African maps have been discovered, which were produced before Columbus and accurately map longitude and latitude. In Mexico, the presence of Egyptian-inspired pyramids, sculptures with African features, wall paintings, and religious philosophies are now being credited to the presence of Ancient Africans — like The Olmec civilization of 1200 BC, which came before any other advanced civilization in the Americas.[29]

It's also been reported that Egyptian artifacts and words have been found in the Grand Canyon.[30]

For society to fully embrace the "true history" behind the greatness of Africa, it would have to reverse the entire course of world history as we have been traditionally taught. Young black male, regardless of whether this is ever done, you can make the mental shift in reprogramming your mind right now to embrace the incredible legacy of our heritage. We are royal descendants of the original man of brilliance, innovation, and greatness.

This original man who was the first to travel all across the world and create the foundation for everything man-made in this world, is a black powerful man just like we are. So young black male, know that you always have the power to create a new world for yourself, mentally and physically. Feel free to go anywhere you feel in your heart you are destined to go.

Melanin – Awesome Attributes & Adaptation

The sun is the most vital source of energy to every living organism on our planet. It's extremely important to the vitality of the human body, and was even more critical to the human body thousands of years ago when people did not have access to the plentiful food and vitamin supplies we have today. Our body needs to absorb the sunlight through our skin to produce vitamin D, but our skin also has to protect us from not absorbing too much ultraviolet rays from the sunlight, which can be very harmful.

Melanin is our primary source for regulating how we absorb energy from the sun. Melanin is the pigment associated with darkness, which gives our skin, hair, and eyes its color. Melanin allows for the absorption of sunlight energy necessary for the body to produce vitamin D for maintaining a healthy body and strong bones, while creating a skin shield that protects the body from too much exposure to harmful ultraviolet rays.

Traditional science teaches us this fundamental role of melanin in humans. However, further studies and theories support even more advanced biological attributes of melanin. Heat and electrical energy have incredible effects, especially from a source as powerful as the sun. Melanin theorist Dr. Carol Barnes, author of *Melanin: The Chemical Key to Black Greatness*, states, "Melanin gives humans the ability to feel, because it is the absorber of all frequencies of energy." He refers to melanin as an "organic superconductor" information processor that can function with no resistance.[31]

As a superconductor and semiconductor with insulation qualities, melanin possesses incredible attributes for attracting, absorbing, regulating, and most importantly transferring the powerful properties of heat and electrical energy throughout our body. All activities of the body are controlled by the brain. Melanin refines, stimulates, regulates, and communicates from the central nervous system, so that messages of naturally impulsive and intuitive properties are sent from the brain to other areas of the body extra fast.[32] The more melanin one has, the more rapid energy-based messages from the brain are naturally sent throughout the body. This is a powerful function of stimulation and feeling, which drives us as beings.

In the book, *The Science and the Myth of Melanin*, by physiological psychologist Dr. T. Owens Moore, he states "Melanin helps to heighten mental awareness, it speeds reaction time, and it greatly enhances the capacity of the brain to transmit neural impulses."[33] Melanin is a chemical stimulated by hormones secreted and regulated in the brain. Hormones stimulate specific cells or tissues in the body into action. Thus melanin amplifies and accelerates the brain's processing and communication of energy to stimulate rapid, focused action in the body.

Melanin has its own unique hormonal properties just as dopamine in the brain does, which it is associated with. As discussed earlier, drugs like cocaine are used to stimulate hyperactivity of hormones like dopamine in the body. Steroids are used to stimulate more production of muscle mass through proteins, while generating more fuel energy to work out even more, without getting tired and feeling the muscle breakdown that normally makes people stop. Melanin however is not unnatural or illegal. It's possibly the most powerful natural use of unlimited energy to stimulate action in our universe.

Melanin has also been referred to as "Dark Matter" and "The Black Dot."[34] Melanin functions in our body as a conductor of energy in a similar way to how dark matter functions in the universe, and how chlorophyll functions in plants.[35] According to Black History and Metaphysical Educator Bobby Hemmitt, melanin is composed of carbon molecules just like our DNA, which is our life-defining genetic code.[36] Carbon is recognized as one of the primary keys to life and is found in all organic compounds throughout the universe.[37] Earth's carbon substance is considered crude oil, which is arguably the world's most important natural resource.[38] The powerful universal properties of carbon make up a significant composition of our melanin.[39]

Blacks in all of our various skin shades have the highest level of this powerful melanin source.[40] This is profound biological support for why our excellence is so noticeable in areas like athletics and rhythmic dance. Melanin allows for our brains to operate at extremely fast levels, based on an accelerated and advanced psychological, physical, emotional, and even spiritual energy flow. Melanin enhances the rapid stimulation of feelings and activation of actions. It contributes to what gives us "Soul."

Young black male, this is a phenomenal biological and cosmic trait that we've inherited from our great lineage of African ancestors, which we all share. We can confidently maximize upon transformative attributes stimulated by our melanin in performing our best in every realm of life from the physical to the spiritual. All ethnicities have unique attributes to be proud of, and it's extremely important that we as strong phenomenal blacks recognize the scientific truth about our own great attributes in understanding how special we are. We're naturally the farthest from anything remotely close to inferior.

Young black male, we possess a natural quality that gives us the ability to achieve the following: running the fastest, jumping the highest, dancing the most graceful - as well as speaking with the most articulate level of passion, discovering the greatest of medical breakthroughs, creating the most astounding entertainment, marketing the most successful businesses, building the strongest of happy families and communities, charismatically leading the greatest of nations, treating others with the highest levels of love and compassion, becoming in tuned with the highest realms of spirituality, along with ANYTHING else that can be conceived in the mind and activated through the body. We don't need to over-indulge ourselves in a superiority complex, but we should embrace an all-powerful innate ability to be as great as we want to be. #BLACKLIVESMATTER and always will because BLACK LIFE IS MATTER – infinite, universal, and everlasting.

Evolution of Europe

Due to the great amount of sunlight given off in the hot African environment, darker skin with more melanin was most common and advantageous. Darker skin directly exposed to the sun allowed for an ideal balance of absorbing the right amount of sunlight while simultaneously protecting the body from too much. The proper balance of sun absorption in various environments is reflected through the evolving of various skin complexions of humans throughout history.

Some geneticists believe humans migrated out of Africa over 50,000 years ago.[41] The environment affects how humans physically evolve and adapt. As Africans migrated all over the world, various environmental conditions influenced different physical adaptations including skin complexion.[42] Europe is much colder and darker with much less sunlight available than in Africa, leading to a risk of less vitamin D production in the body for those with darker skin during this time.[43]   In this harsh climate, the mutation of lighter skin with less melanin became more common and advantaged because the bodies of those with fairer skin could adapt and function better under conditions with minimal sunlight.[44]

Those Africans with genetic traits of lighter skin adapted better to this environment versus darker skin, which under these conditions prevented production of enough vitamin D. Over the course of thousands of years, this skin adaptation to the lack of sun and colder climate in addition to a change in diet, led to the evolving of more fair-skin populations in Europe, people considered Caucasian and white.[45] Geneticists estimate that sometime between 6,000 to 12,000 years ago, Europeans lost a significant level of pigmentation from the initial Africans of darker skin shades.[46]

The different environments of the world — from its deserts, rain forests, tropical islands, to its mountains — all presented various conditions in which the human body had to adapt and evolve differently. Each new environment favored some genetic traits over others for survival. These mutations through natural selection were just that, biological adaptations.

One of the most brilliant and beautiful elements of human existence is our diversity. Each of our unique sets of biological traits and cultures, influenced by our unique environments, lead to why the science of mankind is extraordinary. However, mankind's worst mistake is seeing these unique differences as a means of creating a superior versus inferior complex that has brutally separated what should be an incredibly united human race.

Ancient Greece & Rome

Traditional history recognizes Ancient Greece as a highly advanced empire that established the foundation for western civilization, achieving its greatest political and cultural period within the capitol of Athens between 600-336 BC.[47] Greece fully developed a democratic system of government, a city-state infrastructure (similar to the United States), aristocratic societies of powerfully rich families, advanced philosophical ideologies, educational centers, and a sophisticated patriotic cultural identity during what is known as the Golden Age of Athens.[48]

Africa had a significant influence on Ancient Greek civilization and culture. The black Phoenicians, African descendants from the land of Canaan, traveled to Europe with a powerful navy and advanced skill for trading and nation building.[49] Black

Phoenicians taught Greeks their alphabet in order to have a unified language to conduct business.[50] Greeks adopted this alphabet and also passed it along to the Romans. The Phoenician alphabet is regarded as the ancestor of almost all modern alphabets and is where the English language derived.[51] The black Phoenicians also gave a system of weights and measures to the Europeans.[52] The Greek philosopher Thales, considered the "Father of Western Philosophy," studied in Africa and learned the science of philosophy from Egyptian priests.[53]

War is a very prevalent part to Ancient Greece, with expansive conquests of more regions led by conquerors such as Alexander The Great. Large militaries were built engaging in intense wars and constant fighting amongst the Athenians, Persians, and Spartans. War created a large system of slavery in which it's estimated about 80,000 slaves lived in Athens.[54]

Rome built upon these previous cultures, sciences, and ideologies, originally inspired by Africans, in an even more focused manner to build and organize their empire. The famous quote, "Rome was not built in a day," refers to the sophisticated development of its empire. Advancements were made to develop stronger architecture and public buildings, highly competitive events such as gladiator battles at the Coliseum, road networks expanding throughout the entire empire, luxury social classes, a population counting census system, and a very progressive legal system and government with a large Senate under Roman Law.[55] Julius Caesar was Rome's most well-known dictator and military leader – killing, enslaving, and uprooting millions in his conquest of power and wealth.

Rome enforced brutal laws of governmental control to maintain its power and eliminate any threats of division. In addition to the many wars of conquest, there was also an emerging level of attacks against opposing religions, specifically Christianity. Romans persecuted Christians for over 250 years, including the crucifixion of Jesus.

The Roman Empire grew too big to effectively govern and began to break down. Several factors in its decline include corrupt rulers that weakened the government, a debilitated army due to the hiring of many foreign soldiers mostly motivated by money versus a movement, and economic breakdown leading to high levels of unemployment and poverty. The Roman Empire fell and was conquered by Anglo-Saxon Germanic tribes by A.D. 476.[56]

The Greek and Roman empires expanded the systematic structures of gaining power through economics, government, civilization, and military. Their conquest and empires reflect a very focused leverage upon complex systems to rule and dominate. These empires based on such systematic dynamics also reflect a viral growth of power aggression channeled in greed to become bigger, wealthier, and more powerful in taking over as much land and resources as possible while forcing a particular way of life upon others. This becomes an even more prevalent thread of vicious domination in human civilization and global evolvement.

Dark Ages

As more countries and various rules of power emerged within Europe, numerous nations emerged such as Germany, Spain, Portugal, France, Italy, and England. However, in what is considered the Dark Ages, there was a drastic decline in culture within Europe following the end of the Roman Empire in 476 AD for about 500 years through 1000 AD. This time period is characterized by stagnant cultural growth, constant wars, and horrendous plagues reducing the population.[57]

Black Moors

The Black Moors from North Africa in Morocco invaded Spain in 711 AD and ruled in Europe for 700 years through the 14th century.[58] The Moors introduced advancements to European society such as paper, new agricultural crops (lemon, orange, sugar cane, silk, and rice), astronomy, modern surgery, chemistry, physics, mathematics, and architecture.[59] According to the *Atlanta Black Star* article, "When Black Men Ruled The World: 8 Things The Moors Brought To Europe," the Moors established the capital city Cordoba, which is recognized as one of the most important cities of this time.[60] It was amazingly built and technologically advanced with hygiene products, fashion, urban utilities, street lights, hospitals, public baths, and the hydraulic engineering of pipelines that carried water from the mountains to the city.[61]

The incredible accomplishments of the Black Moors sparked a period of cultural enlightenment in Europe that led them out of the Dark Ages and on to further global explorations that helped shape the world to what it is today.[62] One of the most remarkable uncovered findings about the Moors is the existing evidence that suggests they sailed to the Americas centuries before Christopher Columbus.[63]

It's documented that these Moors of African origin sailed westward across the Atlantic Ocean from a Spanish port. After a long time they returned from a "new strange land" with many goods they had acquired.[64] Ironically, the same year the Moors were conquered in Spain, Columbus later sailed to the New World of America in 1492. It's also historically documented that men of African origin in Spain were brought along to accompany Columbus on this voyage.[65] This suggests that the Black Moors had already sailed to America and had the knowledge to show Columbus how to get there for "his" first time, not theirs.

European Exploration Out of Desperation

By the 14th century, Europe became extremely overpopulated for such a relatively small area. There was simply not enough "land" to support the massive amount of people there. In the 1798 "Essay On The Principle of Population," Thomas Malthus stated, "if humans reproduce so greatly beyond the limits of available resources needed, they can reach a point of catastrophe, which under these conditions of survival and scarcity is inevitable."[66]

In Europe, a low quality of life and malnutrition existed due to agricultural exhaustion, crop failures, and food shortages, which all led to massive epidemics. A series of famines and plagues, such as the Black Death, swept across Europe killing huge portions of the population. These horrible conditions were aggravated by civil unrest, revolts, and constant wars of close proximity during the late Middle Ages in Europe.

Such drastic conditions created a desperate urgency to begin exploring the entire world for new land, resources, and ways of building a stronger economic base for power. Economics would be the pivotal core to this movement. Advanced systems of trade and commerce were developed to expand their ability to get more resources, conquer more land, build more wealth, and evolve in becoming perpetually more dominant.

Emergence of United States – Capitalism and Democracy

Spain and France colonized numerous land areas in the Americas through violent conquests of natives using a more advanced production of guns and steel for weaponry along with the spread of diseases they had become immune to. However, England won several wars in the 17th and 18th centuries making it the dominant colonial power overseas in North America. Great Britain established thirteen colonies in America. The costly wars Great Britain fought during this time left its economy weakened with a huge debt.

To pay the debt off, the British Parliament began passing laws that heavily taxed the American colonists. Americans rejected the British monarchy and overthrew the rule of Great Britain in winning the American Revolutionary War. America won its independence and became the United States of America.

America's fight was fueled by the desire for freedom. In 1776 during the American Revolution, the United States had drafted a Declaration of Independence for the purpose of protecting all citizens' civil rights to life, liberty, and the pursuit of happiness. This is the fundamental ideology for which the United States of America was founded. A new form of government based on a democracy for the people by the people was created. The Constitution was drafted defining how the U.S. government and laws work under the three branches — executive, legislative, and judicial. This democratic system ideologically created freedom for all, but in reality was enforced to govern a particular style for gaining power and wealth.

World history has taught us that powerful civilizations are anchored by its core economic foundation. A country's ability to generate money and wealth is the foundation for building up its civilization, military, and subsequent power. America's key to establishing its version of a working democracy was through capitalism, a free-market economy. Capitalism idealistically stimulates greater innovation and prosperity through the freedom of uninhibited competition and free trade. Unfortunately, the drive to achieving unlimited growth and economic prosperity for one group of people comes with the risk of a growing parallel to the brutally limiting oppression enforced upon another.

New land was the greatest asset to exploring, conquering, and colonizing in America. With all of the farmland for agriculture in the new land of America, the natural resources of crops such as tobacco, sugar, and cotton became the economic drivers for building prosperity through international trade. Field hands were needed to work the fields.

The capitalistic goal of "maximizing profits" in fulfilling huge global demands led to the inhumane act of exploiting slaves for cheap labor. The more slaves who could work the plantation fields with no pay, the more crops could be cultivated to sell and make enormous profits for white owners. The stronger the unjust racist treatment towards a particular group of people as inferior, the more a prejudice rationale could be applied globally to systematically enslave a people for maximum productivity and wealth creation in acquiring greater power.

Slavery

Whites in America initially tried to enslave Native Americans, but too many were either dying from epidemic diseases brought to the Americas from overseas or escaping because they knew the area much better. The enslavement of other whites was frowned upon as well, especially in a country promoting freedom for their fellow man. This led to the strategy of enslaving Africans, due to Africa's known history of slave trading. Ignorantly discriminating against a darker people was also determined to be an easier means for gaining white European support.

The Trans-Atlantic Slave Trade became a global economic system, anchored between the points of England, Africa, and America across the Atlantic Ocean. This "triangular trade" involved America sending farm crops to England, England trading manufactured goods to Africa for slaves in addition to capturing slaves, and England sailing back to America to deliver the African slaves. Various estimates of African slaves captured during the entire Trans-Atlantic Slave Trade range from 12-80 million. Millions of African slaves died during the passage, due to diseases on the ships, being thrown overboard, slave raids, or suicide. The Trans-Atlantic Slave Trade Based estimates 10.7 million slaves survived the horrific Middle Passage and were sent to North America, the Caribbean, and South America.[67]

The systematic perpetuation of capitalistic ambitions and oppressive racism to build a global empire by the U.S. led to this New World Slave system, which is the most horrible treatment of humans ever in world history. African men, women, and kids were captured and stolen from their homelands. They were sold, stripped naked, shackled in iron chains, and "packed like sardines" at the bottom of the ships.[68] The space was so cramped they were forced to crouch or lie sideways with often only about 16 inches of width.[69] The air was terribly foul as they were forced to lie amongst their own feces and vomit in suffocating heat. There was a constant threat of malnutrition, epidemics and diseases. Women and kids were exposed to violence and sexual abuse from the crew members as well.

Our captive ancestors had to try to survive in these unbearable conditions on the slave ships for 2 months until they reached America.[70] For over 200 years, the inhumane institution of slavery existed in America. Whites engaged in severe racism, perpetuating false stereotypes of black inferiority and white superiority to drive a ruthless economic system for building a nation. The forefathers of the United States created a nation based on life, liberty, and the pursuit of happiness — for white citizens. On the other hand, then insane oppression of slavery systematically denied every civil liberty imaginable to blacks.

Blacks were denied an education, property, wealth, civil rights, and most of all freedom. Our African ancestors were brutally cut off from family and an extraordinary African culture of great royalty, language, religion, and the advanced civilization which birthed mankind. They were forced to work tirelessly in the fields of plantations predominantly in the South for long hours daily with no compensation. They were maliciously discriminated against, beaten, whipped, raped, hung, and killed. This was all acceptable by U.S. law and enforced by the country's constitution, which considered blacks only three-fifths of a human being.

Slavery Economics

Why did the U.S. engage in such a gross level of oppression towards blacks with slavery? Often I thought it was all because of the hate towards a people of a different skin color, which is hard to argue against given the facts. However, this institutionalized racism was also a capitalistic means to an end. The United States quickly grew from a new nation with minimal global influence to one of the most powerful countries in the world during this time.

Between 1790-1860, the U.S. went from zero production of cotton to 2 billion pounds.[71] By 1860, the U.S. produced 75 percent of the world's cotton and generated $200 million a year, all due to a population of 4 million black slaves.[72] Cotton accounted for 60 percent of total U.S. exports.[73] Cotton was the central raw material for all European economies, and the U.S. became the biggest beneficiary in capitalizing upon this huge global demand. As an enormous demand for cotton grew, a directly correlating demand for black slaves grew. The inhumane slave system of exploiting the tireless work of black slaves on cotton plantations literally catapulted the U.S. to becoming the most powerful nation in the world today.

This drove a system of slavery in which blacks were exploited as profit-maximizing commodities, and dehumanized to an object or animal. Men were valued and sold based on physical strength and procreation ability, while women were valued and sold based on child-bearing ability. This was all done to drive the growth of this highly profitable slave-based economic system. Families were frequently torn apart forever, when a family member was chosen to be sold by their slave owner.

Making of a Slave

Divide and conquer tactics were also used to pit blacks against blacks. In the "Willie Lynch Letter: The Making of a Slave," a slave owner reportedly gives a speech about how to break a black slave and keep them in bondage for centuries.[74] White slave owners raped black women to cross-breed and create children of lighter complexion. This dynamic was used to create a division between light-skin and dark-skin blacks.

Other tactics of division were pitting the younger generation against the older generation, house workers against field workers, and most destructively the black man against the black woman. The black man was beaten and broken down physically to emasculate him to a point of frozen fear.[75] This was done to make him mentally weak, removing him from the natural protective role of family leader, despite being physically strong. The black women would become unnaturally independent in fear of how the black man could be destroyed and helpless, applying this mind-set in raising similar-minded girls and weaker boys in the process.[76] Sadly, certain broken conditions in the black home and community today can be tied to these malicious effects of slavery.

Internalizing Slavery

How Were Slaves Able To Be Captured in Africa – The Great Humanism Cancer

As young black males, one of the most troubling questions we ask ourselves is, "how could Africans who were so great and powerful be captured as slaves for so long?" This is a heartbreaking question that has been a great source of pain for me as a black man. Reflecting on how such an atrocious system of slavery could be accomplished against our ancestors makes us contemplate negative thoughts of "Are we inferior? Are we not smart enough to avoid traps set against us? Was our race meant to be doomed?"

After deep contemplation, conversations, and study, my confident answer to these questions is "ABSOLUTELY NOT!" Jesus being crucified made him no less an extraordinary being. Martin Luther King Jr. and Malcom X being assassinated made them no less the extraordinary black men they were. Black Africans being enslaved made us no less an extraordinary people. All were just victims of what I call society's GHC - "Great Humanism Cancer."

Cancer is the out-of-control growth of abnormal cells in the body, creating a viral disease state. A person with cancer is not bad or any less extraordinary a person, they're just infected with a disease that is manipulating their body in a very harmful way. Cancer makes use of healthy working cells in disrupting a system, by duplicating them out of control in a destructive manner. The genetics, habits, and behaviors of a person can contribute to becoming vulnerable to cancer. But an outbreak of cancer or any other disease is a product of internal elements being exploited by other out-of-control phenomena that spread virally like wildfire.

In the same regard, this "Great Humanism Cancer" of racism and oppression, functions as a very similar disease within human society. Capitalism at uncontrolled levels of overly-duplicated greed becomes this maliciously viral cancerous disease. Money and maximized profits becomes "God" to the oppressor. It's all that matters, like the relationship between a crackhead and crack. With this type of rampant blinded sickness anything else other than money is collateral damage. This includes human life.

Africans during this time were internally susceptible and externally bombarded due to their own cancerous slave trade system, which represents the worst disease ever upon the continental body of a great people. The out-of-control disease of inhumane greed for wealth and power led to a cold-blooded cancerous slave invasion and exploitation of Africa.

A cancer is very systematic and depends on a working system already in place. It can't spread without certain inherent cancerous conditions internally that allow for its uncontrollable growth to occur. The unfortunate reality is whites couldn't have enslaved Africans without Africans themselves playing a major role in it. The following internal conditions in Africa contributed to this GHC and exploitation of blacks:

1. Internal war and lack of unity between African tribes
2. Trade undervaluation of Africa's own people and resources
3. Naive complacency with global exploration and competition.

Africa is a large continent, with many other countries that had thousands of different tribes. They never felt they were one united people. They were disunited, embracing their own separate languages, agendas, and cultures. They continuously engaged in war amongst each other and had their own system of enslaving those in tribes they defeated. Although this slave system was less harsh and inhumane, it was a product of a divisive cancerous element that enabled whites to target this continent in "duplicating" its slave trade on a larger level. Thus, whites were able to get over on local African rulers with hateful war conflicts against each other, and eventually engaged in the exploitation of Africa's own resources.

The undervaluation of Africa's own people and resources for trade was also an internal cancerous element. Undervaluing something special you have can lead to becoming a "sell-out," literally selling out something that shouldn't be sold. This occurred in Africa. Whites had no ability to overpower Africans initially for slaves. They could secure forts on the African coast, but had no knowledge or power to penetrate

Africa without African Chiefs allowing them. In the beginning of the Trans-Atlantic slave era, whites came to Africa peacefully to trade. Africans had all the leverage and power for trading on their own land, but began to hugely undervalue its greatest resources — people.

The science of trading is normally to get something you don't have enough of for something you have plenty of. However, there has to be an accurate valuation for what you have in order for your trade to be profitable in the long run. If I have 100 million iPhones worth $500 each, I might be inclined to trade one for a new pair of exclusive Jordan kicks worth $150. Even though it's $350 less, it's worth it if I have millions of iPhones and can never access exclusive Jordans when they're released. But even if I have 100 million brothers and sisters that I'm constantly beefing with, I should always recognize they're family and never trade even one of them for even an infinite amount of new Jordans.

In a nutshell, Africa started trading its brothers and sisters they were beefing with for fancy sneakers. At the time Africa had a civilization of 100 million people.[76] African rulers saw the intriguing goods from Europeans and lost sight of their most valuable resource on the planet — people! Our most valuable resources have always been and will always be our people.

Sadly, for petty financial and trade value gain many Africans continuously assisted whites in capturing other Africans as slaves. They never recognized how badly they were "selling-out" their own people and souls until it was too late. An entire global community of whites exploited this for economic gain. This short-sightedness has also led to the loss of control of many other natural resources on Africa's rich fertile lands over time including oil, natural gas, gold, and diamonds.

Africa also experienced a decline in global exploration and competitiveness during a time where the rest of the world was obviously changing. Africa had been able to sustain an advanced tribal and communal way of life, but many other parts of the world were transforming into other advanced means to global economic growth. Despite Africa's historical greatness as the pioneer to all of civilization, other nations had begun out-exploring and out-competing Africa on a global level, through the development of a global economy.

The rise of an industrial revolution sparked a competitive, unified network amongst European nations and America to "capitalize" in every way possible on opportunities for wealth and power. To be quite frank, Africa was caught sleeping and became unaware of the global plot by the rest of the world to exploit them for their most precious human capital. While a Great Humanism Cancer was growing rapidly on their watch, Africa became too isolated and did not actively explore what was going on globally. Therefore, they did not catch the cancer growing systemically within that which was destroying their own continent, until it was too late and the GHC had gotten out of control.

What gradually followed these initial cancerous conditions was an uncontrollable spread of this GHC disease, aggressively taking over the entire continental body of Africa. Overwhelming white global support, manipulation, and violence were used to dominantly attack Africa from the inside out. Whites had gained an incredible amount of knowledge about Africa from Africans themselves. Over time, whites learned how to penetrate Africa by any and every means.

European trading companies became powerful military forces in their own right. Their strongest military advantage was the mass possession of the newly invented gun. This was the most fatal weapon created to this point, able to summon instantaneous death. At this time, Africans did not have guns or any other weaponry as powerful. Whites now had a superior arsenal of fatal weapons, along with a well-machined enslaving system, to raid Africa by themselves in order to capture slaves. The Africans' only way of obtaining guns for war was by trading even more slaves with whites. This perpetuated an even stronger cancerous spread of uncontrollable dependency, more sell-out tendencies of Africans at the expense of their own, and inevitable self-destruction.

A new virally explosive economic form of maximal power and wealth through an extreme dehumanizing of a people was now out of control. Americans, Europeans, and even Africans were "selling out" at uncontrollable economic proportions in every catastrophic way you could imagine. As America prospered greatly as a new global powerhouse entirely due to the wealthy economy it built solely off slavery — it became uncontrollably demented and addicted to inflicting the most wicked disease known to mankind. With money and capital gain as the "New God," America led the entire global community in victimizing the people of Africa - epidemically resorting to the out-of-control human oppression of our people. This is the real Great Humanism Cancer.

Black Revolutionaries & Heroes

Despite this terrible form of enslavement, we have countless legendary black history heroes who led rebellions and fought courageously against the oppressive powers during this time. On the slave ship La Amistad, Africans rebelled in taking control over the ship and crew. Many others led rebellions against slave plantations, such as Nat Turner. Harriet Tubman was an abolitionist who escaped slavery and helped numerous other blacks escape through a network called the Underground Railroad. Frederick Douglass was a former slave and leader of the abolitionist movement whose brilliant speeches, writings, and initiatives inspired many whites across the nation to begin considering the abolishment of slavery.

Toussaint Louverture was the leader and military genius behind the Haitian Revolution, which took place between 1791-1804. This black revolution is considered the most successful slave rebellion ever. Black slaves overthrew the French colonial government, leading to the founding of the Republic of Haiti as a free black-controlled nation.

Young black male, our history is full of great black ancestors who fought militantly, intellectually, politically, and economically to destroy the slave system so that centuries later we could experience the freedom we enjoy today.

Slavery Ended

Many white abolitionists, predominantly in the north, began supporting the black fight to abolish slavery. When the Civil War broke out between the North and the South, President Abraham Lincoln eventually abolished slavery with the 13th Amendment to the Constitution in 1865. This was a strategic war tactic to ruin the South's agrarian slave-based economy and force the South to surrender.

This was also to unify the entire country around the North's more industrialized economic system. At the end of the day, President Lincoln felt ending slavery would be best for the U.S. in gaining more wealth and power from a booming economic industrial revolution. The industrial revolution supported a reliance on machines and technology more so than human slaves for maximizing profits in a new economy. Morality was not the No. 1 priority for ending slavery, a more superior way of capitalism was.

Our African Ancestral Rally Cry

Slavery was not the beginning of our history, nor could it end us as a great people. Our African ancestral bloodline is the extraordinary beginning and the greatest influence on the best human civilization has ever had to offer. This history and TRUTH is a source of great pride as a black man.

The part of our history as slaves is a painful chapter. Unfortunately, the damaging effects after slavery known as "post-traumatic slave syndrome" are visible today, when we see the breakup of the black family home, black men neglecting their roles as fathers, black-on-black crime, drug addictions to escape reality, misguided criminal lifestyles of young black men seeking a rebellious form of power and respect, black teen dropouts, black teen pregnancy, black women selling sexuality for money to the highest bidders, poverty and high rates of unemployment in the black community, conflicts within our community showcasing a "sell-out" mentality, prominent black people turning their back on the black community, and any other forms of black self-hate. The effects of over 200 years of institutionalized slavery still exist as generational systemic challenges from an out-of-control Great Humanism Cancer we must all strive to overcome and cure.

The history of our enslavement is important to understanding critical lessons as to how our greatness can be minimized and stolen if WE allow it. As a beautiful, intelligent, marvelous people of African descent, we are our most valuable resources. We should never lose sight of this truth or allow any internal division to allow another to break us apart as a people. No delusional level of money, power, manipulation, greed, or internal conflict should ever force us to "sell out" our own people — or ever be defenseless to anyone trying to destroy us.

Slavery is also a testament to our unstoppable strength as a people to survive and thrive. We, African-Americans are descendants of Africans who survived the most horrible treatment ever against mankind. Our ancestors were stolen from their homeland and culture, enslaved, beaten, raped, hung, and dehumanized to the lowest extent. However, as a people, they survived and did everything it took so that generations later we could exist today with the opportunity to channel our inner greatness as descendants of a royal, powerful, and overcoming lineage.

Young black male, we have the most unique bond of brotherhood in all of mankind. We're the products of strong rocks who endured an immense level of pressure and fire to shine as the diamonds we are today. Our incredible biological DNA make-up and perseverance amidst the harshest circumstances ever imposed upon a people are nothing short of miraculous.

Young black male, we are a wonder admired throughout the entire world. It's very evident that something special occurred to us as a people through the Trans-Atlantic Slave Trade. Black History and Metaphysical Educator Bobby Hemmitt stated, "all the DNA ancestry services that are so popular today are in place just to study us!"[77] Young black male, WE have been recognized as the new, fascinating evolution of man. Evolution is taking place now right before mankind's eyes more rapidly than ever before, and WE are the undisputed human evolutionary trendsetters. Young Black Male, you are and have always been the most glorious form of history in the making.

CHAPTER 13

The Movement: Breaking the Shackles

The next 100 years after the abolishment of slavery represent what I consider the most critical emergence of a people — the evolution and revolution of Black History. Although slavery was supposedly ended, racism and discrimination was still institutionalized in America to a horrible extent. The shackles of oppression weren't as visible in chains, but they were heartlessly visible within every other part of American society as blacks were continuously denied equal rights and freedom. During this important time in history, the world witnessed the rise of a people that represented an awesome level of brilliance, courage, and perseverance. This incredible time period was an awesome movement and emergence of the African-American.

Reconstruction

The period following the end of the Civil War between 1865-1877 is known as Reconstruction. America tried to "reconstruct" the country in bringing all of the states in the North and South together again under one unified nation. African-Americans began to strive for experiences of freedom through greater levels of cultural acceptance, political equality, economic opportunity, and collective self-determination to rise above oppressive conditions as a people. During Reconstruction, the Civil Rights Act of 1875 was passed as a legislation giving more equal rights to blacks. Over 1,500 African-Americans held a political office within the U.S. government during Reconstruction.[1]

Jim Crow

Reconstruction and the advancements of blacks in American society aroused fears among many whites, mostly in the South. They felt the advancement of blacks took away from their economic, political, and social privileges. After 1876, this Reconstruction period ended. White supremacy control was once again instituted in America, specifically in the South. Racial segregation laws were put back into effect within most cities and states down South. These were the "Jim Crow Laws." Under these oppressive laws, blacks were denied economic, educational, and social civil liberties.

This included unfair practices of discrimination towards blacks regarding housing, job employment, bank lending, and new start-up businesses. Jim Crow laws also made mandatory, by law, the segregation of schools, military, restaurants, public transportation, restrooms, and water fountains. Black entities did not receive the same amount of privilege or resources as whites. They were made not only separate but far from equal.

These practices were enforced throughout all levels of government to ignorantly promote white privileged supremacy and black disenfranchised inferiority. White supremacy organizations such as the Ku Klux Klan, cowardly disguised in white sheets, engaged in violent group attacks and the lynching of blacks to wickedly promote this criminally accepted brutal racism against blacks. A study by the Equal Justice Initiative found that nearly 4,000 black men, women, and children were killed by lynching in the southern states alone between the years 1877-1950.[2]

The Great Migration

To escape this brutal discrimination and institutionalized segregation of Jim Crow laws in the South, many African-Americans embarked upon a geographic movement known as the "The Great Migration." It's estimated that 6 million African-Americans relocated during this time from the South to cities in the North, Midwest, and West for several decades from 1916-1970. Greater opportunities for a better life were courageously pursued by blacks. A factory wage during this time in the North was on average three times more than the South.[3] The Northern cities most impacted by a rise in black population were New York, Chicago, Philadelphia, Washington, D.C., and Detroit. Black newspapers like the *Chicago Defender* became very instrumental in communicating the opportunities and new emergence of black urban culture during this migration.

The Black Renaissance

Despite the discrimination that began to grow in the North from a growing senti-ment of dislike by whites due to the population booms of blacks during "The Great Migration," blacks were still able to build a new enlightening and empowering environ-ment for themselves economically, politically, philosophically, artistically, and cultur-ally during the Black Renaissance era also known as "The New Negro Movement" from 1918-1930s. This movement, which spanned all across the newly black-populated cit-ies, was mostly spearheaded by the artistic and cultural influenced movement of the Harlem Renaissance in New York. A formerly white neighborhood in Harlem had be-come populated with 200,000 African-Americans.[4]

The black experience was brilliantly expressed in literature by writers and poets like James Weldon Johnson and Langston Hughes. Music was revolutionized by a new genre of jazz and a trendy "swing-style" by musicians such as Duke Ellington, Louis Armstrong, and singer Billie Holiday. Fashion was also revolutionized, transitioning from a conservative Eurocentric style to a new, colorful ultra-stylish urban couture. The entire movement reflected a revolutionized culture rooted in African pride. Today's hip-hop culture is strongly influenced by the Black Renaissance.

This new black Renaissance Movement was so powerful, because it stimulated in-credible pride and a culture unique to blacks that became admired all over the world. Despite the racial oppression of the country towards blacks, this transformational movement of African-Americans, breaking through with a contagiously unique style of intellect and artistic expression, created the re-emerging of a "New Black Culture" — a black culture self-defined for us by us!

Like all black cultural movements, it served as a creative platform for enlighten-ment and empowerment to help challenge racism and stereotypes. Culture unifies a people and provides a source of motivation to evolve into greatness against all odds. This movement served as a proud means of self-identify and "black unification," which created special moments of universal harmony.

Young black male, the greatness African-Americans so vibrantly display in such move-ments are the foundations for our ability to be great in so many ways today. As a people, we have always been brilliant enough to use various forms of enlightenment, like the arts and music, to create breakthrough forms of expression that channel our pain, strength, talents, intellect, and faith. Such an innate ability to drive a movement molds our past history as a people into a new, amazing reality for today and possibility for tomorrow.

We create genius self-defining culture, even amidst the challenges of an oppres-sive one. We create movements, we break through any and all shackles, and we display unstoppable greatness. As African-Americans, that's just what we do! Our swag, our hip-hop, and our trendsetting fashions today are all confident forms of unified power and expression unique to us – emulated and admired all across the world. The Black Renaissance Movement supported the ultimate "Movement" for black freedom and unrelenting, uninhibited emergence of black greatness.

The Black Advancement Movement:

Booker T. Washington "Self-Help/Non-Integration" vs. W.E.B Dubois "Talented 10th"

The discriminatory racist landscape of the Jim Crow era where blacks were being oppressed and lynched, brought upon great philosophical debates amongst black intellectuals regarding how African-Americans should approach overcoming racism in America. During the early part of the 20th Century, some of the most profound debates in philosophy for the advancement of blacks were between Booker T. Washington and W.E.B. Dubois.

Booker T. Washington was born a slave down South in Virginia, and went above and beyond to emerge as an intellectual by means of self-education. His accomplishments include founding the Tuskegee Institute in 1881 to train vocational skills for blacks, delivering the 1895 Atlanta Compromise Speech, writing his autobiography, *Up From Slavery*, and being formally invited to the White House by President Theodore Roosevelt in 1901.[5]

Booker T. Washington's philosophy for the advancement of blacks was based on self-help educational and economic progress in the wake of a white-dominated society of racial discrimination that would not change anytime soon. Rather than trying to force political agendas of integration and equal acceptance from whites, Washington believed it would better serve blacks to focus on working for ourselves by training ourselves to be proficient in real-world jobs by mastering a skilled trade.[6]

Washington encouraged African-Americans to stay isolated from mainstream society, yet unified as a race, by committing to working hard and learning real world trade and entrepreneurial skills. He believed this was a much more empowering alternative to creating value for the black race versus trying to assimilate to a white system that oppressed blacks.[7] He felt this self-help approach would build a demand that would, over time, prove blacks worthy of equal rights.

W.E.B Dubois grew up under a very different background than Booker T. Washington. Dubois was born a free person in the North in Massachusetts. His accomplishments include becoming the first African-American to receive a Ph.D. from Harvard University, writing many books, including *Souls of Black Folk*, leading the Niagara Movement in 1905, and becoming the founder of the legendary NAACP organization in 1909.[8]

W.E.B. Dubois' philosophy for the advancement of blacks embraced a mode of political activism against the system to overcome injustice and inequality. Dubois believed this was the only way for blacks to overcome, and this ability was strongly contingent on an advanced education. He strongly condemned lynching, Jim Crow laws, discrimination, and he even attacked President Woodrow Wilson for promoting segregation.[9] He aggressively fought for the right to vote, social equality, and good education for blacks.

Dubois philosophy also promoted a theory called the "Talented Tenth." This theory was based on assimilation and stated the top 10 percent of the African-American race, the best of the best, should seek higher education through college while integrating with the most elite levels of society.[10] From this experience, these elite blacks could be recognized as intellectual counterparts to whites and thus reach their full potential in American society as brilliant men. Dubois felt this form of assimilation to white and world culture could transcend black men into leaders who could uplift the entire black race through freedom-fighting efforts that could lead to a fully integrated experience.

Dubois strongly disagreed with Booker T. Washington and believed that political justice and fair social integration by the law must be pursued, in order to reverse the inevitable disenfranchisement and destruction of blacks by the United States, which negated any self-help economic initiatives. Dubois felt the responsibility of black leadership should fall on the educated "Talented 10th," who could empower themselves through a higher education experience.

This fully integrated experience with white society would enable elite blacks to learn the ways of the world, to teach and lead blacks to a promised land of equality. On the other hand, Washington and supporters of his self-help philosophy, like Carter G. Woodson, argued that assimilation of white society would only lead to a greater level of brainwashing, minimization of black cultural skill sets, and an epidemic of "elitism" that would encourage the "Talented 10th" to neglect their black communities.[11]

These were two strong philosophies by two incredible men committed to the advancement of the African-American. The ultimate question, which philosophy was the right one? Despite the pros and cons of each, I believe both! Similar to assessing which approach is best for a high school basketball player to play Division I Basketball. Should that basketball player excel on his high school team or excel by play in AAU?

Both are most necessary. That player would need to develop fundamentally sound skills at a specific position as well as meeting the student-athlete standards to excel within the universal system of the high school basketball program. That player would also need to develop the standout athleticism amongst a faster-paced, more elite competitive breeding ground for advanced players all across the country, such as AAU. A rigorous combo regimen of excellence incorporating both programs and approaches, is best and recommended for all basketball athletes seeking to play Division I Basketball. This dual approach can be customized to the individual player and their environment, to best produce and "optimize" a program built for success.

In this same regard, Booker T. Washington and W.E.B. Dubois' distinctly different approaches were both necessary and very empowering towards advancing the African-American race. The "Independently Talented 100th" is what I would call the optimal merging of their strategies to continue their cause for black social and economic justice.

We must explore a unified agenda that trains 100 percent of the black population to become empowered as skill-based entrepreneurs in our own community, as well as intellectual powerhouse professionals within mainstream integrated society. Washington and Dubois' distinguished philosophies became the fundamental blueprints for evolving initiatives from future black leaders, which would be very influential in breaking down numerous internal and external shackles to furthering "The Movement."

Marcus Garvey: Black Nationalism & Pan-Africanism Movement

Marcus Garvey, a native of Jamaica and self-educated, was a civil rights activist most inspired by Booker T. Washington's "self-help/non-integration" philosophy. This became the fundamental strategy for his movement of Black Nationalism rooted in creating a prosperous self-sustaining black economic base, along with the movement of Pan-Africanism, which promoted the unification of African descendants worldwide. In 1912, Garvey founded the Universal Negro Improvement Association (UNIA), with the ultimate goal of uniting all African diaspora to "establish a country and absolute government of our own."[12]

Garvey launched several manufacturing businesses and the Black Star Line, a shipping company that established international trade between blacks in America, the Caribbean, South America, Canada, and Africa. These businesses were the economic bases he created for catapulting a newly black unified civilization, rooted in principles and structure, which could evolve into blacks unifying to ultimately create a centralized nation "for us by us" in Africa.

As a highly threatening target, Garvey's movement was derailed by a federal investigation. He was convicted of mail fraud and sentenced to 5 years in prison. Upon his release, he was deported to Jamaica. He continued his activism work in Jamaica and London until his death. Garvey even attempted to have a reparations bill passed in Congress to deport 12 million African-Americans back to Africa, which failed and unfortunately diminished his once popular support.[13]

The "Garvey-ism" movement was incredibly powerful. Its approach had an action-oriented agenda that told America "If you don't like us, fine. We'll leave you and build our own nation on our own terms." In essence it told the U.S., "we don't need you!" It mobilized black economic revolution along with a movement of redefining African pride, to attempt the creation of an entirely new black unified nation to break the shackles of oppression. Marcus Garvey inspired the Nation of Islam and the Rastafarian movement. Garvey-ism proved blacks can strategically create its own economic base and international infrastructure for building a utopian black society. This type of courage, resourcefulness, and nation building intelligence is the reason why I was able to overcome my criminal circumstances to build my own internationally sourced economic base of prosperity through Beautiful Hair 4 U.

Young black male, this ancestral entrepreneur DNA is within you to create your own economic and world-recognized greatness as well. The Garvey-ism within us all is never confined to undesired circumstances. We have an entire world and universe always at our disposal to create our own uniformed culture of happiness and freedom. Garvey's furthering of the movement played a pivotal role as well in the evolution of black history.

The Civil Rights Movement:

Martin Luther King Jr. "Non-Violence" + Malcolm X "By Any Means Necessary"

As American Society evolved through the industrial revolution and so many other advancements during the mid-20th century, the lack of human advancement reflected through the blatant discrimination against blacks reached a highly enraged breaking point. With horrific acts of racial hate continuously committed, such as the murder of 14-year-old black teen, Emmitt Till, for reportedly flirting with a white woman, the bombing of four young black girls in a Birmingham Baptist church, Ku Klux Klan attacks lynching black men, and the use of dogs and water hoses by local police to attack innocent blacks – African-Americans were ready to fight back like never before. This began the emergence of the Civil Rights Movement.

Arguably the most pivotal breakthroughs in black history occurred during this era between the Civil Rights Movement years of 1954-1968. The landmark Supreme Court case "Brown vs. Board of Education" in 1954 ruled that the segregation of public schools was unconstitutional. Yet and still, black students of newly integrated schools required the National Guard to protect them while going to school. Such events contributed to spark a new generation of blacks who courageously ran with the philosophical freedom-fighting torches passed down by great predecessors, such as Booker T. Washington, W.E.B. Dubois, and Marcus Garvey to whole-heartedly revolutionize "The Movement." Two of the greatest men and leaders to ever exist on this planet emerged during this movement — Dr. Martin Luther King Jr. and Malcolm X.

MLK

Dr. King was born in Atlanta in 1929 and was a standout scholar. He entered Morehouse College at the young age of 15 and received his Ph.D. by 25. King eventually became the lead minster at the same church his father and grandfather had previously led, Ebenezer Baptist Church. When Rosa Parks was arrested for refusing to move to the back of the bus in Montgomery, AL, King was selected to lead the Montgomery Bus Boycott. This boycott crippled the bus company financially and forced the changing of the law to make segregated public transportation unconstitutional. King's incredible leadership and life-changing motivational speaking skills during this process catapulted his legacy as an incredibly gifted civil rights activist.

Some of King's other groundbreaking accomplishments in fighting for the rights of blacks also include:

- Founding the Southern Christian Leadership Conference with 60 other ministers and activists, to build community organizing power for civil rights through the church

- Leading the 1963 Birmingham Boycott Campaign to end discriminatory economic policies of local businesses
- Leading the 1963 March on Washington for Jobs and Freedom, gathering over 200,000 people and delivering the famous "I Have a Dream Speech," advocating for racial harmony and economic rights for blacks
- Winning the 1964 Nobel Peace Prize
- Leading the 1965 Selma-Montgomery March, a non-violent protest for black voting rights, which was met with vicious police brutality that sparked widespread public outrage when it was broadcasted all over the country.

King's breakthrough activism led to the passage of the Civil Rights Act of 1964, outlawing discrimination in publicly owned facilities, and the passage of the Voting Rights Act of 1965 outlawing discrimination practices denying blacks the right to vote.

MLK Philosophy: Non-Violence

King's philosophy was inspired by W.E.B. Dubois' approach of aggressively fighting the political system of oppression. It also incorporated Gandhi's "Non-Violent and Civil Disobedience" approach used to liberate the people of India. King believed there are only three ways to overcome oppression:

1. Violence – attack oppressors with violent measures
2. Resignation – cooperate with the injustice of oppressors
3. Non-Violence – resist oppressors with assertive non-violent measures through civil disobedience.

Of the options, King felt Non-Violence through protests was the most effective weapon against a racist and unjust society. The Non-Violence ideology was deeply rooted in a Christ-based method of overcoming hate with an overpowering love. This love was not weak or cowardly in avoiding resistance. It was just a morally superior form of resistance, very dynamic and aggressive in results-driven actions to demand justice, only passive in its refrain from physical violence.

King felt it took more strength for a man to non-violently protest in the face of physical danger with civil disobedience. It showed that no-physical action could stop a morally superior movement to resist oppression with such determined force that it eventually breaks down the oppressive system and commands justice. King stated the willingness to be the recipient of violence without responding with violence "disturbs the consciousness and sense of commitment amongst the oppressor."

The strategy to King's Civil Rights Movement of Non-Violence was to "create a situation so crisis-packed that it will inevitably open the door to negotiation."[14] King showcased this strategy by protesting in racist cities where black men, women, and children were met with such hostile extreme measures of unjust violence that they became huge publicity moments captured by the media and broadcasted to the world. A powerful display of this tactic was the Selma-Montgomery March, which showed — on TV across the country — white state troopers attacking unarmed, peaceful black demonstrators, with tear gas and clubs while beating many unconscious.

Those violent acts along with the news about lynch-mob murders sparked national outcries for justice. This put pressure on government officials, including the President of The United States to fully address changing laws to eradicate such inhumane senselessness in granting the civil right liberties demanded by blacks. King's Non-Violent movement was the casting of a mirror to America to show "the more you try to hurt and kill African-Americans, the more you are really self-destructing and killing America."

Malcolm X

Malcolm X was born Malcolm Little in 1925 in Omaha, Nebraska. His family moved to cities in Wisconsin and Michigan during his early childhood. At the young age of 6, Malcolm's father who was a Baptist preacher and black activist enthusiast of Marcus Garvey's Pan-Africanism movement, was killed. Many suspected it was by a white supremacist group. Soon afterwards, his mother had a nervous breakdown and Malcolm became an orphan along with his siblings.[15]

Malcolm dropped out of junior high school after a white teacher told him his career aspiration to become a lawyer was "no realistic goal for a nigger."[16] He later moved to Harlem where he got caught up in the streets. As a young street hustler, Malcom engaged in drug dealing, gambling, racketeering, robbing, and pimping. Malcolm was sentenced to 10 years in prison for larceny, and breaking and entering. During his imprisonment, he was introduced to the Nation of Islam religion led by Elijah Muhammad. He used those teachings to become committed to re-educating himself, "reprogramming his mind," and becoming an activist within the aggressive black liberation Nation of Islam movement in America.

After being paroled from prison, Malcolm dropped his slave-inherited last name "Little" and became known as Malcolm X, with his official Muslim name eventually becoming El-Hajj Malik El-Shabazz. Malcolm X became such a brilliant and powerful speaker for the Nation of Islam's movement that Elijah Muhammad appointed him minister and national spokesman. Malcolm X became a fearless leader who relentlessly fought for the rights of blacks, accomplishing and creating numerous points of groundbreaking impact, including:

- The establishment and expansion of Nation of Islam temples in Boston, Philadelphia, Harlem, Atlanta, Springfield (MA), and Hartford (CT)
- Significantly contributing to increasing the membership of the Nation of Islam from 400 to 40,000 people[17]
- Forming international alliances with numerous political leaders throughout countries in Africa and the Middle East, to build a unified international support base for black liberation
- Founding the Organization for Afro-American Unity

Malcolm X's incredible contributions amplified a strong black empowering platform for self-asserted justice. His breakthroughs led to an unstoppable surge of power movements to tremendously advance the psyche of black respect and greatness in America, as well as all over the world.

Malcolm X Philosophy – By Any Means Necessary/Black Nationalism
Malcolm X's philosophy of Black Nationalism was inspired by Booker T. Washington's "Self-Help/Non-Integration" approach, and more so Marcus Garvey's Pan-Africanism, which was further formulated by Elijah Muhammad and the Nation of Islam, with a goal of creating a black powerful nation independent of an oppressive America. Malcolm X endorsed a philosophy of segregation and effective self-defense to overcome institutionalized racism in America. This ideology of empowerment encouraged blacks to counter whites committing acts of violence with a full-throttle form of self-defense "by any means necessary."

This included retaliation acts of violence. He felt that in order for a man to be strong, he must be ready to physically and militantly defend himself and his people if danger violently comes their way. This viewpoint was considered controversial by many, including blacks who supported "Non-Violence."

During the initial years of Malcom X's activism, he subscribed to a theory embraced by the Nation of Islam that in order for the whites to enslave, oppress, and murder blacks senselessly in the country for hundreds of years – whites had to be inherently evil. He believed whites in America during this time used "white" as a tool towards brutal oppression and privilege that blacks should no longer tolerate without a physical fight.

Malcolm saw self-preservation as the first law of mankind, and the Constitution gives men the right to bear arms because of this innate human law that blacks should not forgo in the wake of ever being attacked. Malcolm stated, "I wouldn't call on anyone to be violent without a cause. But the black man, above anyone, due to the discrimination of America, is justified...to defend against violence by any means necessary."[18]

Malcolm X taught blacks that "it's our duty to organize ourselves and warn the government that if they don't stop the racial injustices and wrong doings, we'll do something to stop it ourselves." He believed historically with nations and mankind in general that the only thing power respects is power, stating "Power never takes a back step, only in the face of more power." In addition, he despised the use of the media to portray the criminalization of blacks to justify a police state that violently abused blacks.[19] To counter, Malcolm X incorporated the disciplined lifestyle of Islam, the economic independence and international scope of Marcus Garvey that was rooted in African pride, and a national military mind-set towards self-defense as a blueprint for the true empowered nation-building advancement of blacks.

Malcolm X founded the Organization of Afro-American Unity with a purpose to "heighten the political consciousness" of African-Americans in accelerating the process of freedom and independence. The primary objectives in his words were to:

1. Fight whoever gets in our way
2. Bring about complete independence of blacks and people of African descent in America and the Western Hemisphere
3. Command the civil liberties blacks are entitled to under the U.S. Constitution and Bill of Rights.

The primary tactics to accomplish those objectives were to gain allies with all blacks across the globe, and to engage in self-defense "by any means necessary."

Turning Points & Unified Fronts for Malcolm & Martin

In the beginning phases of their leadership, Malcolm X's "By Any Means" philosophy directly conflicted with Martin Luther King's Civil Rights Movement of "Non-Violence." The perceived hostile dynamics in Malcolm X's willingness to promote violence as a countermeasure against whites, created a strong rift between the two and their respective followings, regarding the best approach for the advancement of blacks. Harsh words were spoken, as Malcolm X at one point even called King an "Uncle Tom." Despite King's resistance to Malcolm X's approach, he managed to refrain from engaging in any bitter exchanges.

A sharp turning point occurred in Malcolm X's life when he separated himself from the Nation of Islam for reasons of severe internal conflict. Malcolm felt he could no longer righteously endorse the black advancement movement from that platform. He went on an international trip and pilgrimage to Mecca. During this trip, he enlightened himself on a new global outlook and array of alliances, based on how Africans overcame oppression in certain African and Middle Eastern colonies. Also through this spiritual pilgrimage, he deeply worshipped and fellowshipped with people of all races, and gained a life-changing transformation. He then began to believe what he was taught about whites was wrong because . . .

. . . whites were not inherently evil!

Despite the long history and his experience of witnessing horrible acts of racism by many whites in America, he had embarked upon an entirely new experience with whites in total contrast to that. He befriended white men who displayed nothing but love, righteousness, and upstanding character, like men of many other races during the pilgrimage. He gained a valuable understanding that white, black, brown, red, or any other racial color category was just an incidental trait that had nothing to do with actions. For the first time, he 100 percent agreed with Martin Luther King in truly believing within his heart that "a man should not be judged by the color of his skin, but by the content of his character." From his newfound vantage point, this wasn't a dream — it was his newfound reality.

It was after this pilgrimage and revelation that he came back to the U.S. and publicly announced to the world his restructured philosophy, in addition to his separation from the Nation of Islam. He founded the Organization of Afro-American Unity. Malcolm still maintained his core belief in self-defense "By Any Means Necessary" along with a black nationalism agenda to overcome racial injustice in America. But one of his biggest changes in approach was becoming willing to work with Civil Rights leaders like Martin Luther King. Even if they supported Non-Violent protests, he wanted to become more "unified" with them in advancing the movement for black freedom.

Malcom X and Martin Luther King met once briefly in Washington, D.C., in 1964. Both were in attendance at the Senate's debate on the Civil Rights Bill. Malcolm X in the past had refuted political activism or integration, but now began encouraging political activism to complement the Civil Rights movement led by King, which promoted integration and full equality for African-Americans. Malcolm X even came to Selma, AL, while King had been locked up during a protest to deliver a speech to inspire the movement behind the voting rights protests.

In Selma, Malcolm mentioned that he sent a message to the main white racist agitator threatening Dr. King, stating, "If your presence causes harm to Dr. King or any other black in Alabama trying to enjoy their rights, then you and your Ku Klux Klan will be met with maximum retaliation from those of us not handcuffed by the non-violent philosophy."[20] Martin Luther King and Malcolm X were both on the brink of breaking new ground for black advancement through "Non-Violence" and "By Any Means Necessary" approaches to establish a way to dominantly unify and co-exist.

One of the common-ground breakthrough anchors, which they both embraced during this time of potential epic philosophical merger, was "black economics." Martin Luther King gained an even greater value for the Malcolm X/Marcus Garvey approach to creating and leveraging black independent wealth. They both understood the mass power of black purchasing power that drove the economy. The power of collective economic withdrawal by blacks was a potent tool that they were beginning to recognize could be the ultimate "Non-Violent/By Any Means" breaking point of engagement.

This black economics philosophy promoted boycotting companies that did not embrace black agendas or employment — along with strengthening black communities by investing in black-owned businesses, such as banks, insurance companies, and more, to build a powerful economic base.[21] This would, as King stated, "put pressure where it hurts" by supremely fighting the true source of the oppression of blacks — capitalism and money![22]

The Ultimate Sacrifice – Courage of Two Great Men

After countless death threats, including the bombing of his house, Malcolm X was assassinated while delivering a speech in Manhattan at the Audubon Ballroom on February 21, 1965. He was gunned down by men of his very own race and previous religious organization, with many sources linking a connection to the FBI or CIA. Three years later after receiving countless death threats as well, Martin Luther King Jr. was assassinated on a hotel balcony in Memphis, April 4, 1968. FBI and CIA involvement has been highly suspected in his death as well. Both were only 39 years old.

At the time of their murders, Martin Luther King Jr. had four children, and Malcolm X had four children with twins on the way. Malcolm X once stated, "The Price of Freedom Is Death." He even mentioned in his autobiography that he didn't expect to live to see it published, which he didn't. In King's last speech he stated, "I might not get there with you, but we as a people will get to the promised land." If what defines a man is what he's willing to die for, these two men are possibly the greatest men to ever exist.

These men laid their lives on the line in the face of the most globally powerful and cold-blooded killing machine of oppression that has ever existed. Why would they choose to sacrifice their lives like this? Why would they choose a path that would leave their wives widows and their kids fatherless?

They sacrificed their lives and a happy future for their family to enjoy the presence of a living husband and father, so that decades later people like ME and YOU could live in a much better world. They dedicated themselves to a cause where they would be sacrificed from their own children, so that their children's children and generations afterwards could have a greater chance at living in a better world. They had the vision and foresight to see that sacrificing their life for "OUR MOVEMENT" would be a breakthrough. They knew their sacrifice would "break the shackles," so that we could have a greater chance to experience "life, liberty, and the pursuit of happiness" with an uninhibited freedom 50 years later.

By leading, speaking, marching, protesting, debating, fighting, educating, empowering, and sacrificing to a point of a violent death – they created a future landscape for me and you to confidently be a man! Walk like a man, talk like a man, become educated like a man, explore employment like a man, love like a man, fight like a man, party like a man, challenge the system like a man, use a public bathroom like a man, eat at a restaurant like a man, create hip-hop like a man, vote a black President into office like a man, start up our own business like a man, and live life to the absolute fullest...like a FREE MAN! In my opinion Martin Luther King Jr. and Malcolm X are the epitome of everything men of relentless courage can be.

The Black Triangle

Who was right? Which philosophy was best? Who advanced blacks the furthest? Who was most necessary for fighting oppression of blacks in America? Martin or Malcolm? The answer once again — BOTH!

No other culture is provoked to have two people viciously clash with each other constantly except black culture. We're always marginalized as a culture to believe we must be divided in choosing one man or one way over the other. It's an internally divisive microcosm of the ignorance, propelled within the same "superior-inferior" complex, society has historically used to validate having to declare a winner and loser between black and white. When divisively confined to black culture, one black man has to be right and an opposing black man has to be wrong. One black way of advancement has to work, and the other way won't. That sort of conflicting disunity has hindered us as a people since the beginning of time.

Who's boxing style was best, Ali or Frazier? Sure I can have a preference of one style and fighter over the other when they faced off. But in the greater scheme of life, if I wanted to build the best boxing school, needed the best fighters to defend me, or wanted to use the best fighters for furthering a movement – the best "optimal" decision would be to use BOTH. Both are two of the best fighters ever, with two very distinctly different styles. However, both men had the same goal of relentlessly outboxing their opponent to win. If ever I could create a situation to have both fighting on the same team for the same cause - that would be the best-case scenario.

Kobe was the best guard in the world, and Shaq was the best big man in the world during their run in the early 2000s, when they won three championships together. Would you want to stick with Kobe or Shaq? My answer, BOTH! They were the most incredible inside-outside 1-2 punch in basketball. Nobody could stop Kobe on the perimeter, nobody could stop Shaq in the post. If those men and the Lakers organization could've creatively found a way to keep them united instead of splitting them up, there is no telling how many more championships they could've won.

Our universe often operates off dual dynamics, incorporating two elements to make a whole. Day and night must both occur for the earth to completely rotate once. Two people must be together to create a child. We have two arms, legs, hands, feet, eyes, ears, and nostrils so we can function as humans at an "optimal" level. Two separate yet parallel elements are often required for optimal performance.

The great pyramids were created in the shape of a triangle. The perfect triangle requires two separate lines upwardly extending from "opposite sides" of the same base to reach the highest optimal point of union in the middle. Martin and Malcolm were two separate men with two different upbringings and philosophies. However, their strength was in a common base of the African-American experience in a country denying us justice. Their highest optimal point of union was their desire for freedom for YOU and ME!

WE are the highest point in the middle, supported by their great leverage of sacrifice. Martin Luther King's courageous life work and sacrifice was to fulfill a dream, in which WE "non-violently" reached an optimal promised land, where we're not judged by the color of our skin, but by the content of our character. Malcolm X's courageous life work and sacrifice was to fulfill a dream in which WE built and defended such a right to optimal freedom "By Any Means Necessary!" They both were extremely needed so that WE could fulfill unified greatness through seeing so much and standing so high on the shoulders of such strong sacrificial giants.

Many people say, "We need a new leader in the black community. Where is our next Martin and Malcolm." My response is every black man we see should be that leader, as an evolved manifestation of a new Martin + Malcolm. The corrupt powers that be were so intimidated with Martin and Malcom's powerful leadership, which catapulted the black greatness movement, that their main focus became their assassination. Kill the movement by killing the two leaders before they become even more powerful and unified.

However, now there will no longer be just one, two, or a few greats carrying the burden of sacrifice in advancing such a powerful movement. There will be an entire nation, an entire army of black men with too many names to count and entirely too much unified power to kill off. Young black male – YOU, I, and every other black male WE see must be a leader within this movement. It is our greatest inherited calling and destiny.

CHAPTER 14

Unity

"The Movement," catapulted during the Civil Rights era, inspired the evolution of numerous organizations to follow, which leveraged upon the ideologies of the great black leaders before them to advance the fight for black justice. These organizations of black activism include the Black Panther Party founded by Huey P. Newton and Bobby Seale in 1966, the Black Liberation Army led by Eldridge Cleaver and Assata Shakur during the 70s, the Rainbow PUSH coalition founded by Rev. Jesse Jackson in 1971, the revived Nation of Islam under the leadership of Minister Louis Farrakhan beginning in 1981, and the National Action Network founded by Al Sharpton in 1991. Many other new-age activist groups have also formed, including Black Lives Matter, in addition to the Dream Defenders led by Phillip Agnew. Both which launched in 2008 in protest to the murder of Trayvon Martin.

Many intellectual leaders in the black community emerged to further the movement, such as Dr. Cornell West, Michael Eric Dyson, Dr. Boyce Watkins, and Dr. Umar Johnson, to name a few. The common thread behind all of these individuals and organizations is the fight for the justice of black people through "unity." A unified stance for political, legal, socio-cultural, and economic justice. Our ability to be unified as a people is our greatest opportunity and our greatest challenge. We have proven time and time again that we're our strongest when unified, and our weakest when divided.

No one can do anything great for a sustained period of time by themselves. No one can achieve victory consistently by themselves. Young black male, we can never overcome all the obstacles to experiencing our greatness in its most free and liberated expression by ourselves. We need a unified team, we need a unified family, we need a unified black race, we need a unified human race, so we ultimately need each other.

Two of the greatest benefits to experience as a human being in this world are the feelings of pride and privilege. Pride is a confidence that comes from being a part of something bigger than self. Every culture and every nation relies on this unified group dynamic. During the Olympics fans cheer for their home country and gain a sense of national pride in supporting a team that represents them in pursuit of victory. When someone makes it out of the same hood that we're from and becomes successful, we gain a sense of pride knowing that they are cut from the same cloth we are.

Unfortunately, all of the oppressive tactics used against us as a people have been done to detach ourselves from our historical greatness and remarkable story as a people. This is done to reduce pride for ourselves, which reduces our collective power against injustices. This breaks us to where we don't want to cheer for one another, support one another, congratulate one another, or build with one another, because we feel disconnected from our fellow black brothers and sisters.

Young black male, our "true" story as a race is incredible. We have just as much reason to be supremely proud of our strong team of black and African-American greatness as any other culture. Our ancestors have accomplished and endured more than any to create the greatest opportunities for us to make the absolute most of this world. There is a strong sense of black pride we must always maintain to continuously overcome and revolutionize our culture to its highest degrees of greatness!

Privilege is also a big element of the human experience. Even a young kid feels entitled when they tell another kid this is "My Mommy, My Daddy, My Toy, or My House!" They are expressing a special sense of love, security, and exclusive rights they feel they have that validates how special and "privileged" they are from every other person in the world.

Races, religions, and class systems all are categories designated to create a special experience of various forms of entitlement for certain groups of people. Luxury cars and homes are designed to make certain people feel "privileged" in being able to afford or spend a lot of money on desired items that others aren't able to. In the same manner - oppressive tactics such as legal injustices, economic disparity, urban school-to-prison pipelines, police brutality, and the criminalization of blacks within the media have been used against blacks to perpetuate a lack of privilege that makes others feel "more privileged."

However, young black male, our ability to be unified amongst each other enhances our own revolutionized privilege that we exclusively share with each other. We can uniquely create our own diverse platforms and experiences of privilege in the forms of our own networks and alliances. Most things are a certain way in this world just because a group of people determined that's what they wanted to say and believe for their benefit.

Young black male, what do we want to stand for and believe in to assert true authority of our world and affairs? How do we want to make an unprecedented dent in the universe? Whatever we decide as a unified force, it's all possible. But only when we're unified as one.

Young black male, in summary of this amazing unified journey we have taken together in this book, I want to leave you with five points of commitment for being a successful Black Man and leader for the continuous revolution of our culture:

5 Points of Commitment

    1.0 Black Love – "Love one another"
    2.0 Black Power – "Fight for one another"
    3.0 Black Wealth - "Create wealth with one another"
    4.0 Black Excellence "Be the best amongst one another"
    5.0 Black Unity "Forever unite with one another"

1.0 Black Love – "Love one another"

Young black male, life is about love. Happiness is the common factor that drives us all to do anything we do. There is no sustaining purpose of self, family, race, or human civilization without love. Love drives mankind and everything else we have faith in.

Love of Self

So our revolution must continue to be rooted in love, as all black movements have been. This starts with love of self. Young black male, YOU must always know that YOU were created for a divine purpose. There is nothing that has ever been created in this universe as unique as YOU, and there never will be. Your purpose and your mission in life can only be carried out by YOU! If you don't get it jumping, it won't jump off.

Young black male, unconditionally love yourself and your life. YOU are that dude, YOU are the MAN! Love the fact that YOU are uniquely capable of accomplishing anything you want in this world. Look yourself in the mirror and always be proud of yourself in every way. Your great ancestral lineage from the beginning of mankind was driven to produce YOU.

There is no other person in this world worth loving and believing in more than you. This becomes the foundation for how you can unconditionally love anything else. How you look, what you currently have, and what you currently do – whether perceived as good or bad, is a strategic plan of destiny to prepare you for all of the greatness YOU are divinely intended to be.

Whether you feel society currently labels you as rich or broke, successful or a failure, strong or weak, good or bad, blessed or cursed, privileged or underprivileged, free or incarcerated, liberated or oppressed, loved or hated — YOU are the only author to your story. YOU don't always control how the story starts off, but YOU are the sole controller of how your success book ultimately plays out. YOU have every right to love your current situation as a platform of immaculate change to live out the grandest version of your greatest vision to being the best YOU.

Love of Family

Manhood is a prominent level of leadership for one's family. Young black male, we're the rock for protecting and providing for our family. A man's ability to create stability with love and strength is the backbone to a family. As fathers of mankind, we're evolutionarily built to be great fathers and great husbands. One of the most powerful tools for disrupting the black race has been removing the black man from the home. Our unconditional love and most disciplined commitment to our families are mandatory to move forward as a people.

We must learn to love our own so deeply that we avoid the removal of our physical presence in the home by any means. There is no greater gift for a man than his own family created through a union of love. A boy is most prepared to become a great man through the active presence and love of his father. A girl is most prepared to be a righteous woman through the active presence and love of her father. A wife is best able to shine as a beacon of beautiful womanhood through the active presence and love of her husband. There is nothing more important than this role of a man. It drives our culture. When the black family is lovingly supported by an actively present strong black man who provides and protects in every way, it instills the internal foundation for multi-generational black cultural greatness.

Love of Black People & Culture

Everything there is to love about this world was either created or influenced by black people and black culture. Every empire and civilization that has ever existed has emerged from the powerful muscle and creative mind power of African descendants. Our greatness is reflected everywhere in everything we do. In the midst of oppressive circumstances, we have also been able to take voiceless situations and create the most powerful voices like a Martin, Malcolm, and Tupac. Our black is beautiful, powerful, extravagantly vibrant, sensationally viral, and always the highest standard for greatness. This is a phenomenal truth we should always know, love, and be proud of.

As stated earlier in this book, if you don't love yourself your neighbor is in trouble. Young black male, our closest neighbor is the young black male right next to us. Living right beside us on our own block in the community and competing right beside us in our own line of ambition is someone who looks most like us and is a part of our very own culture. To be so blinded as to see him as our worst enemy is the most naive thing we could ever do in contributing to the self-destruction of our own race.

We can compete, disagree, and even fight – but that should only be a means towards collective improvement. Iron sharpens iron, and black iron sharpens black iron. Black iron should not seek to destroy another piece of black iron made up of its very own substance. The young black male should never engage in the senseless killing and destruction of another young black male. That can only occur as an act of self-hate: an act based on not loving yourself and taking it out on someone else closest to you, who becomes a threat in your mind because their similar makeup exposes the insecurities you have about your own self in connection to your own people. Even in this case, hate is just an inverted, infected, twisted version of love.

Love must come with real trust and respect. That love is only cultivated in a pure mind, pure body, and pure seeking environment. The elimination of negative perspectives, substances, and lifestyle activities helps to stop the self-destruction of a great race YOU and YOUR BLACK BROTHER are integral parts of.

Our love and knowledge of self must extend beyond our inner circle to our entire circle as a people. The stronger and more unified this entire circle is in love, the more powerful we are to mobilize into further collective prominence. We may choose to embrace our own preferred circles of ideals and affiliations for expressing black prominence, as we see fit. But we should always understand the overlapping team and cultural unities of black love that encompass them all. We're only as strong as our weakest link. So by linking every young black male within the fabric of the black community chain as strongly as possible through the power of love, we are unbreakable and unstoppable.

Love of Human Race

Any acts of anger and hate are misguided emotions of immaturity and ignorance. Every act of hate that has ever been committed against blacks reflects a victimized state of weakness within the oppressor more so than the blacks targeted to be oppressed. The most superior minds in mankind have always overcome any fear with a stronger level of confident love. A love rooted in the knowledge and understanding that, as humans, we are diverse evolutions of one source to mankind.

This love has been reflected throughout the course of history as many whites have loved, fought, and even died for the equal rights of blacks. All across the world, and within America, are people of all colors and creeds, who embrace this unified love for all of mankind. Our ultimate purpose in the movement for black freedom and empowerment is to unify the entire world, so that every human can live a free and happy life. When these moments of universal love are evident in all its diversity it signifies the absolute greatness of the human race.

Young black male, our strength and love in being Pro-Black never has to be a conflict, creating the need to be Anti-Anyone, Anti-Any Race, or Anti-Anything. That would make us weaker than any other ignorant racist who has discriminated against blacks. During a lecture, black activist and psychologist Dr. Umar Johnson stated, "The biggest white oppressor you have to kill is the one within yourself." The damage of oppression is only truly done when we internalize any notion of black inferiority within ourselves. That's the most destructive oppressor, that one we allow to cancerously grow within ourselves, neglecting our own inherited black greatness which is fully connected in love with the human race.

Black love in its purest form is human love for all. Young black male, you are entitled to display your power to love in whatever righteous way you feel fit. The browning of America and the world through the growth of mixed families and cultures is one of the most beautiful expressions of evolution. However, your decisions to display love throughout the human race should never denounce or dehumanize black people in any way, especially when YOU are and will always be black – along with anything else that is created from you.

Your diversity, experienced in whatever realms of work, family, or social life, should never create an elitism that takes away from an ability to show an ultimate black love, which at your core is love of self. If ever there are discouraging thoughts making you despise opportunities to love a black woman, befriend a black male, reunite with your black family, enterprise with a black business, live amongst a black community, celebrate black culture, or fight for a worthy black cause for justice – that is a problem to check. Young black male, any generalization you make to reject black culture is a self-defeating means to ultimately rejecting YOU.

In an interview with legendary hip-hop artist KRS-1, he stated, "The deepest part to being black is being African. The deepest part to being African is being human. The deepest part to being human is being God. The deepest part to being God is being love." Young black male, our voice, our story, our cause, our fight, and our movement shines as a light of oneness we give to the world as the ultimate life teachers to mankind. The ultimate purpose of the teaching of this life lesson by hardcore demonstration is to prove that the only thing that should matter and the only energy that truly exists is love.

2.0 Black Power – "Fight for one another"

Black love fuels black power with the strength and energy required for breakthrough and liberation. The Black Panthers have historically been misinterpreted as a militant and violent group. Their entire mission rose from a love for righteousness and justice so deep for blacks and mankind that they built a zero tolerance for injustices against blacks. This led to a development of armed soldiers to courageously protect blacks in the community from wrongful acts of racial violence and police brutality. Even with this military defense platform, community social programs were at the core of their organizational platform. This included "Free Breakfast for Children" programs and community health clinics.

The Black Panther Movement, just like many other movements fighting for the freedom of blacks, was driven by the power of unified organization. Our most powerful movements have been the most organized. They have strategically planned, documented, articulated, and activated organized blueprints for action. The Black Power movement amplifies black pride and black values that "express a range of political goals from defense against racial oppression, the establishment of social institutions, and a self-sufficient economy."

Our black revolutionary and civil rights forefathers have shown us that the first step in power is taking a courageous stand for an urgent cause that goes beyond self-interests in benefiting others within our race. The time is always now to flex our unified black power through rally and protest whenever one of our black brothers or sisters is wrongfully discriminated against, abused, or murdered. The time is always now to vote to remove politicians from office when they fail to represent the best interests of equal rights for blacks. The time is always now to challenge laws and social institutions that fail to represent the best interests of equal rights for blacks. The time is always now to support great black-owned businesses and withdraw from spending with any non-black-owned businesses that neglect the best employment, consumer, or cultural interests of blacks.

Young black male, YOU are powerful beyond measure. YOU are the epitome of iconic. YOU are constantly studied, admired, and sadly targeted by the most powerful global forces in the world. YOU are wrongly dissected, projected, and destructed in multi-faceted ways you couldn't even imagine. However, YOU are not alone.

WE are in this together. WE are soldiers with an innate power stronger than the forces that have ever opposed us. That is why we survive and find ways to thrive time and time again. When we intelligently unify all of our collective spiritual, physical, mental, economic, political, social, and cultural black power we prove over and over that we are truly dominant in the face of any opposition to our greatness.

3.0 Black Wealth - "Create wealth with one another"

Black Wall Street

One of the wealthiest all-Black communities in America was the Greenwood community in Tulsa, Oklahoma, established around 1910, also known as "Black Wall Street." It was the home to numerous successful black businessmen, doctors, lawyers, realtors, and multi-millionaires. This 35-square-block area was populated with 11,000 African-Americans who were unified in overcoming segregation by establishing their own incredibly prosperous and prominent black community.[1]

In an article written by Jeffrey L. Boney, he states Black Wall Street had its own bus line, thirteen churches, four hotels, three drugstores, two high schools, two theaters, two newspapers, a hospital, a library, and 200 commercial buildings for professional offices.[2] One of the most astounding and powerful economic stats about Black Wall Street is the black dollar circulated 36 to 1,000 times within its own community.[3]

Meaning, for example, that when a black teacher got paid, they spent some of that money at the black grocery store, the black grocery store owner spent some of that money with the black banker, the black banker spent some of that money with the black doctor, the black doctor spent some of that money with the black movie theater, the black movie theater owner spent some of that money at the black clothing store, the black clothing store owner spent some of that money at the black beauty salon or barbershop...and on and on up to 36 to 1,000 times. This type of money flow circulation within one small economy of people is amazing. As Boney states, Black Wall Street became "the envy of America, producing a sense of accomplishment, pride, and self-sufficiency."[25] Black Wall Street was the epitome of Black Economic Power.

During one of America's worst acts of racial violence in June 1, 1921, Black Wall Street was burned to the ground by a mob of angry whites in an outbreak known as the "Tulsa Race Riot." Dr. Boyce Watkins, who is producing a movie about Black Wall Street, refers to it as "The Tulsa Race Massacre," due to the horrendous bombing and killing that took place.

Three-thousand blacks were killed, 600 black businesses were destroyed, over 1,000 houses were destroyed, and an estimated 10,000 blacks were left homeless.[4] Although the mob attack was reportedly done because of wrongful claims that a black boy sexually assaulted a 17-year-old white girl, the unbelievable degree of damage and killing suggests that much more powerful malicious national forces conspired to destroy this thriving all-black community.

Black Wall Street was such a powerful threat because it showed the U.S. establishment how great blacks can be in a segregated environment where blacks were self-sufficient and independent from any needs to assimilate into White America. One of the biggest critiques of the Civil Rights Movement for equal rights and integration is it significantly reduced our power as a great, unified people to further build an independent economic, socio-cultural, and educational base run and controlled by ourselves. Black Wall Street never re-emerged, partly because integration laws influenced more blacks to assimilate into white-operated customs by spending our dollars and sending our talent outside of the black community.

According to Boney, "the dollar circulates almost ten times within the Jewish community before it reaches outside. The dollar circulates almost six times within the Asian community before it reaches the outside. The dollar circulates an infinite number of times within the white community in general, but sadly the African-American dollar does not even circulate one time within its own community. The black dollar only stays in the black community less than 6 hours."[5] If money is power, it's very easy to see how we so quickly give ours up to everyone else but ourselves.

Trillion-Dollar Black Power

Despite the circumstances of poverty in the black community, we're collectively one of the most prosperous groups in the world. The Nielsen African-American Consumer Report released in 2014 estimated that African-American buying power is over $1 trillion. That is $1,000,000,000,000 with 12 zeros. This figure would make African-Americans the 16th largest economy in the entire world if we were a country.[6] This figure supports the fact that we're not only a major driver of the U.S. economy, but the global economy as well.

Dr. Boyce Watkins stated, "Having political power with no economic power is like having a driver's license with no car to drive." A civilization's economic wealth is the core anchor to develop its infrastructure for building an empire. A civil rights movement without a strong economic movement won't move much at all.

When someone is addicted to a substance, they experience a serious withdrawal and extreme adverse effects when it's taken away. Thus, for the most powerful nation addicted to dominating by means of possessing the greatest wealth, often overvaluing money as a "god" (despite the misleading "In God We Trust" words printed on it) – our greatest tool of leverage as African-Americans is our unified economic purchasing power and collective economic withdrawal.

Our unified buying power of over $1 trillion has equated to massive annual consumption, with billions of black dollars spent per industry for products such as food, automobiles, gas, bank accounts, shoes, healthcare, alcohol, tobacco, and sports/recreational products to name a few. If for only 30 days every African-American chose to withdraw their money from a national bank like Bank of America, stopped buying groceries at Walmart, stopped buying gas from Exxon Mobile, or stopped buying Nike gym shoes I think the entire stock market could crash.

There would be national headlines everywhere of the U.S. stock market falling drastically, with a threatened recession on the brink. These Fortune 500 companies would all be facing extreme dangers of bankruptcy. Young black male, that is power! Collectively, as a people, we have economic power that could bring the entire country and most dominant global forces down to their knees.

Here are some of the powerful actions that could be taken with our collective trillion-dollar purchasing power:

- 20 cents of every black dollar spent could eliminate every external debt of every African country, enabling many African nations to emerge as global powerhouses
- 1.5 cents of every black dollar could rebuild Haiti's reconstruction costs of $14B
- If 2 cents of every dollar spent by black Americans was put aside for scholarships, it would total $20B and could pay for every black college student to go to college on a full scholarship.

These are all statistics to prove that our black purchasing power can be used to transform the black community and the entire world. It's our most powerful weapon, more so than thousands of weapons of mass destruction and machine guns. Our collective buying power of $1 trillion used strategically could literally turn this economic-driven world upside down. It could be the answer to reparations for blacks, a larger base of more black-owned businesses, more job sources for blacks, better schools for blacks, and the foundation for our own version of a black global empire constructed however we see fit. It's also a powerful tool of leverage to demand changes in the political, social, and economic system to better provide equal rights for us all.

We did not create this current U.S. and global economic system, so we aren't able to control it in every way that we would like. In past situations where we have gained control of our own economy like Black Wall Street, we also know how malicious the world can be in literally plotting to burn us down. However, we are economically empowered as a unified whole to such a wealthy extent that we can create our own liberating options.

Everybody goes after the black dollar in the black community. If money is the major end goal for our capitalistic society, then that is our loudest voice and most powerful weapon. This power begins with taking control of our personal spending on an individual basis, and then unifying on a collective basis to demonstrate even greater power.

Even 100 homeless blacks with only $20 to their name to waste on liquor can make an impact. If they came together to stop buying $20 worth of whiskey every month from the neighborhood liquor store that always treats them like crap, that's a consistent $2,000 a month taken out of that liquor store owner's sales. That $2,000 a month turns into $24,000 a year, which is a serious dent. If that liquor store was a chain of 10 stores all throughout black neighborhoods in the city, and 100 homeless blacks per neighborhood stayed united with this boycott, that would be $240,000 a year taken out of that liquor store's bank account annually. Nearly a quarter of a million dollars is a big hit to any business. It could force them to do major layoffs, lose key liquor accounts, close down a store, and possibly go out of business. This can all be done starting with one homeless man with 20 wrinkled up singles.

Bob Law stated during an interview, "Every other group in the world is comfortable with dealing along the principles of nationalism and working to make sure their group is protected and empowered first before entering into alliances with other groups." Every ethnicity in the world knows you must take care of self and your own people first. That's the only smart way to engage in the global capitalistic game.

It makes no sense for me to build up everybody else's home using my one-bedroom apartment rent money. However, after I build a mansion for myself and a block of mansions for my family and people, I can more confidently integrate and share my wealth, to build up homes all over the world for others — having a much stronger base to intelligently enterprise with and continuously generate more money to recycle back into my community.

We drive the U.S. and global economy in so many ways and get the least benefits from it. We no longer have to play this game this way, and our first line of defense is taking full control of our own spending. We must unify by pulling our dollars out of businesses that don't support us, reinvest back into our communities, nor value our collective agenda. We must then unify by putting our dollars into black-owned businesses that will support, employ, educate, promote, reinvest, lead, and value us to the fullest.

In addition, we must become less consumer-minded and blinded, so we can become more supplier minded to generate maximum black wealth and economic control interdependently through working exclusively together. It takes work, but we have a trillion dollars' worth of seed money to work with, which begins with black economic investment one black dollar at a time. By coming together to build one unified economic front, we can create our greatest opportunities for freedom and wealth. This can spark a greater revolutionary movement for the epic development of our own 21st century Trillion Dollar Black Wall Street.

4.0 Black Excellence — "Be the best amongst one another"

During an epic face-off scene in HBO's critically acclaimed series *The Wire*, jack boy Omar is caught off guard by Brother Mouzone, a hitman, he severely hurt who returned unexpectedly with a gun. In a trash-talking sequence between the two, Omar stated, "Even when I miss I don't miss!" Despite the street context, I love that line and believe it embodies the current state of African-Americans.

Even when we are misjudged, we are iconic. Even when we are mis-educated, we are brilliant. Even when we are oppressed, we are powerful beyond measure. Even when we are dehumanized, we are the alpha and omega. Even when we are misguided in self-destructive ways, we are immortal.

Young black male, you are admired all over the world. You can go to any continent on this planet and you will find people staring at you in awe. People will stop in their tracks in broad daylight to study the way you look, the way you walk, the way you talk, and the way you effortlessly move with excellence in everything you do. Your hair, your skin, your smile, your style, your swag, your body, your mind, and your soul give off a powerful energy that can never be denied. Despite all the twisted ways in which the world and the media criticize this energy, it exemplifies an undeniable mark of excellence...black excellence.

Young black male, the truth of our greatness is the most idolized and feared amongst the most profound global circles of politics, economics, biology, history, and power. We epitomize the most potent manifestation and evolution of mankind. We represent the most extraordinary talents and source of opportunity within the most unordinary challenges of oppression. We're the most inherently empowered, yet the most targeted for disenfranchisement from power. Young black male, we're the most loved and the most hated because we represent the greatest, most explosive energy to ever exist within mankind.

Young black male, when we commit to putting in the work and going hard, we become the undisputed best. When we emerge as a great businessman, engineer, doctor, lawyer, educator, activist, entertainer, athlete, and President - time stops as the entire world pauses in awe of our greatness and supreme level of excellence. We become the best in the world and best in class when we commit our mind, body, and spirit to excellence.

That's why it's so important for us to break the shackles of injustice and disadvantage by becoming the absolute best at whatever we do. We must become masters of channeling an unbreakable level of confidence and passion to drive ourselves towards excellence. There is at least one positive and productive activity in this world that you're best built to dominate as No. 1. It must become your life mission to discover this in pursuit of achieving ultimate greatness. During this life process, we develop the discipline, appetite, and skills to become the best. Once you master the art of overcoming any obstacle to becoming the best, you position yourself for overcoming any obstacle to becoming a master of the world. At that point you can best make an impact for changing it.

That's why education is not a game. Mastering math, science, reading, writing, and history, along with other real life applications to an extent far beyond traditional schooling gives you a foundation for intellectual breakthrough that you will continuously be able to use. Young black male, you are already brilliant. You just have to put in the time to apply your mind so strongly that you become an expert at breaking down problems and creating solutions. You go from being tested to being the only one who can create a test worthy of challenging yourself to being the best. That is self-mastery.

To become the best and the standard of excellence in your field - non-stop training, work, and sacrifice is mandatory. Young black male, get used to it! That's the only way to fulfill your destiny. Break through the illusions of fear, resistance, failure, and limitation. Find your zone. Find your unique expression of excellence. Put in those 10,000 hours of perfect practice and training to become an expert. Master the art of completing a task perfectly. Then master the ability to complete it perfectly 100 times. Then master the system of being able to duplicate that process of perfection flawlessly 1,000 to 1,000,000 times.

Whether this is in the form of excellence with perfect school exam scores, advancements in computer technology, scientific inventions, creative marketing, business strategies, ground-breaking entrepreneurship, legit hustle economics, million-dollar revenue operations, wealth creation, motivational speaking, political policy and debates, spiritual leadership, body building exercises, athletic dominance, music innovation, or artistic genius — YOU can become the best at whatever it is you put your mind to. No one but you can ultimately control the power of your thoughts and mind to create whatever form of excellence and success you can envision. This unlimited power can fuel your actions and work ethic so that you bring these visions into reality. This dedication to excellence begins right where you're at in life now, and can carry you through the evolving points of greatness where you want to be.

Young black male, you are fearless, relentless, and masterful. When you put in the unrelenting work to break through you prove time and time again that you are unstoppable and unbreakable. You know this and you see this in every way possible through every form of black excellence visible within yourself. Young black male, this shared experience of black excellence is also a powerful common bond we share amongst each other. When you become the best at what you do in your own unique way, and I become the best at what I do in my own unique way, we breed a culture of black excellence that every other young black male can build from. We then become a Dream Team.

We become a legion of unified powerful superstars capable of the highest levels of performance, dominance, and greatness. Iron sharpens iron, black iron sharpens black iron, and black excellence sharpens black excellence. This sharpening process of excellence eliminates all the BS, weakness, and excuses for evolving and overcoming as the best black men we can possibly be. This includes being the best students, the best workers, the best soldiers, the best professionals, the best executives, the best sons, the best brothers, the best fathers, the best husbands, the best leaders, and the best unified group of great ambitious men to ever exist. Young black male, this is black excellence!

5.0 Black Unity — "Forever unite with one another"

Synergy is defined as when the sum of the parts is greater than the whole. So for example let's say I have $1,000, you have one $1,000, and another young black male has $1,000. Based on the premise of synergy, we should be able to unite in producing something greater than the sum of our money pulled together which is $3,000. That is the power of unity under a synergy principle, and that's why it makes so much sense to unite. We don't unite so we have $3,000 to split amongst each other. With nothing additional added to the group mix, that would still leave each of us with what we had to start, $1,000. But if by uniting we could create a synergistic effect that produced $30,000, that split would be $10,000 for us which is 10Xs what I had by myself. That's the ideal form and purpose of unity, when it creates synergy. It's a unified front that creates so much more for the individual as well as the group.

From an economic, political, and social perspective, this is the most powerful way to advance as blacks. We must create synergy through unyielding unity. It takes a strong level of love, trust, respect, and support to create the unified synergy we need to overcome. But it's most necessary to create this sense of unity because it has and will always be our greatest unfulfilled option.

Our current generation doesn't know what it feels like to be kings and queens of human civilization as blacks, but it has been done. We don't know what it feels like to have a prosperous self-sufficient black-run economy unified like Black Wall Street, but it has been done. We don't know what it feels like to put a government-run agency out of business for discriminating against us for being black, but it has been done. We don't know what victory feels like when completely overthrowing a system of oppression, but it has been done. Moments in history have proven this, and even glimpses of this are visible today when we're unified. However, the most recent historical moments and glimpses have been too few and far between, considering the task at hand.

Young black male, what will we do to finally unite whole-heartedly as a people. How many more unarmed black males have to be killed at the hands of cops before we unite once and for all? How many more politicians have to take office without ever changing the laws that hurt us as a people before we unite? How many more non-black-owned businesses have to dominate our communities and our dollars without ever supporting our interests before we unite? How many more black elites must become multi-millionaires while distancing themselves from the plight of millions of blacks unable to experience the American Dream before we unite?

How many more generations of courageous black leaders must be sacrificed before we fully unite as a people populated with millions of black leaders too powerful and plentiful to stop? How many more young black males must be murdered at the hands of another black before we finally decide to eradicate that self-destructive BS of killing our own and finally unite as one? To all of these questions the answer is "NO MORE!" Young black male, we must become absolutely unified NOW!

The reality is this, We're All We Got!" No one else will do it for us; we must do it for ourselves. We must break the cycle of black disunity and create ultimate black unity amongst our families, networks, alliances, businesses, ideas, communities, leaders, and culture because "We're All We Got!" I believe in my heart that once we reach a level of seamless black unity we will finally prove to ourselves and the world that "We're All We Need!" To achieve this great possibility of black utopia, we must unite! We can no longer tear each other down and tear our culture apart. Any greatness we can accomplish as individuals can be increased a million times more by unifying together as one.

Below are 10 Commitment Points to Black Excellence & Unity:

10 Commitment Points to Black Excellence & Unity

1. Empower your mind through continuous education and your soul through spirituality
2. Train and maintain your body as a divine weapon controlled by disciplined thought to avoid any unproductive behaviors and lifestyles
3. Fight with every inch of your soul to be a strong leader of your family as a devoted and exceptionally active father and husband
4. Master a talent and skill to perform and monetize as "The Best" while contributing to the greater good of black culture
5. Fall in love daily with the past, present, and future greatness of black people and black culture with an all-encompassing love for humankind
6. Go above and beyond to support your fellow black brother & sister, in all areas of life while minimizing conflict
7. Identify the political and social causes & organizations for black liberation you will align with and fight for
8. Identify the personal and unified ways in which you will create black-ownership & wealth, support black-owned businesses, and withdraw spending with non-black businesses that don't represent our best interests

9. Build upon a black mentoring relationship as a mentor and mentee
10. Think Black Unity, Feel Black Unity, Speak Black Unity, & Act Black Unity

Our hope is that these commitment points can be new ground for an unprecedented breakthrough as unified African-Americans exemplifying unconditional greatness and freedom to our most paramount capacity.

War On The Young Black Male – "Tale of The Wolf"

The Dead Prez classic hip-hop album, *Let's Get Free*, begins with an intro track called "Wolves." It's a snippet from a lecture a black activist gives about the hunting technique of certain indigenous people in the arctic when hunting a wolf:

"They'll put blood on the blade, and they'll melt the ice and stick the handle in the ice, So that only the blade is protruding, and that a wolf will smell the blood and wants to eat. It will come and lick the blade trying to eat. What happens is when the wolf licks the blade, of course he cuts his tongue and he bleeds. He thinks he's really having a good thing. He drinks and he licks and he licks, and of course he is drinking his own blood and he kills himself."

This tale of the wolf is used as an analogy to describe the enemy imperialistic tactics used against blacks to break down our community. Cultural traps have been set to trick us into licking the blade of drug addiction, crack cocaine distribution, black-on-black crime, white assimilation at the demise of black unified empowerment, and many other destructive traps. These traps delude us into thinking we're getting ahead in an environment in which we're only trying to survive, but it's the ultimate death trap as we end up killing ourselves like the wolf.

There is undoubtedly a war on the young black male. With all the attempts of mass destruction and killing this world has historically orchestrated to annihilate the young black male, we're at war. Unfortunately, we're not fairly protected either. The murders of unarmed young black males like Sean Bell, Oscar Grant, Trayvon Martin, Michael Brown, Eric Garner, Tamir Rice, Tony Robinson, Walter Scott, Freddie Gray, and countless others killed at the hands of cops show that there is a violent, calculated war targeted against us. Police officers kill black suspects twice a week in the United States, on average 96 times a year. Young black teenagers are 21 times more likely to be shot dead by police than white teenagers.

Young black male, we have to intelligently fight for ourselves and more importantly become fully united in fighting for our entire black race as a whole. To successfully do this, we must refrain from self-destructive traps of addiction, assimilation, and senseless internal conflicts that only lead to the perpetuated disunity and death of young black males. We are active soldiers at war, but we're engaging in the worst form of war and mutiny against ourselves.

Black gangs were initially created as a defense for protecting the black community. They were rooted in political and economic black interests that required a military agenda only for those black protective purposes. However, over time they have transformed from platforms of black revolution to dissolution of black culture.

Petty beefs over gang turf, drug corners, and material possessions have created a "crab-in-a-barrel" co-existence, creating the most lethal, self-destructive weapons to kill young black males — thus carrying out the oppressive agenda. We have allowed our best friend and closest ally to become our worst enemy in the black community. We must wake up and realize that "We're All We Got!" We cannot kill ourselves; we must heal ourselves and totally unite as one, to rebuild ourselves into the greatest culture of blacks we can be. Black suicide must be transformed into being black unified. Young black male, let's throw away the blade and "Let's Get Free" through black unity.

Dope Black Boy 2 Rich Black Man

My story as a dope boy hustler was full of self-destructive, misguided experiences. I dropped out of school, did drugs, sold drugs, committed crimes constantly, and did my fair share of damage in poisoning black culture as well as myself. Society failed me and counted me out as another young black male to criminalize, victimize, kill, and destroy. However, despite the harsh realities of my environment and misguided pursuits, my innate ambitions to pursue happiness, freedom, and success prevailed above all.

A broken home couldn't stop me. A broken education system couldn't stop me. A white-dominated broken social system of black discrimination couldn't stop me. A broken street environment offering crime as the only way to survive couldn't stop me. Nor could the prison system that economically thrives off the disproportionate incarceration of blacks stop me. No white man and no white system could stop me. The only person who could stop me was me. My entire journey as a misguided dope black boy hustling ambitiously in the streets was a lesson of self-discovery leading me to a full awareness that I had all the power. I was the sole master of my mind, body, and soul. I was the master of my fate. I am a FREEMAN.

I reprogrammed my mind as well as my body and spirit to turn my life completely around. I channeled every source of energy, talent, intelligence, and hustle within me to become the best black man I could be. I'm still hood, I still wild out and have fun from time to time, and I'm still always improving as a person. But through it all, I know that I am destined for greatness. Young black male, so are YOU!

I used every hustling quality of passion, business savvy, leadership, charisma, and desire for greatness that I used as a dope black boy to fully transition into becoming a rich black man. I was always built for greatness and success, but I was blinded by the short-term trap of the streets that can only lead to death — the death of your dream, the death of your family, the death of your freedom, the death of your manhood, the death of your culture, and the death of your future. This leads to the ultimate suicidal death of your own self, and the death of your potential greatness as a black man.

But just as the greatest savior known to mankind rose from the dead, we too are capable of rising from the dead as powerful young black men. My success in building Beautiful Hair 4 U into a multi-million dollar company from the ground up and contributing as a pioneer to a black takeover of the virgin hair industry is not just my personal success. It's the success of our people made possible by our black ancestors and black power movement forefathers sacrificing their lives so that I could make it along with countless others like me. They paved the way and passed the torch for us to build upon for greatness in continuing a journey from being a Dope Black Boy to becoming a Rich Black Man.

Young Black Man, this book reflects your journey as well. YOU can be from the hood and be the best. YOU can use every skill that creates short-lived come-ups in the streets to go legit and takeover a professional industry in creating long-term success. YOU are just as capable of becoming successful in your own right as an empowered black man. YOU have the key to unlocking any and every shackle that could ever exist to making any dream YOU can imagine a reality. Together WE are the never-ending unified circle of black power, wealth, enlightenment, and freedom built to create the greatest black civilization. With this we have the power to eradicate the sickness of discrimination and oppression, leading to the greatest human civilization of all races to ever truly unify and exist.

YOU In 200 Years

What will the version of YOU look like 200 years from now? YOU will be alive through an offspring that looks just like YOU with your own blood running through its veins.

How will that version of your future culture work together to represent greatness? What sacrifice will YOU make today and for the rest of your life so that your YOU 200 years from now is the greatest YOU that could ever be, in being a part of the greatest black civilization and human society to ever exist?

Third and Long

This book serves as the essential playbook and rally cry for the Young Black Man. As the authors of this book, we have spent countless hours forming a united brotherhood amongst two Young Black Men to draw up the best playbook we can for every Young Black Man to WIN! At this special moment in time we are all on the same page. We must all unite as Young Black Men together in the game of our lives on this field of revolution. Our opposition is incredibly fierce. We have experienced extreme pain, setbacks, turnovers, injury, loss, and temporary moments of defeat. But we are built for GREATNESS and built to WIN. We can change the course of history. Our opportunity for legendary revolution is NOW!

We're on the football field of life and down to basically one play to make it happen. For the Young Black Man, we have been knocked back numerous yards behind the line of scrimmage, and it's now "third and long." Yes, it's a challenge; no, it is not fair; but as a team, our backs are against the wall and this is the pivotal situation at hand.

The closing of this book is the departure from the huddle where we have looked each other in the eye – and verbally as well as intuitively communicated our unified commitment to do everything it takes to make the necessary play to get a first down, score a touchdown, and make a victorious comeback to WIN!

When it's "third and long" there's no question what must be done, you gotta GO DEEP! Young black men, WE must GO DEEP to stay unified on the frontline to protect our black families, communities, and culture. WE must GO DEEP with a passionate strategic running route to get as far down the field of black liberation as possible. WE must GO DEEP with the mental IQ, physical arm strength, and spiritual faith-powered accuracy to throw the ball deep into the hands of black greatness. Losing is not an option. In the words of Olivia Pope in the most riveting black liberation episode of *Scandal*, "Stand Up, Fight Back, No More Black Man Under Attack!"

When we unify to make this "third and long" reception, we survive another set of downs to fight and win for black culture. Regardless of the circumstances, nobody can ever stop us! We're way too talented, brilliant, and powerful, especially when united.

Young Black Man, I love you as our brother, and there is no greater man I'd rather fight on the front lines with for black justice than YOU. Young black man, I am ready for whatever and I know YOU are too.

The time is NOW. YOUNG BLACK MAN, GO DEEP!

Notes and References

Chapter 2:   Own Mind

1. Safdie, Ben and Safdie, Joshua. *Lenny Cooke.* Shop Korn Productions, 2013.
2. "The World's Billionaires," *Forbes Web Site.* [Online] 2015. [Cited: August 14, 2015.] http://www.forbes.com/billionaires/list

Chapter 3:   Greatness, Dominance, & Killer Instinct: Stages 1-4 (PERSPECTIVE/ PASSION/TALENT/WORK)

1. Dahl, Darren. "Top Companies Started During A Recession," *The Huffington Post.* [Online] August 11, 2011. [Cited: August 14, 2015.] http://www. huffingtonpost.com/2010/05/10/top-companies-started-during-a-recession_n_923853.html.
2. Grover, Tim S. *RELENTLESS.* New York : SCRIBNER, 2013.
3. Sharp, Andrew. "Kobe Bryant is not totally human, and now we have (more) proof," *SB Nation.* [Online] March 2016, 2013. [Cited: August 14, 2015.]   http://www.sbnation.com/nba/2013/3/6/4071142/ kobe-bryant-las-vegas-workout-reddit.
4. Sharp, "Kobe Bryant is not totally human, and now we have (more) proof."

Chapter 4:   Greatness, Dominance, & Killer Instinct: Stage 5 (MASTERY)

1. Schultz, Michael. *The Last Dragon.* TriStar Pictures, 1985.
2. Schultz, *The Last Dragon.*

3. Schultz, *The Last Dragon*.

4. Tzu, Sun. *The Art of War*. Boston : The Denma Translation Group, 2001.

5. Gladwell, Malcolm. *Outliers*. New York : Little, Brown and Company, 2008.

6. Welch, Paul. "Becoming A Master - 10,000 Hours to Master Your Craft," *Paul Welch Blog*. [Online] February 1, 2012. [Cited: August 14, 2015.] https://sacredthief.wordpress.com/tag/philosophy/.

7. Mike Tyson vs Muhamad Ali - Who Wins? *YouTube*. [Online] ThisIs50.com, September 3, 2012. [Cited: August 2015, 2015.] https://www.youtube.com/watch?v=MF17mkqyf44.

8. Ali, Muhammad and Ali, Hana Y. *The Soul Of A Butterfly*. London : Transworld Publishers, 2004.

Chapter 5: Greatness, Dominance, & Killer Instinct: Stages 6-7
(DECISION/IMPACT)

1. "Barack Obama's keynote address at the 2004 DNC," *YouTube*. [Online] CNN, November 7, 2012. [Cited: August 14, 2015.] https://www.youtube.com/watch?v=dYAr4lhPb_s.

2. "Barack Obama's keynote address at the 2004 DNC."

3. Shyamalan, M. Night. *After Earth*. Overbrook Entertainment, 2013.

4. Dhall, Atima. "Mandela's Leadership Lessons," *Thirstt*. [Online] [Cited: August 14, 2015.] https://www.thirstt.com/droplets/Mandela-s-Leadership-Lessons/53dd0956e72d9a1f3d9ab4af.

5. Mendoza, Dorrine. "9 simple ways to keep Nelson Mandela's legacy alive," *CNN*. [Online] December 16, 2013. [Cited: August 14, 2015.] http://www.cnn.com/2013/12/16/living/keeping-mandelas-legacy-alive/.

6. Gunawardana, Gamini N. "Transformational Leader - Nelson Mandela," *Mirror Business*. [Online] 2015 9, July. [Cited: August 14, 2015.] http://www.dailymirror.lk/78885/transformational-leader-nelson-mandela.

7. "Statistics," *The Fatherless Generation*. [Online] [Cited: August 2015, 2015.] https://thefatherlessgeneration.wordpress.com/statistics/.

Chapter 6: Education

1. "The first 20 hours -- how to learn anything | Josh Kaufman | TEDxCSU," *YouTube*. [Online] March 14, 2013. [Cited: August 14, 2015.] https://www.youtube.com/watch?v=5MgBikgcWnY.

2. "11 Facts About High School Drop Out Rates," *DoSomething.org.* [Online] [Cited: August 14, 2015.] https://www.dosomething.org/facts/11-facts-about-high-school-dropout-rates.

3. Rampell, Catherine. "College Degree Required by Increasing Number of Companies," *The New York Times.* [Online] February 19, 2013. [Cited: August 14, 2015.] http://www.nytimes.com/2013/02/20/business/college-degree-required-by-increasing-number-of-companies.html?_r=0.

Chapter 7: Million $ Transition: How Dope Boy Skills Translate to a Successful Entrepreneur

1. Luo, Benny. "Rick Ross: How I Made $2 Million A Day On The Streets," *NextShark.* [Online] August 13, 2013. [Cited: August 14, 2015.] http://nextshark.com/rick-ross-a-former-drug-kingpin-talks-about-making-2-million-dollars-a-day-how-to-keep-people-loyal-and-taking-risks/.

2. "Spending on illegal drugs," *Worldometers.* [Online] [Cited: August 14, 2015.] http://www.worldometers.info/drugs/.

3. Kosoff, Maya. "How One Nonprofit Is Transforming Ex-Convicts and Former Drug Dealers into Entrepreneurs," *Business Insider.* [Online] August 21, 2014. [Cited: August 14, 2015.] http://www.businessinsider.com/defy-ventures-transforms-ex-cons-into-entrepreneurs-2014-8.

4. *Defy Ventures.* [Online] [Cited: August 14, 2015.] http://defyventures.org/.

5. Chun, Janean. "Jeff Henderson, The Henderson Group: What Drug Dealing Taught Me About Running A Business," *Huffington Post.* [Online] July 6, 2012. [Cited: August 14, 2015.] http://www.huffingtonpost.com/2012/07/06/jeff-henderson-what-drug-dealing-taught-me-about-business_n_1601526.html.

6. Chun, "Jeff Henderson The Henderson Group: What Drug Dealing Taught Me About Running A Business."

7. "The Millionaire Ex-convict...Uchendi Nwani," *M.O.V.E. WITH KENNY.* [Online] December 11, 2011. [Cited: August 14, 2015.] http://kehindeajose.blogspot.com/2011/12/millionaire-ex-convictuchendi-nwani.html.

8. *Millionaire Barber.* [Online] [Cited: August 14, 2015.] http://millionairebarber.com/.

9. "From drug dealer to entrepreneur: The Block to the Boardroom," *YouTube.* [Online] CNN, September 1, 2014. [Cited: August 14, 2015.] https://www.youtube.com/watch?v=PI4qYHLwBhk.

10. Hovitz, Helaina. "The Powder Broker: From Teenage Drug Dealer to Real Estate "It" Guy," *Observer.* [Online] February 19, 2013. [Cited: August 14, 2015.] http://observer.com/2013/02/the-powder-broker-from-teenage-drug-dealer-to-real-estate-it-guy/.

11. *Jay Mr. Real Estate.* [Online] [Cited: August 14, 2015.] http://www.jaymrreal-estate.com/.

Chapter 8:   Thug Life vs. Real Life

1. Burrell, Tom. *Brainwashed.* New York : SmileyBooks, 2010.

2. Joseph, Jamal. *Tupac Shakur Legacy.* New York : Atria Books, 2006.

3. Smith, Jacquelyn. "America's Best Paying Blue-Collar Jobs," *Forbes.* [Online] June 5, 2012. [Cited: August 14, 2015.] http://www.forbes.com/sites/jacquelynsmith/2012/06/05/americas-best-paying-blue-collar-jobs-2/.

Chapter 9:   The Trap Pt. 1: Prison & Death

1. "U.S. Department of Justice - Bureau of Justice Statistics Prisoners in 2013," *Bureau of Justice Statistics.* [Online] September 30, 2014. [Cited: August 14, 2015.] http://www.bjs.gov/content/pub/pdf/p13.pdf.

2. "U.S. Department of Justice - Bureau of Justice Statistics Prisoners in 2013,"

3. Alexander, Michelle. *The New Jim Crow.* New York : The New Press, 2010.

4. Kerby, Sophia. "The Top 10 Most Startling Facts About People of Color and Criminal Justice in the United States," *Center for American Progress.* [Online] March 13, 2012. [Cited: August 14, 2015.] https://www.americanprogress.org/issues/race/news/2012/03/13/11351/the-top-10-most-startling-facts-about-people-of-color-and-criminal-justice-in-the-united-states/.

5. Michelle, *The New Jim Crow.*

6. Kerby, "The Top 10 Most Startling Facts About People of Color and Criminal Justice in the United States."

7. Kerby, "The Top 10 Most Startling Facts About People of Color and Criminal Justice in the United States."

8. Kerby, "The Top 10 Most Startling Facts About People of Color and Criminal Justice in the United States."

9. Kerby, "The Top 10 Most Startling Facts About People of Color and Criminal Justice in the United States."

10. Kerby, "The Top 10 Most Startling Facts About People of Color and Criminal Justice in the United States."

11. Kerby, "The Top 10 Most Startling Facts About People of Color and Criminal Justice in the United States."

12. "Black Boys Viewed as Older, Less Innocent Than Whites, Research Finds," *American Psychological Association.* [Online] March 6, 2014. [Cited: August 14, 2015.] http://www.apa.org/news/press/releases/2014/03/black-boys-older.aspx.

13. "Fair Sentencing Act," *Wikipedia.* [Online] [Cited: August 14, 2015.] https://en.wikipedia.org/wiki/Fair_Sentencing_Act.

14. Michelle, *The New Jim Crow.*

15. Michelle, *The New Jim Crow.*

16. Michelle, *The New Jim Crow.*

17. "Prisoners and Prisoner Re-Entry," *United States Department of Justice.* [Online] [Cited: August 14, 2015.] http://www.justice.gov/archive/fbci/prog-menu_reentry.html.

18. Pelaez, Vicky. "The Prison Industry in the United States: Big Business or a New Form of Slavery," [Online] March 31, 2014. [Cited: August 14, 2015.] http://www.globalresearch.ca/the-prison-industry-in-the-united-states-big-business-or-a-new-form-of-slavery/8289.

19. Pelaez, "The Prison Industry in the United States: Big Business or a New Form of Slavery."

20. Pelaez, Vicky. "The Prison Industry in the United States: Big Business or a New Form of Slavery,"

21. Pelaez, Vicky. "The Prison Industry in the United States: Big Business or a New Form of Slavery,"

22. Pelaez, Vicky. "The Prison Industry in the United States: Big Business or a New Form of Slavery,"

23. Pelaez, Vicky. "The Prison Industry in the United States: Big Business or a New Form of Slavery,"

24. "CIA Involvement in Contra Cocaine trafficking," *Wikipedia.* [Online] [Cited: August 15, 2014.] https://en.wikipedia.org/wiki/CIA_involvement_in_Contra_cocaine_trafficking.

25. "The Secret Rap Meeting That Changed Rap Music and Destroyed a Generation," *Hip Hop Is Read.* [Online] April 24, 2012. [Cited: August 15, 2015.]

http://www.hiphopisread.com/2012/04/secret-meeting-that-changed-rap-music.html.

26. "The Secret Rap Meeting That Changed Rap Music and Destroyed a Generation."

27. "The Secret Rap Meeting That Changed Rap Music and Destroyed a Generation,"

28. Schoettler, Jim. "Jacksonville man helpless as Buckman Bridge accident victim cried out to his family, Jesus, before dying," *The Florida Times Union*. [Online] July 21, 2014. [Cited: August 15, 2015.] http://jacksonville.com/news/crime/2014-07-21/story/jacksonville-man-helpless-buckman-bridge-accident-victim-cried-out-his.

29. Schoettler, "Jacksonville man helpless as Buckman Bridge accident victim cried out to his family, Jesus, before dying."

30. Schoettler, "Jacksonville man helpless as Buckman Bridge accident victim cried out to his family, Jesus, before dying."

Chapter 10:   The Trap Pt. 2: Drugs, Alcohol, & Dope Boy Hollywood

1. "Your Brain On Crack Cocaine," *YouTube*. [Online] AsapScience, November 20, 2013. [Cited: August 15, 2015.] https://www.youtube.com/watch?v=vxI7PTVRfhQ.

Chapter 11:   Intimacy: Bridging the Gap Between Love & Sex

1. Deida, David. *The Way of the Superior Man*. Boulder : Sounds True, Inc., 2004.

2. Baines, John. *The Science of Love*. New York : John Baines Institute, Inc., 1993.

3. Baines, *The Science of Love*.

4. Jaslow, Ryan. "CDC: 110 million STDs among U.S. men and women," *CBS News*. [Online] February 14, 2013. [Cited: August 15, 2015.] http://www.cbsnews.com/news/cdc-110-million-stds-among-us-men-and-women/.

5. Jaslow, Ryan. "CDC: 110 million STDs among U.S. men and women,"

6. "11 Facts About Teens and STDs," *DoSomething.org*. [Online] [Cited: August 15, 2015.] https://www.dosomething.org/facts/11-facts-about-teens-and-stds.

7. Lowe, Jeneatte. "Herpes Statistics: How Common is Genital Herpes (HSV-2)," *Just Herpes*. [Online] January 16, 2013. [Cited: August 15, 2015.] http://justherpes.com/facts/genital-herpes-statistics-us-hsv2/.

8. "Genital HPV Infection - Fact Sheet," *Centers for Disease Control and Prevention.* [Online] [Cited: August 15, 2015.] http://www.cdc.gov/std/hpv/stdfact-hpv.htm.

9. "Genital HPV Infection - Fact Sheet."

10. "HIV in the United States: At A Glance," *Centers for Disease Control and Prevention.* [Online] [Cited: August 15, 2015.] http://www.cdc.gov/hiv/statistics/basics/ataglance.html.

11. "CDC Fact Sheet - HIV among African Americans," *Centers for Disease Control and Prevention.* [Online] [Cited: August 15, 2015.] http://www.cdc.gov/nchhstp/newsroom/docs/cdc-hiv-aa-508.pdf.

12. Barnes, Mo. "Top 25 cities with high HIV and AIDS rate," *Rolling Out.* [Online] May 24, 2014. [Cited: August 15, 2015.] http://rollingout.com/2014/05/24/top-25-cities-high-hivaids-rate/.

Chapter 12: Our World History in Black & White

1. "Whole Genome Association Studies," *National Human Genome Research Institute.* [Online] [Cited: August 16, 2015.] https://www.genome.gov/17516714.

2. "Race in a Genetic World," *Harvard Magazine.* [Online] May-June 2008. [Cited: August 16, 2015.] http://harvardmagazine.com/2008/05/race-in-a-genetic-world-html.

3. Knight, Michael M. *Why I Am A Five Percenter.* New York : Penguin Group, 2011.

4. Knight, *Why I Am A Five Percenter.*

5. Mayell, Hillary. "Oldest Human Fossils Identified," *National Geographic.* [Online] February 16, 2005. [Cited: August 17, 2015.] http://news.nationalgeographic.com/news/2005/02/0216_050216_omo.html.

6. Schmid, Randolph. African's have world's greatest genetic diversity. *NBC News.* [Online] April 30, 2009. [Cited: August 17, 2015.] http://www.nbcnews.com/id/30502963/ns/technology_and_science-science/t/africans-have-worlds-greatest-genetic-variation/#.VdFd6ZeLWik.

7. Mayell. "Oldest Human Fossils Identified"

8. Windsor, Rudolph. *From Babylon to Timbuktu.* Atlanta : Windsor's Golden Series, 1969.

9. Windsor, *From Babylon to Timbuktu.*

10. Windsor, *From Babylon to Timbuktu.*

11. Windsor, *From Babylon to Timbuktu.*

12. Asante, Molefi K. *The Egyptian Philosophies: Ancient African Voices From Imhotep to Akhenaten.* Chicago : African American Images, 2000.

13. *African Holocaust.* [Online] [Cited: August 17, 2015.] http://www.africanlegends.info/.

14. Jarus, Owen. "Step Pyramid of Djoser: Egypt's First Pyramid," *Live Science.* [Online] September 10, 2012. [Cited: August 17, 2015.] http://www.livescience.com/23050-step-pyramid-djoser.html.

15. Asante, *The Egyptian Philosophies.*

16. *African Holocaust.*

17. *African Holocaust.*

18. *African Holocaust.*

19. *African Holocaust.*

20. "Cleopatra," *Wikipedia.* [Online] [Cited: August 17, 2015.] https://en.wikipedia.org/wiki/Cleopatra.

21. "History of ancient Egypt" *Wikipedia.* [Online] [Cited: August 17, 2015.] https://en.wikipedia.org/wiki/History_of_ancient_Egypt.

22. Wolchover, Natalie. "How Much Would It Cost to Build the Great Pyramid Today?," *Live Science.* [Online] February 22, 2012. [Cited: August 17, 2015.] http://www.livescience.com/18589-cost-build-great-pyramid-today.html.

23. Wolchover. "How Much Would It Cost to Build the Great Pyramid Today?,"

24. Wolchover. "How Much Would It Cost to Build the Great Pyramid Today?,"

25. Moore, A. "Who is Black? Striking Images of the World's Dark-Skinned People Inaccurately Considered Non-Black," *Atlanta BlackStar.* [Online] March 6, 2014. [Cited: August 17, 2015.] http://atlantablackstar.com/2014/03/06/black-striking-images-various-types-black-people-around-world/.

26. Sertima, Ivan V. *They Came Before Columbus: The African Presence in Ancient America.* New York : Random House, 1976.

27. Chengu, Garikai. "Before Columbus: How Africans Brought Civilization to America," *Global Research.* [Online] October 12, 2014. [Cited: August 17, 2015.] http://www.globalresearch.ca/before-columbus-how-africans-brought-civilization-to-america/5407584.

28. Chengu. "Before Columbus: How Africans Brought Civilization to America."

29. Gordon, Taylor. "10 Pieces of Evidence That Prove Black People Sailed to the Americas Long Before Columbus," *Atlanta BlackStar.* [Online] January 23,

2015. [Cited: August 17, 2015.] https://atlantablackstar.com/2015/01/23/10-pieces-of-evidence-that-prove-black-people-sailed-to-the-americas-long-before-columbus/2/.

30. Gordon. "10 Pieces of Evidence That Prove Black People Sailed to the Americas Long Before Columbus,"

31. "Science of Melanin Shatters Neanderthal-Caucasoid Genetic-Superiority Paradigm! | Carol Barnes," *YouTube.* [Online] Ocotber 3, 2013. [Cited: August 7, 2015.] https://www.youtube.com/watch?v=Sf2w29ProWI.

32. "Science of Melanin Shatters Neanderthal-Caucasoid Genetic-Superiority Paradigm! | Carol Barnes."

33. Moore, T. Owens. *The Science & The Myth of Melanin: Exposing The Truths.* s.l. : EWorld Incorporated, 2010.

34. "Bobby Hemmitt- What you need to know about melanin," *YouTube.* [Online] April 9, 2013. [Cited: August 17, 2015.] https://www.youtube.com/watch?v=x9xtGsokcUM.

35. "Bobby Hemmitt- What you need to know about melanin."

36. "Bobby Hemmitt- What you need to know about melanin."

37. "Difference Starts With Melanin," *Alkha Life.* [Online] [Cited: August 17, 2015.] http://alkhalife.info/content/difference-starts-melanin.

38. "Bobby Hemmitt- What you need to know about melanin."

39. "Difference Starts With Melanin."

40. "Bobby Hemmitt- What you need to know about melanin."

41. Knight, *Why I Am A Five Percenter.*

42. Knight, *Why I Am A Five Percenter.*

43. "Understanding Genetics," *The Tech Museum of Innovation.* [Online] October 7, 2009. [Cited: August 17, 2015.] http://genetics.thetech.org/ask/ask330.

44. "Understanding Genetics."

45. "Understanding Genetics."

46. "Understanding Genetics."

47. "Ancient Greece," *Wikipedia.* [Online] [Cited: August 17, 2015.] https://en.wikipedia.org/wiki/Ancient_Greece.

48. "Ancient Greece"

49. Windsor, *From Babylon to Timbuktu.*

50. Windsor, *From Babylon to Timbuktu.*

51. Windsor, *From Babylon to Timbuktu.*

52. Windsor, *From Babylon to Timbuktu.*

53. Windsor, *From Babylon to Timbuktu*.
54. "Slavery in ancient Greece," *Wikipedia*. [Online] [Cited: August 17, 2015.] https://en.wikipedia.org/wiki/Slavery_in_ancient_Greece.
55. "Ancient Rome," *Wikipedia*. [Online] [Cited: August 17, 2015.] https://en.wikipedia.org/wiki/Ancient_Rome.
56. "Germanic Wars," *Wikipedia*. [Online] [Cited: August 17, 2015.] https://en.wikipedia.org/wiki/Germanic_Wars.
57. "Dark Ages," *Wikipedia*. [Online] [Cited: August 17, 2015.] https://en.wikipedia.org/wiki/Dark_Ages_%28historiography%29.
58. "Moors," *Wikipedia*. [Online] [Cited: August 17, 2015.] https://en.wikipedia.org/wiki/Moors.
59. "When Black Men Ruled The World: 8 Things The Moors Brought To Europe," *Atlanta BlackStar*. [Online] October 7, 2013. [Cited: August 17, 2015.] http://atlantablackstar.com/2013/10/07/when-black-men-ruled-the-world-moors/.
60. "When Black Men Ruled The World: 8 Things The Moors Brought To Europe."
61. "When Black Men Ruled The World: 8 Things The Moors Brought To Europe."
62. Windsor, *From Babylon to Timbuktu*.
63. Sertima, *They Came Before Columbus: The African Presence in Ancient America*.
64. Sertima, *They Came Before Columbus: The African Presence in Ancient America*.
65. Sertima, *They Came Before Columbus: The African Presence in Ancient America*.
66. "Crisis of the Late Middle Ages," *Wikipedia*. [Online] [Cited: August 7, 2015.] https://en.wikipedia.org/wiki/Crisis_of_the_Late_Middle_Ages.
67. "Gates, Henry L Jr. How Many Slaves Landed in the US? *The Root*," [Online] January 6, 2014. [Cited: August 2015, 17.] http://www.theroot.com/articles/history/2012/10/how_many_slaves_came_to_america_fact_vs_fiction.html.
68. Rediker, Marcus. *The Slave Ship A Human History*. New York : Penguin Group, 2007.
69. "The Holocaust," *Essays By Ekowa*. [Online] [Cited: August 17, 2015.] http://www.essaysbyekowa.com/Holocaust%20Maafa.htm.
70. Rediker, *The Slave Ship A Human History*.

71. "Without Slavery, Would The U.S. Be The Leading Economic Power?," *Here & Now.* [Online] November 19, 2014. [Cited: 17 2015, August.] http://hereand-now.wbur.org/2014/11/19/slavery-economy-baptist.

72. "King Cotton," *Wikipedia.* [Online] [Cited: August 17, 2015.] https://en.wikipedia.org/wiki/King_Cotton.

73. "King Cotton."

74. *The Willie Lynch Letter And the Making of A Slave.* s.l. : Classic Books America, 2009.

75. *The Willie Lynch Letter And the Making of A Slave.*

76. "The Enslaved - What They Endured," *Humboldt State Univerity's Department of History.* [Online] [Cited: August 17, 2015.] http://users.humboldt.edu/ogayle/hist110/enslaved.html.

77. "Bobby Hemmitt- What you need to know about melanin."

Chapter 13:   The Movement: Breaking the Shackles

1. "Reconstruction Era," *Wikipedia.* [Online] [Cited: August 17, 2015.] https://en.wikipedia.org/wiki/Reconstruction_Era.

2. "Lynching in America: Confronting the Legacy of Racial Terror," *Equal Justice Initiative.* [Online] [Cited: August 17, 2015.] http://www.eji.org/lynchinginamerica.

3. "Great Migration," *History.* [Online] [Cited: August 17, 2015.] http://www.history.com/topics/black-history/great-migration.

4. "Harlem Renaissance," *Wikipedia.* [Online] [Cited: August 17, 2015.] https://en.wikipedia.org/wiki/Harlem_Renaissance.

5. "Booker T. Washington," *Wikipedia.* [Online] [Cited: August 17, 2015.] https://en.wikipedia.org/wiki/Booker_T._Washington.

6. Woodson, Carter G. *The Mis-Education of the Negro.* s.l. : The Associated Publishers, 1933.

7. Woodson, *The Mis-Education of the Negro.*

8. "W.E.B. Du Bois," *Wikipedia.* [Online] [Cited: August 17, 2015.] https://en.wikipedia.org/wiki/W._E._B._Du_Bois.

9. "The Rise and Fall of Jim Crow," *PBS.* [Online] [Cited: August 17, 2015.] http://www.pbs.org/wnet/jimcrow/stories_people_dubois.html.

10. "Booker T & W.E.B," *PBS*. [Online] [Cited: August 17, 2015.] http://www.pbs.org/wgbh/pages/frontline/shows/race/etc/road.html.

11. Woodson, *The Mis-Education of the Negro*.

12. "Marcus Garvey Biography," *Bio*. [Online] [Cited: August 18, 2015.] http://www.biography.com/people/marcus-garvey-9307319#founding-the-united-negro-improvement-association.

13. "Marcus Garvey Biography."

14. King, Martin L Jr. Letter From Birmingham Jail. June s.l. : Liberation, 1963.

15. "Malcolm X Biography," *Bio*. [Online] [Cited: August 18, 2015.] http://www.biography.com/people/malcolm-x-9396195.

16. X, Malcolm and Haley, Alex. *The Autobiography of Malcolm X*. New York : The Ballantine Publishing Group, 1964.

17. "Malcolm X Biography."

18. "Malcolm X - The Last Speech - February 14, 1965," *YouTube*. [Online] December 6, 2012. [Cited: August 8, 2015.] https://www.youtube.com/watch?v=5fnPXw-Tn6I&feature=youtu.be.

19. "Malcolm X - The Last Speech - February 14, 1965,"

20. "Malcolm X - The Last Speech - February 14, 1965,"

21. "Martin Luther King on Black Economic Empowerment (Coca Cola Boycott 1968)," *YouTube*. [Online] [Cited: January 1, 2011.] https://www.youtube.com/watch?v=RkmJcCGfuzo.

22. "Martin Luther King on Black Economic Empowerment (Coca Cola Boycott 1968),"

Chapter 14:   Unity

1. Boney, Jeffrey L. "The Black Wall Street-Case Study," *Atlanta Metropolitan Black Chamber of Commerce*. [Online] February 1, 2015. [Cited: August 18, 2015.] http://ambcc.org/black-wall-street-case-study/.

2. Boney. "The Black Wall Street-Case Study,"

3. Boney, Jeffrey. "From Black Wall Street to the Black Dollar Project," *Forward Times*. [Online] May 4, 2014. [Cited: August 18, 2015.] http://forward-timesonline.com/2013/index.php/state-local/item/1320-from-black-wall-street-to-the-black-dollar-project.

4. Boney, "From Black Wall Street to the Black Dollar Project."

5. Boney, "From Black Wall Street to the Black Dollar Project."

6. Boney, "From Black Wall Street to the Black Dollar Project."

Authors

Christopher Freeman is a self-made entrepreneur and business owner of Beautiful Hair 4 U - one of the leading and fastest growing distributors of virgin hair in the nation. The Beautiful Hair 4 U enterprise currently includes a store in his hometown Jacksonville, FL - in addition to Orlando, Tampa, Atlanta, and Charlotte. Christopher is author of *"Crumbs to Bricks,"* and a motivational speaker for at-risk youth and ex-convict re-entry programs. In his spare time Christopher enjoys staying "on point" through boxing training.

www.beautifulhair4u.com

Instagram: @beautifulhair4U   @mrbeautifulhair

Facebook: @beautifulhair4you

Marcellus Womack is a MBA brand strategist/PR consultant and business owner of MPerfect Marketing Solutions. Marcellus has created successful marketing campaigns and executed transformational business strategies for numerous small businesses and global Fortune 500 companies. The Chicago native is also a dedicated mentor plus a hip-hop and hooping enthusiast.

Twitter: @CellPR23

LinkedIn: Marcellus Womack

Printed in Great Britain
by Amazon

56817284R10169